The
Startup
Playbook

The Startup Playbook

Founder-to-Founder Advice from Two
Startup Veterans

Rajat Bhargava
Will Herman

WILEY

Published by John Wiley & Sons, Inc., Hoboken, New Jersey.
Published simultaneously in Canada.

Limit of Liability/Disclaimer of Warranty: While the publisher and author have used their best efforts in preparing this book, they make no representations or warranties with respect to the accuracy or completeness of the contents of this book and specifically disclaim any implied warranties of merchantability or fitness for a particular purpose. No warranty may be created or extended by sales representatives or written sales materials. The advice and strategies contained herein may not be suitable for your situation. You should consult with a professional where appropriate. Neither the publisher nor author shall be liable for any loss of profit or any other commercial damages, including but not limited to special, incidental, consequential, or other damages.

For general information on our other products and services or for technical support, please contact our Customer Care Department within the United States at (800) 762–2974, outside the United States at (317) 572–3993 or fax (317) 572–4002.

Wiley publishes in a variety of print and electronic formats and by print-on-demand. Some material included with standard print versions of this book may not be included in e-books or in print-on-demand. If this book refers to media such as a CD or DVD that is not included in the version you purchased, you may download this material at http://booksupport.wiley.com. For more information about Wiley products, visit www.wiley.com.

Library of Congress Cataloging-in-Publication Data:

Names: Bhargava, Rajat, 1964- author. | Herman, Will, author.
Title: The startup playbook : founder-to-founder advice from two startup veterans / Rajat Bhargava, Will Herman.
Description: First Edition. | Hoboken : Wiley, 2020. | Series: Techstars | Includes index.
Identifiers: LCCN 2020007526 (print) | LCCN 2020007527 (ebook) | ISBN 9781119708513 (hardback) | ISBN 9781119708551 (adobe pdf) | ISBN 9781119708537 (epub)
Subjects: LCSH: New business enterprises–Management. | Entrepreneurship.
Classification: LCC HD62.5 .B4863 2020 (print) | LCC HD62.5 (ebook) | DDC 658.1/1–dc23
LC record available at https://lccn.loc.gov/2020007526
LC ebook record available at https://lccn.loc.gov/2020007527

Cover Design: Wiley
Interior Illustrations: Rocio Hedman

Printed in the United States of America

SKY10020386_081020

To AHA & RMB
—Rajat

For Sandra, without whom none of this would have happened.
—Will

For all the gutsy entrepreneurs building the next great startups
and to the mentors who help them.
—Rajat and Will

Contents

Foreword

As an entrepreneur and venture capitalist for over 30 years, I've had the opportunity to help create many companies. I've been a part of wildly successful companies like Harmonix (creators of *Guitar Hero*), Zynga, and Fitbit, and I've been involved with many other companies that are growing and profitable. I have also been involved in many businesses that ultimately failed. Through these experiences, I've seen firsthand how the qualities of a founder and founding team can make or break a company.

There isn't a magic formula for success—I don't know of one and neither does anyone else. If there were a magic formula, creating a successful company would just be a matter of copying and executing it. But you'll often hear successful entrepreneurs say that building a successful business is a combination of skills, talents, chemistry, hard work, and luck.

They're right about that, but how does a first-time founder figure out which combinations are relevant? How can an aspiring entrepreneur get up to speed on what to do, what not to do, and what to expect at various stages of growth?

Look no further than *The Startup Playbook: Founder-to-Founder Advice from Two Startup Veterans*. Will and Rajat have taken the mystery out of starting a business and they have shined a light on the black box of entrepreneurship, and anyone who reads this book will be light-years ahead of their competitors.

In an engaging, authentic, and easy-to-read style, Will and Rajat share what they've learned about starting a successful business, they talk candidly about their failures, and they distill complex topics into the essentials. Reading *The Startup Playbook* is like having a trusted person guide you through the practicalities and nuances of building a successful business.

We see all sorts of founding teams at Foundry Group and Techstars who have great ideas and solutions but struggle with creating a profitable business. It's why we focus on the team as a key factor in the potential success of a company. When we make an investment in a founding team, we see it as a long-term partnership. We work with the team to help fill in gaps by sharing what we've learned from many other startups. Once we've made our investment, we sit side-by-side with the team, not on the other side of the table. Now, with *The Startup Playbook*, we have an additional resource to provide founding teams that will accelerate their learning.

I've known both Rajat and Will for much of my professional life. Will and I met when I was at MIT, and we later made our first angel investment together in 1994 in NetGenesis, Rajat's first company. Since then, I've started a few companies with Rajat and have invested in several of his startups. Will and I have made many investments together, and we have been on boards together, including several of the companies that Rajat started.

Having worked with them over the last 25 years, I've seen and been involved in many of the ups and downs that Rajat and Will have had. Throughout the good and bad times, they've approached everything they've done from the founder's point of view, which is what they do in this book.

If you are a first-time founder, or an entrepreneur at any stage, increase your chance for success by reading and following Will and Rajat's advice in this book.

Brad Feld
Managing Director, *Foundry Group*
March 2020

The Startup Playbook

Introduction

The fact that I (Will) was essentially bankrupt wasn't even the bad part. The bad part was I had to admit that my parents might have been right about what a stupid idea joining a startup was and, to add insult to injury, I had to ask if I could move back in with them.

You see, as a sophomore in college, I was so convinced that the startup path was right for me that, against my parent's pleadings, I quit school to join a fledgling company. As far as I could tell, everything was going incredibly well, and I'd made a great decision—until the day the company announced it was folding. What? It didn't make sense. And, to make matters worse, no one could explain what caused the meltdown. It wasn't even clear if anyone really knew.

Despite the failure and with no idea why the company crashed and burned, I thought I could do better. So, I acquired some of the assets from the failed company and created my own startup, DataWare Logic. I was sure I'd find success where the last company hadn't.

It didn't turn out well. In eighteen months, the new company was dead, and I went home with my tail between my legs.

After two failed startups, I still had no idea what had gone wrong or how either unraveled. There were customers,

1

computers, and contracts, but no more cash. Not only was there no one to ask—I didn't know anyone who had even tried a startup—but I didn't even know *what* to ask. I had no wisdom, no knowledge, and no help.

Starting a Company Is Easy. Starting a Sustainable, Growing Business Is Hard. Really Hard.

Starting a company is shockingly easy. There are almost no barriers and no costs standing between a would-be founder and a company on paper. Creating a sustainable business that provides real value to its customers, employees, and investors—now that's incredibly hard. Unfortunately, Will's story, above, is far from unusual. The fact is, nine out of ten startups fail.*

Yes, you read that right. Only 10 percent succeed, and we think that's being generous. Some would-be successes are really just among the walking dead. They haven't failed yet, but they're getting there slowly. Others are surviving but can't find a way to make money for their founders and investors. In our experience, when thinking about companies that have succeeded in all dimensions, the success rate is closer to just a few percent.

So, what do you do when you want to start a company and the odds are so clearly stacked against you? How do you ensure you are among the few percent who succeed when you don't have the knowledge, experience, or help to take a new, fledgling company from inception to success? As with most things, surrounding yourself with people who have the wisdom of experience born from both successes and failures increases the odds of success.

The Startup Playbook is our personal how-to guide for building your startup from the ground up. In it, you'll find a collection of the major lessons and shortcuts we've learned that will shift the odds in your favor. We're sharing our tips, secrets, and advice in a frank, founder-to-founder discussion with you.

In the following pages, we focus on the fundamentals you need to create and run a successful business. We provide a framework for how to think about the startup journey and specifically how to validate whether you have an idea that can be successful. We also hit the major points—points that many books and advisors ignore—that you need to blend and balance to take an idea and turn it into a successful business. We'll share the nitty-gritty details that are often skipped over when talking about building a business. Unfortunately, those details are often the ones that trip up entrepreneurs the most.

We both became founders in the early days of the tech startup boom. Will co-founded his first successful company, Viewlogic Systems, a few years after failing with DataWare Logic. Will and Rajat met when Rajat was starting NetGenesis in 1994 when Will became one of his first angel investors.

While we certainly can't make the claim that we've done and seen everything, we've learned an awful lot and enjoyed long, successful careers as entrepreneurs and tech startup founders. Between us, we've started over a dozen high-tech software companies, raised over $500 million in investment capital, acquired over thirty-five companies, had three of our startups go public, sold six of them, and we made a lot of money for shareholders. We've also advised and mentored over two hundred companies and actively worked with venture capitalists (VCs), incubators, and accelerators to help launch many other new startups.

We've seen the other side of the startup world, the investment side, too. We've directly invested in over one hundred companies and hundreds more through angel networks and venture capital funds. We've done this work together and independently for over twenty years.

And yes, amid our successes, we've also crashed and burned. We've failed at building companies and products, been a breath away from bankruptcy, and some days, we've wanted to walk away from the very concept of startups. We've had turmoil in our founding and management teams. We've dealt with lawsuits, intense competition, and we've been blindsided by market shifts.

As investors, we've also made bad investments and thrown good money after bad more than a few times. We certainly never wished for these scars, but we've learned so much from them. The tips, strategies, and advice in this book are here to help you avoid the mistakes we've made.

We make no bones about our bias. We're on your side, the founder's side, and you'll hear that perspective. There is no doubt that venture capitalists, investors, and accelerators/incubators have great value in the startup ecosystem, but this book isn't about their points of view. We'll tell you where our interests as founders diverge from those on the other side of the table, including investors, bankers, advisors, board members, and others. We mean no disrespect to these critical and important constituents in the startup process, but we feel the tribal knowledge of building a business is being lost.

We want to share with you the true, honest, and unabridged version of what it's really like to start and grow a company – everything we've learned. The real, uncensored truth isn't a glamorous story. Even the highly visible, successful founders everyone knows by name had a bumpy ride at many points along their journeys.

We realize this book probably isn't the first stop on your journey to learn about how to deal with startup challenges. You've likely already encountered a staggering amount of information: some good, but much of it likely bad, incomplete, or biased. The internet megaphone doesn't distinguish between the expert and the poseur. In fact, many legitimate experts (and there are many of them now) don't trumpet their knowledge or success. Most entrepreneurs are busy starting and running companies, after all, and don't have the time to share their stories.

Unfortunately, there are also people in the ever-expanding entrepreneurial ecosystem who have had some level of success with a single venture and feel motivated to promote themselves as experts. Often, these people try to capitalize on their limited success by promoting themselves as having knowledge and wisdom that applies to all startups and at all stages when, in fact, they simply know how one set of decisions worked. While wisdom can be gleaned from the experiences of any entrepreneur, failed or successful, be wary of extrapolating too much advice from people who have only seen a small number of the challenges that a startup might face.

There's even a larger group of so-called experts who haven't even been a founder, built a startup, or succeeded at any entrepreneurial venture. They will offer and even advertise their "advice" through blogs, social media, and any other outlet they can find. We'll be even more direct in this case. Don't listen to those people.

Hopefully, *The Startup Playbook* becomes your startup manual – a manual you can read now and come back to time and time again to help you think through challenges as your business grows.

How This Book Is Organized

In *Part 1: I Want to Start a Company*, we cover subjects many experts gloss over if not avoid entirely, like what it really means to be a founder. In these chapters, we discuss the reasons why people become founders; common traits, characteristics, and habits founders need to have; and their must-play roles in the company. This section is designed to make you think, reflect, and consider whether becoming a founder is the right path for you. Hint: it's most definitely not for everyone.

In *Part 2: Getting Off the Ground*, we move into generating an idea for a company, creating a business model, validating it, building a founding team, which we strongly favor, and the nuts and bolts of forming a company. We can't tell you how many mistakes are made at this stage. Conventional wisdom says you need a brilliant idea to succeed, but we'll debunk that myth. What happens after the seed of an idea is far more important than the idea you start with.

In *Part 3: Funding Your Startup*, we discuss what most founders incorrectly think is the most important milestone on their startup path: raising money. In our experience, it's not. Still, having money accelerates your efforts, which can be an important component of your success. In these chapters, we'll walk you through the available funding resources and give you a way of thinking about what the best ones are for you and your startup. We'll discuss the process of figuring out how much money you'll need, how to develop a comprehensive plan for investment, and, ultimately, how to approach and close investors, including reviewing term sheets, setting your valuation, and what to negotiate. Our goal is to demystify the funding process and to add a realistic founder's perspective to the venture-capital-dominated narrative you hear about every day.

Finally, in *Part 4: Running Your Company*, we detail how to transform your vision and preliminary business model into a great business. After all, the work, risk, and uncertainty that we talk about in the first three parts of the book will amount to nothing if you can't actually create a vibrant, sustainable business. In the chapters of Part 4, we offer you our secrets to building a product or service that resonates with customers, how to create a killer sales and marketing strategy, how to identify and connect with your target audience, and how to manage your business. Successful entrepreneurs will tell you time and again that great execution is crucial to success. In fact, it's the single most important factor in creating a successful company in our opinion. So, we'll break down what that means into how you run your business including thinking about your culture, building your management process, recruiting top-notch talent, and creating momentum with your team. In short, this section is the CliffsNotes® to running your business.

Our Assumptions

The explanation of the startup journey is a complex one, and we could easily get mired in exceptions and nuances. Covering each of these at every turn would make this book thousands of pages long and really wouldn't serve anybody. While we'll try our best to point out the exceptions where it makes sense, the following are some assumptions we've made to make the book easier to read.

Assumption 1: The startup process is linear. We all know that it isn't. The startup process is messy. People start and stop, founders join and leave, teams move forward and fall back, and the competitive environment is quirky and somewhat unpredictable. But, for the purposes of this book, we're going to lay out the startup process in a fairly logical, step-by-step fashion. The book will start with why you should create a company and what that company looks like, whether a person can and should be a founder, how a founder creates a business concept, the process of validating and starting the business, and how to bring an offering to market and then grow it. Sometimes, those parts happen in a different order; often, they take place in parallel. Since each situation is unique, we'll generalize a logical case.

We've written the book so you can jump around and read any chapter in any order. If you're reading it straight through, you'll see that we take a complex process and make it linear for readability. Believe us, we know it's easy to get lost in the startup process since so many things happen at the same time.

Assumption 2: There is a founding team, not just one founder. We see many individuals attempt to create and build companies alone. They are at a huge disadvantage if they try to do so. Well-rounded founding teams do far better. They move faster, avoid more problems, and take advantage of more opportunities than individuals. As a result, accelerators often only take on teams of founders, and investors prefer to invest in startups with multiple founders. This is why we believe that having multiple founders is the only way to go.

Assumption 3: One of the founders is also the CEO. It can happen that an external CEO is brought into a company, but for the purposes of this book, it's a founder who plays that role. We'll explore that more in Chapter 29 to help you decide whether you should bring in an outside CEO.

Assumption 4: Founders are the management team. It isn't strictly the case that the team is just founders at the early stages of a company. We often see founders hire their first employees or part of their management team early on. That being said, we assume that for at least a reasonable amount of time, the founders are also the management team and responsible for operating the business on a day-to-day basis. This will help us illustrate some of the founders' key responsibilities. We will, though, actively discuss how and who to recruit to join the startup team, from executives to individual contributors.

Assumption 5: Products and services are the same. Most of the principles we discuss in this book apply to companies that offer products as well as those that sell services. To make things simpler throughout the book, we refer to the offerings of all companies as products. There are some key differences between the two, and we will point those out where applicable.

Assumption 6: Incubators are accelerators. We mention incubators and accelerators throughout this book. While there can be differences between accelerators, incubators, and the myriad of other startup programs, for ease of reading, we call them all accelerators.

Who Should Read This Book?

This book is written for entrepreneurs who are eager to start and run their first company. Founders come in all shapes and sizes. We think of founders as building at least three different types of organizations: local businesses, nonprofits, and startups. The local business is a restaurant, dry cleaner, or home contractor with a geographically local customer base. Nonprofits are clearly entrepreneurial and focus on a return to society rather than a financial return. Startups are businesses with aspirations to expand rapidly by creating a scalable and repeatable model. While *The Startup Playbook* is applicable to all three, it's this final category, startups, where we focus most of our attention.

In addition to founders, this book can be an invaluable resource to anyone in the community surrounding the founding team, both inside and outside the company. It's great for the extended startup team because it will give the members of that team a window into how founders think about their problems and how to grow their businesses. It will also point out the red flags that indicate behaviors and actions that should be avoided and that they should be keenly aware of. In fact, it makes sense for all employees, not just the early ones, to get a complete understanding of what it takes to build a successful startup by reading this book.

But it goes even further than that. It's not only helpful for those who are engaged in the actual business, but those who are close to the founding team outside of it. Significant others, relatives (especially parents who might otherwise think you're out of your mind for risking everything), and even friends can get a better understanding of what you're trying to do, what you need to do to optimize for success, and the risks you need to take to make it happen.

Finally, if you're just dabbling with the idea of becoming a founder and starting this journey, then this book can help you determine whether it's the right path for you.

Let's Get Started

This playbook is what we wish we had when we began building companies. Hopefully, the pages that follow will give you a way to think about the startup journey and process in a way that works for you.

Many founders fail because all they focus on is the product they're creating. Successful founders realize that it's finding the right combination of their team, value proposition, distribution strategy, the quality of the product, and the sales and marketing approach that makes a successful company. We think of this as the company's business model, the framework you use to guide your actions. Your differentiation can come from any one of the components that make it up or even from combinations of them.

Even if you do all of this right, as a founder, we guarantee you'll make mistakes. And, that's great; it's a part of life and especially a part of business. Those mistakes will fuel your learning and help you build a better business. It means you're pushing hard to figure things out.

Of course, there is no right way or only way to build a company. That's true, but we believe there is one important underlying principle in building a business. We're not being preachy about it, we're just saying that it makes everything else a lot easier.

Be clean and honest.

We've encountered people who cut corners in big ways, but that approach rarely works in the long run. If you lack clean books and financial statements, it will haunt you. If you decide to have the cheapest manufacturing, use bad parts, or outsource to countries that use child labor all in the name of saving money, it will haunt you. If you create a fraternity house culture at the office, it will haunt you. If you aren't focused on being inclusive with employees, it will haunt you. All of this is bad business. And, there's no reason for you to build your startup under these circumstances.

In this book, we'll show you how to create a company with integrity and honesty from the get-go.

We know you're feeling intense pressure to succeed, perhaps believing that success will be yours only if you become that next unicorn that exits (via an IPO or the sale of the company) for billions of dollars. The pressure you're feeling is most likely driven by external sources, which define success as building that one gigantic company that will sell for $10 billion or more. We urge you not to believe the hype. For example, in the technology sector over the last ten years, 88 percent of the few companies that exited were bought or acquired for less than $100 million.[†]

A key perspective you'll hear from us throughout this book is to figure out the right thing to do for your customers, your investors, and your business without getting fixated on the external narrative of the time. Building a business is a powerful, long-term journey that is about more than how much money you make. It's an experience that can transform who you are and create a legacy for you and your family. And, who knows, you may create something that even changes society.

Success is for you to define. And, we'll help you think through what that means for you.

Success to us has meant many things, and these have changed along the way. We've built some interesting products that have changed industries and created new categories. We've returned significant dollars to shareholders. And, we've built incredible teams where people have transformed their lives personally, professionally, and financially. We've watched people we've worked with go on to start their own ventures, and that may be one of our most gratifying achievements of all.

Look, we're not saying personal financial success isn't a great achievement. It is, and it's so much better than the alternative. We're just saying there's so much more you can get out of starting a company.

Although we can't and won't guarantee that you'll sell your company for millions of dollars after reading this book—no one can give you such assurance—we know this book will help to increase your odds of success.

In the end, all any founder can ask for is the best chance to take the seed of an idea, turn it into a much-needed product, and create a thriving company.

Good luck building your business!

Part 1

I Want to Start a Company

Chapter 1

What Is a Startup?

Can you create a high-growth startup by combining a bunch of small businesses or what some people call local businesses—those with a geographically limited customer base? I (Rajat) tried to do exactly that with my third startup—combine a number of local businesses. I was a co-founder of a company called Interliant that focused on acquiring and integrating small web hosting companies.

In three years, Interliant acquired over thirty of these types of companies and tried to combine them into one high-growth, scalable startup. While most of the companies that we acquired weren't startups themselves, our goal was to inject a startup ethos into them and their teams so that we could create one of the largest web-hosting firms in the world.

In Interliant's case, we took a nontraditional path to building a startup. We created a very fast-growing company that eventually went public (and was subsequently acquired for pennies on the dollar during the dotcom downturn) using individual building blocks that weren't, themselves, startups. We never felt confined to any particular startup model, which contributed to the fast growth of the company.

While we probably wouldn't recommend this particular model of a startup for first-time entrepreneurs because of the degree of execution difficulty, it does serve the key point: startups come in many different flavors.

The Definition of Startup

What is a startup? There is no agreed upon definition of what exactly a startup is. Of course, the academics do their best to define it in a "scientific" way, but if you ask ten entrepreneurs to define a startup, you'll hear ten unique answers. A quick search of the internet proves equally unsatisfying. Famed serial-entrepreneur and teacher Steve Blank says there are six different varieties of startups: lifestyle, small business, scalable, buyable, social, and inside a large company.[*]

In an article for *Forbes*, Neil Blumenthal, co-founder and co-CEO of Warby Parker says, "A startup is a company working to solve a problem where the solution is not obvious and success is not guaranteed."[†] Jan Koum the co-founder of WhatsApp, says a startup is a feeling.[‡]

Confused yet?

We think of a startup as a high-growth company that is scalable, focused on continuously growing, and one where the founders develop an exit strategy that results in either a sale of the company or an IPO (Initial Public Offering). This definition isn't unique, but we see it as one that eliminates some ambiguity and that creates a better framework for thinking about the business.

A startup is a high-growth company that is scalable, focused on continuously growing, and one where the founders develop an exit strategy that results in either a sale of the company or an IPO.

Let's break this definition down further.

Scalable. Scalability in a startup refers to its ability to grow—usually at a fast pace and over the long haul—and with minimal incremental cost. This means a company has a large-enough market or opportunity in a market, the ability to quickly expand into that market, and then, eventually, to generate ever-increasing profits. At a minimum, scalability means there are enough customers in the target market who can purchase from the startup, and the opportunity is significant enough with each customer to build a large and expanding business. Of course, what amounts to enough and large are in the eye of the beholder, but a simple rule of thumb is that if there aren't enough potential customers for your business to justify continuous growth over time (this is often referred to as TAM, Total Addressable Market), or it's going to be too costly to get access to those customers, you probably don't have a scalable business. Remember your TAM isn't just the size of the overall market you play in, but the actual size of the market you can reasonably address.

High growth and continuous growth. Growth is a core part of any startup. If a startup isn't growing, it will struggle to stay ahead of its competition, attract key employees, and get additional funding. Most successful startups grow fast, especially at the beginning. Every industry has their own definition of what high growth means, but according to research by the venture capital firm IVP, successful companies grow at about a 133 percent annual rate between $0 and $25M in revenue.** These are, of course, averages. Keep in mind that a consumer smartphone app business, enterprise software company, and hardware device supplier, as a few examples, will all have different growth characteristics. In the end, you'll need to judge what high growth means for your startup, but it should be within the norms of what your successful peers are doing and what your investors are looking for.

Growth also changes over time. Growing by multiples per year is possible early on, but as the size of the business increases, it isn't realistic to grow as fast. According to the previously mentioned IVP research, growth rates drop in later stages, down to about 73 percent for companies between $25 and $50M. For startups, the quest for growth never ends. Continuous growth remains one of the primary benchmarks of startup success.

Exit strategy. Our belief is that every startup, by definition, will have an exit at some point in time. At the very least, the founding team should be thinking about selling the company, doing an IPO (Initial Public Offering), merging with another company, or finding another type of financially positive exit. Regardless of the type of exit, the goal is the same: to get a positive return on the investment—their money and time—for the investors and founders. It could be many years or even decades away from happening, but having an exit is fundamental to the very nature of a startup. Creating a payday that represents a significant return for the investors, founders, and the team is part of what makes a startup in the first place.

We could join others in the startup world and present an even stricter definition of a startup, but we don't think it's necessary. There are many types of startups and even more ways to implement them.

You might be asking why labels matter, or why you should care whether your company is called a startup, a local business, a lifestyle business, or anything else. Does the label actually change anything? Yes, it does. At the very least, what you call your business affects people's perception of it, which, in turn, will affect fundraising, hiring, and even the customers you attract. Knowing what type of business your company is will also affect how you capitalize the business, what expenses you take on, your financial model, your go-to-market plan, and much more. So, for us, the term *startup* is really shorthand for a specific type of business.

Startups Exist in Many Sectors

While the technology sector attracts the most attention, especially in the media, startups come from many industries and sectors. If you're just beginning to think about a startup, consider what type of company you want to start, and then open your mind to the opportunities in all fields and industries. Some of the most exciting new companies in the last few years have been in existing industries and older markets ripe for disruption.

Uber is a case study in this. It's easy to point to Uber as a technology startup and, certainly, they are leveraging technology. However, at its core, they are really just a service provider, helping people get to where they need to go. That doesn't sound startup-like, but it is. And, who would have ever thought that the taxi industry was ready for disruption or could support a high-growth business? Uber is building a valuable worldwide business in one of the sleepiest industries that anyone could imagine. Interestingly, many entrepreneurs are using Uber's model and applying it to other markets and sectors.

Uber is just one of many companies we're watching that have burst onto the scene in a variety of non-tech sectors. Here is a quick snapshot of a few non-tech startups selling products:

- Clothing (Trunk Club, Blank Label, Rent the Runway, and Peach)

- Shaving/skin care (Dollar Shave Club, Harry's, and Birchbox)
- Furniture (Leesa, Burrow, and Casper)

High-tech or not, startups are disrupting just about every market, and sometimes it's not only the products that they disrupt, but the way products are purchased as well. Just think about an Amazon Prime membership, and you'll know what we mean.

We also see loads of service-oriented startups in markets like:

- Grocery delivery, food preparation, and beverages (Blue Apron, HelloFresh, and Drizly)
- Health clubs (ClassPass and Exhale Spa)
- Travel (Airbnb, HomeAway, and Hopper)

While each of these startups use technology, for sure, their customers don't get too involved with it. Instead, their customers see better delivery of a service than they could have gotten before these companies were founded.

Each of these companies fit our criteria for a startup—scalable, for sure, and trying to achieve and maintain high growth. Since they have all taken money from outside investors, we'd wager some kind of exit strategy is almost assuredly part of their long-term plan.

These are just some examples of what startups look like today and what industries we find them in, but there are tens of thousands of other examples of companies operating in fields many people wouldn't think of—from philanthropy to life sciences. This should inspire you. You don't have to deliver the next innovative technology to get going in the startup world.

Think out-of-the-box about what market and industries can be improved. When you do this, you've taken the first step in launching a potentially successful startup.

* * *

While the definition we use for a startup isn't necessarily universal, it has the key, common elements broadly understood by most people involved in the startup ecosystem. Why is this important? By understanding the definition, you can begin to comprehend what it means to build a startup, and it gives you a basis for thinking more about what the broad goals are for a startup company along with some of the challenges to achieving them.

Chapter 2

Why Start a Company?

I (Rajat) was a senior at MIT and started my first company with a group of friends. The World Wide Web had just been introduced, and it seemed like there was tremendous opportunity. I jumped at the chance to start a business, even though I wasn't finished with college.

My journey to becoming a founder didn't happen overnight, but it didn't take long, either. I was fortunate enough to work for Intel during each of my summer breaks during college. While Intel was and still is an amazing company, I quickly realized that I wouldn't have the opportunity to make a significant impact. I believed I could do more, but in the confines of a large, well-structured organization, a junior employee would hardly be trusted with critical decisions and work.

I wanted to be challenged and thought I could do much more with the energy and skills that I had. At the time, I realized my only option to create that work environment for myself was by starting my own company.

The Allure of Startups

Many successful entrepreneurs have become household names. Their journeys and exploits have been written about and movies have put them on pedestals. Soon, we'll have action figures of the most successful startup titans. Can you imagine a Mark Zuckerberg or Steve Jobs bobblehead doll? With the intense interest in these icons and the companies they created, it's easy to see why many people want to do the same thing.

Or, at least, achieve the same status.

That status was achieved only after a tremendous amount of work and dedication—most of this glossed over by the media. Apparently, years of long days and nights filled with many successes and a reasonable number of failures don't make for exciting stories. In the end, those successful founders each had tremendous energy and passion for what they were doing, and this, along with some brains and a lot of luck, is what elevated them to their superhero status.

Without the curiosity, passion, and drive to accomplish their goals—the internal fire to fill a hole in the market, exploit an opportunity, to do the right thing for their community, or to do something no one else ever has—they would have never achieved their level of success or iconic status. Nor will you. Successful entrepreneurs are driven first and foremost by unrelenting passion. They're internally motivated to create something from nothing.

If you're starting a company because you think it's cool or fashionable or because you think you'll make bags of money quickly or even make money at all, you may want to reconsider your motivation.

Think about it: Facebook took almost 10 years to go from inception to IPO. We guarantee you that those weren't 10 easy years. Of course, very few companies even reach Facebook's level of success, and you probably shouldn't plan on it. But, less success doesn't imply a shorter path unless, of course, you don't make it. Even if you find yourself among the 10 percent who do make it, on average, you'll still need about seven years of hard work to get there.* And that's in tech; other markets can take considerably longer. In our experience, planning for about a decade is the smart thing to do. For example, Viewlogic took about ten years to reach an IPO, StillSecure took 13 years to sell, and Quova's acquisition happened ten years after its founding.

Being an entrepreneur can certainly be fashionable and cool. But, those things won't support you when your company goes off the rails for the tenth time or when things aren't looking good in year five. And, the money, well, let's just say you'll pay yourself almost nothing—at least initially. One survey of 11,000 founders discovered that 73 percent pay themselves less than $50,000 per year.† According to that same survey, 66 percent of founders in Silicon Valley pay themselves less than $50,000 per year, and a full three-quarters make less than $75,000.‡ As we mentioned earlier in the book, there's no guarantee you'll ever become the next Zuckerberg or Jobs, not when 90 percent of all startups fail.**

Any way you cut it, the chances of you making money are substantially higher when you work for someone else. Not that any of this really matters if you have the startup bug. True motivation only comes from within. If you're not working to build something you deeply believe in, then the tangible returns alone won't drive you. As Frederick Herzberg, known for his work on motivational theory and management, said, "The bottom line is that none of these things [tangible returns] are motivators."††

Why Should *You* Start a Company?

Becoming a founder and growing a successful company is hard work (funny how we keep bringing that up, right?). We've noticed a pattern in those founders who have reached an exit milestone. Many of them share a common set of reasons why they started their companies in the first place. Virtually all the reasons were deeply motivational on an individual level and were driven by a strong passion for what they were doing. For our part, we've been driven by various reasons during different parts of our lives and careers, but the thing we've always come back to is our deeply driven desire to have an impact on the world, on people, and on our own lives.

The reasons listed below are some of the most powerful that we've seen, and by many accounts, they give founders the edge when a likely but unexpected twist or setback inevitably happens.

As you read through them, ask yourself if they apply to you. Do you think they will sustain you through the difficult periods during your startup journey? We encourage you to be as honest as possible with yourself when evaluating each one. It might also help to discuss them with someone close to you to validate your thinking.

I'm on a Mission

Some people have a vivid vision of how the world should be in the future, and they're compelled to try and make it a reality. Or, they have a vexing problem that just must be solved. It's a passion for shaping the world as they see it could be. This may be a shift for mankind on a global scale, a smaller change that alters an industry or even a community, or perhaps it just solves a previously unsolved problem.

It's the notion that you have an idea that must be unleashed, and you're driven beyond fear to create a new world. From our perspective, this is a prerequisite. Being on a mission, regardless of how small or large, is what sustains a founder through the dark times, of which there will be many.

I'm Entrepreneurial by Nature

Being an entrepreneur is more than a job title; it's a way of life for certain types of people. Just as many people who choose accounting as a profession have certain characteristics, so do entrepreneurs. For one, there's a sense of fearlessness despite risks. It's not that entrepreneurs are ignorant of risk, it's more like they're missing the gene that makes others feel worried. At their core, these entrepreneurs are driven to experiment and to find new ways of solving problems, whether by creating a product or service or a company. Their need to constantly learn and adapt outweighs the inner voice that tells most people to run and hide from a risky situation in the first place.

Entrepreneurs have an inner confidence and faith that if things don't work out with their idea or company, then somehow, in some way, they'll land on their feet; they'll rebound regardless of what happens. They know that the next thing—an idea, a company, an opportunity—is around the corner. This confidence gives them the fuel to risk starting a company.

When you have these attributes, it makes taking risks—of which there will be quite a few—more palatable and easier.

I Want to Be My Own Boss

Sick of being under the thumb of *the Man?* Some people do better when they aren't taking orders or being managed by other people. These individuals don't necessarily need to manage or be in charge of the office, but they do need to be in charge of themselves. Starting a company is a great way for you to have the autonomy and independence you need and crave. Yet, if this is your singular motivation, you may want to question whether it's enough without one or more of the other drivers in this list. While this might seem like a good reason now, it might not be quite as motivational after five years of round-the-clock worries.

I Want to Have a Big Impact

When you work at a large company, it can take many years to learn the business, to make key decisions, or to have a significant impact on the company or the customer. In large firms (and many medium-size ones, too), your level of responsibility and ability to move up the ranks is often tied to your tenure with the firm and experience in the field. Many entrepreneurs bristle and rebel against this approach, preferring to connect duties with performance. As a founder, you get to skip to the front of the line (of course, you also get all the responsibility and negatives of being in charge, too)! From day one, you can have a profound impact on the company. You can make your work matter in a way that you can't at larger companies.

I Also Want to Make Money

Don't get us wrong, wanting to make money isn't a bad thing. It's just that on its own, making money doesn't consistently motivate successful founders—not when the sacrifices and challenges of starting and growing a company are so high. But, when you mix wanting to make money with some of the other reasons on the list above, then it becomes a powerful tool for success. For sure, money may not buy happiness, but it's certainly a nice reward.

We run into many entrepreneurs who think of little more than how rich their startup is going to make them. As we say, this can motivate you for a while, but when you're in year seven of your company, and you're still struggling to reach profitability, venture capitalists won't return your calls, and you have a new baby at home, then what's going to drive you to brush off the challenges and continue to charge forward with the same energy you had on day one? It's not likely to be the prospect of making money, at least not by itself.

* * *

Starting a company can be a life-changing experience. You can change the world and learn while doing it. You'll meet many people, potentially affect many lives, and maybe even make some money or become famous. While these are wonderful outcomes, the sacrifices you make when you're building a startup can be significant. If, at your core, you aren't aligned with the personal trade-offs you'll make when building your company, then success will be tough to achieve. But, if you can find a mission you're incredibly passionate about—better yet, obsessed with—then that will become the fire you need to give the startup a real chance for success.

If you're considering starting a new company, ask yourself why. What is your internal motivation? Do you share any of the same motivations that we listed above? Do you have other deep desires or goals that you can draw strength from when this path gets rocky?

If you can find that inner fire, then go for being an entrepreneur. If you can't discover any strong motivating factors, then you may want to look for another path, another job, or another career to apply your energy to.

Chapter 3

Am I Cut Out to Found a Startup?

I (Will) am not a visionary. There, I admitted it in print. But, that just doesn't matter when it comes to being a successful founder. In every company that I've co-founded, I've been part of a team that had at least one person with strong visionary skills. And, that's what matters. Vision is a critical skill for the team to have. It's not critical that everyone has it individually.

I brought my own strengths to the founding teams I was a part of—strong cultural beliefs, management and people skills, the ability to drive execution, and a complete lack of interest in trying to do it alone. My deep-seated competitive drive certainly helped along the way as well.

I have plenty of weaknesses when it comes to being a textbook company founder, but I've always been part of a team that filled in for where I was weak. Because I also made a habit of surrounding myself with people who are smarter or more experienced than me, I learned along the way and kept myself from making the same mistakes too many times.

The First Question You Should Ask

Before diving into the basic principles of starting and running a company, we want to address a basic question that almost never gets asked, "Are you cut out to be a founder?" Often, would-be startup founders jump into developing their idea and building a company without taking a moment to reflect on whether they have the personality, discipline, and habits that will help them succeed at the endeavor.

We're not throwing down a gauntlet here. This isn't a challenge to step up and be something that you're not. We're just recommending that you ask yourself honestly if starting your own company is the best choice for you. Just because you want to start a company doesn't mean you can or should, and it's better to know this now before traveling too far down the path.

Yeah, we know. You're about to skip this chapter because you think that questioning your entrepreneurial cred is patently absurd, right? But, hear us out. Even if you're totally equipped to do a startup, you may still learn something about yourself in this chapter that will help you become even better at starting and growing a company. We'll introduce you to the basic habits you'll need as a founder—among them, working smart, being persistent, and focusing on the right things. We'll repeat the habits in this chapter often throughout the book. If you take this to mean that we think they're important, you're right.

Honestly, most people aren't cut out to be founders, and few of them ever even try. Think of all the people you know—college friends, co-workers, relatives. How many of those people do you think could start a successful company? Not many, right? The long hours, emotional ups and downs, the extreme stress, and humbling experiences are difficult for most people to grasp and come to terms with, let alone actually live through every day.

Still, there isn't one cookie-cutter mold for a successful founder. They come in all shapes, sizes, and backgrounds. There are no specific prerequisites to be a founder, including special degrees, education, or even work experience. No Harvard MBA required.

We should probably mention a brief definition of a startup founder. A founder is part of the initial team of people responsible for the creation of the idea, the transformation of that idea into a real plan to form a business, and ultimately, the execution of that plan—at least initially. Initially because you'll soon add people to the team, including other key management members and, potentially, even a CEO (more on these topics later in the book).

> A founder is part of the initial team of people responsible for the creation of the idea, the transformation of that idea into a real plan to form a business, and ultimately, the execution of that plan—at least initially.

Every founder brings a variety of skills to the startup as well as different personalities, core beliefs, business networks, and, of course, energy. In fact, by taking advantage of the differences in founder characteristics, the best founding teams are created.

Yes, we said teams, because while it's possible to be a sole founder, most startups have at least two founders, and many have several. In our experience, startups that have multiple founders with a variety of additive skills have a higher chance of success than those with just one founder.

And, it's not just skills that matter. Almost no one has the fortitude to go it alone over the long haul. As we pointed out earlier, building a company isn't only more difficult than you think, it'll also take you a lot longer than you think. You'll encounter problems along the way that will be difficult for you to handle by yourself, while they will be much easier to handle after you take on someone with complementary qualities. Now, multiply that by three to five people, and you get to understand why a team is better than an individual.

Not convinced? What are the odds that you, as an individual founder, won't need some serious downtime over the coming years? Need a vacation? Do you get sick? Do you have a family? Dedicating time to such things is almost impossible if you're a single founder, where a team can just roll with such events and priorities. Even the unplanned ones.

Still not enough? Consider this. The vast majority of accelerators and venture capitalists refuse to invest in single-founder companies. Paul Graham, the creator and founder of Y Combinator, a hugely popular startup accelerator, lists having a single founder as the first mistake in his article, "The 18 Mistakes That Kill Startups."* It's not that you can't build a company with a single founder; it's just that it's insanely hard and risky to do. It also makes it substantially harder to get investors to back you and accelerators to help you. These entities want to hedge their bets, and teams of founders almost always represent a safer investment. "At Beachwood Ventures, we're rather opposed to investing in single-founder companies—that's not to say we won't in circumstances where the founder is a repeat entrepreneur with past success, we just prefer a team with at least two founders," says Adam Callinan, entrepreneur and venture investor.†

Keep in mind that when we talk about founding teams, that doesn't mean that the group has to magically form around an idea for the company at a point in time. A single founder can certainly come up with an idea and then recruit others to join them as the idea is fleshed out and turned into a real business. That works, as long as the team is built early and around the nascent idea of the startup so that everyone is deeply involved in its creation, not just its day-to-day operation.

So, circling back to our question at the beginning of this chapter: Are you cut out to be a founder of a startup? Perhaps the real question you should ask yourself is "Are you cut out to be part of a founding team?"

The founding team is a group of founders working together at the inception of a new company. They have complimentary skills, knowledge, and even some behaviors; are all driven to make the startup a success; and work together well as a group.

The founding team is a group of founders working together at the inception of a new company. They have complimentary skills and knowledge, are all driven to make the startup a success, and work together well as a group.

Now that we've got you thinking about the idea of a founding team, we'll discuss the roles that successful founding teams play in the company.

Roles of the Founding Team

In the early stages of a startup, the founders do everything. Every day, the founding team works from scratch to raise money, to develop the product, to create visibility, and to sell the startup's wares. The amount of progress made is directly proportional to the work the founding group puts in. If the product has problems, they fix them. If there's a sales call, the founders do the talking. If there are no more Post-It Notes or coffee, one of the founders runs out to the store. Yeah, founders do everything.

Eventually, you'll hire employees to handle certain responsibilities; however, there are four critical areas the founding team must cover:

- Leading the business
- Creating a strong vision
- Setting the culture
- Building the startup team

Now, you may say, "Well, surely I could delegate some of those things to the employees I hire." Yes, that's possible, but we'd argue, at least initially, the founding team needs to own these responsibilities, and it's likely the founders will own them to some degree forever. Each responsibility is just as important as another.

Leading the Business

One of the first tests of any startup is who is in charge. When a group of founders comes together, this can sometimes be a significant challenge. Whether it's easy to choose a leader or not, you need to have one—preferably a good one!

For the purposes of this book, we assume one of the members of the founding team is the initial CEO of the company. Most often, that individual remains CEO for the life of the company, but sometimes one of the other founders takes that role, or a non-founder is brought in as the CEO by the founders and sometimes by the venture capitalists funding the company. Think about how Eric Schmidt was brought on by Google's founders and venture capitalists. Eventually, one of Google's founders, Larry Page, took over as CEO. And, recently, both founders left and another non-founder was promoted to CEO. The transitions and roles worked out well for them.

These days, such transitions are in the minority, and a member of the founding team, generally speaking, remains at the helm of the company. Of course, every company is different, but the view is that a founder has more passion and commitment to the business while understanding the problem space better.

We started with the discussion about the CEO because every team needs a leader. Note that *leader* is singular here. Very few successful startups have co-CEOs or share leadership in any area. When you choose to share leadership, two things happen. Every decision becomes excruciatingly difficult, and investors will run and hide when they see redundant roles in the company. Not only do organizations with co-CEOs frequently fail, but the fact that the team can't agree on a leader is a bright red flag about its ability to make difficult decisions.

Just say no to co-CEOs.

While the entire founding team is responsible for the successful creation and development of the fledgling company, their efforts are often channeled through the CEO. The CEO needs to be a strong leader who possesses a special skillset that includes excelling at communicating, negotiating, and selling the company's message and position internally and externally. The CEO will be the primary conduit for all the behind-the-scenes work of the founding team and, later, the expanded management team. Additionally, the CEO will be the primary lightning rod for the company when the road inevitably gets bumpy along the way and everyone wants to find someone to blame.

Vision and Direction

The CEO needs to rally the team in the direction of the team's collective vision for the future. A strong vision is one of a future market, not a market that was or is. Having a vision is about imagining a broad way to address an opportunity, including a new product, service, or technology, a marketing methodology, and a sales channel.

It's much more than a kernel of an idea. It's the path to where you want to go.

Not everyone on the founding team must be a visionary, but, together, the team needs to create a compelling vision for how to solve a problem in a unique way. Moreover, the team needs to coalesce behind that decision. While some of the founders may not have initially conceived of the vision, they need to own it like it was theirs and, in fact, it is. It's their company, too, after all.

The clear communication of the vision, both internally and externally, is almost as important as the vision itself. To be successful, a startup needs to explain and sell its vision to others—think investors, prospective employees, potential customers, and partners. While everyone contributes to this communication, the primary broadcaster of it is the CEO. The CEO is also responsible for enforcing the message that the rest of the team sends out to the world. It's critical that the CEO be good at this. So much rides on effectively communicating the startup's vision.

There's no mandate that every founder be a technical wizard. In the tech world, many people believe a founder has to be a technical person. But sometimes, the best founders aren't technical people; they just understand the market. They see the market need and a solution, and they're able to build a team, get funding, and lay the groundwork to build a great company.

Brian Chesky and Joe Gebbia, the founders of Airbnb, the home and room sharing/rental service, are great examples of this. Chesky and Gebbia, industrial designers by trade, were jobless after moving to San Francisco and couldn't afford their loft any longer. With a huge trade show in town, there were no hotel rooms available, so they decided to create a bed and breakfast in their own living room. Without any specific technological knowledge, they recognized a problem, found a solution, and Airbnb was born.

Cultural Leadership

The Business Dictionary defines the culture of a company as the values and behaviors that contribute to the unique social and psychological environment of an organization.[‡] In our opinion, that's too general a view. Culture guides the team in their everyday work. It's the foundation on which people make decisions and take actions. Think of culture as a framework for how you want someone in the company to do their job, make decisions, and behave without having to be told. The sum of all the decisions made and actions taken amounts to success or failure. As the company grows, the vast majority of actions and decisions are made by people outside the founding team, so it's critical to have the right culture in place before the team expands beyond the founders.

> As the company grows, the vast majority of actions and decisions are made by people outside the founding team, so it's critical to have the right culture in place before the team expands beyond the founders.

Creating a culture doesn't happen by sitting in a room and deciding what the company will be like. Culture comes from the core beliefs of the founders, how they act, and how they treat people. Molly Graham, who ran Culture and Employment Branding at Facebook, says that companies are built in the image of their founders and that 80 percent of a company's culture will be defined by its core leaders.** We couldn't agree more.

The culture will primarily mirror the founders and the founders' beliefs. That's not to say the company culture can't be guided by the founders in a literal way—building the culture into something they want it to be. But, it's unlikely that anyone can create a strong culture based on principles that aren't aligned with their core beliefs. That's also why you hear successful founders talk about having cultural alignment on their teams. Generally, the culture will reflect who the founders really are, their emotional styles, and how they act day in and day out.

The startup's culture will, specifically, grow from the actions and reactions that the founding team has, as well as how they treat people, how they communicate, how they conduct their business (hopefully honestly—no shady or underhanded practices), how quickly and easily they step in to help other employees, how they treat the company's customers, and what they reward people for. It's leading by example, but it's also by making strong statements and proving how the founders back those statements up with their actions. It's creating a set of key cultural points that everyone in the company steps into line with, and if they don't, then those people naturally get squeezed out of the organization because they just don't fit.

If, for example, the founding team is generally more open to conflict and public debates, then you can expect the culture to grow into one accepting of people who can thrive in a more argumentative environment. Timid individuals will likely not fit in. If the founding team is an introspective group that perhaps is more data-driven and focuses less on emotional debates, then you can expect that behavior to become part of the culture. Culture is self-reinforcing after it's established. The founding group will hire people that fit, then those people will hire others who are similar, and soon your culture is established.

Building the Startup Team

Startups are created by founders who come up with an idea and lay the initial groundwork for the company. Most often, it's the founders who get the early funding for the company, start serious product development, and perhaps even do the initial marketing and selling of the company's product. That said, one of the first and most important tasks for the founding group, after they have enough financial resources, is to hire people to fill in the holes in skills, capabilities, and other responsibilities that the founding team is too busy to complete.

Together, the founders and the early hires form the startup team.

This team, as a unit, should have a combined set of skills and characteristics to optimize the chances of the startup's success. No one person has all the capabilities that a startup needs, but a well-formed startup team can. The better rounded the startup team is, the greater the chances it has for success.

Hiring the right people is critical. For most companies, people are by far the company's greatest expense. Aside from actual cost, the opportunity cost of hiring the wrong person is huge. If the founding team hires the wrong person, someone they need to fire six months later, for example, for lack of cultural fit or skill, then it's not only the six months of salary they've sacrificed. More importantly, six or more (more because a replacement still needs to be hired, and that will take some time) months of progress are required in that particular area. That lost time can be crucial. Often, early-stage startups may only have one or two people in a particular area of the business. If it turns out that one of those people isn't a good fit, the company has sacrificed a lot of progress.

So, the founding team must hire people who have unique, additive skills to the organization and are a strong cultural fit. We know hiring is difficult. You have a tight schedule, and funding always seems to be running out. Doing this well is often a make-or-break opportunity for a startup.

> The startup team consists of the founding team plus the early hires of the startup—usually those that fill holes of skill, knowledge, or time of the founding team. Together, this group of people will be responsible for accelerating the company and optimizing its success.

***

If, after reading this, you decide that being a founder isn't the right path for you at this time, that's a more than reasonable conclusion. There are alternatives that you might be more interested in now that will help you experience the startup scene without being fully committed to it. You might consider becoming an early employee at a startup or, for even more flexibility, a late-stage startup (one that is already relatively successful, but is still small and nimble). Both will give you a taste of what the startup life is all about. If you enjoy it, you can become a founder in a startup later.

If you don't love being an entrepreneur, if this work doesn't sustain you deeply on a mental, emotional, and physical level, then you're likely to experience a lot of pain and misery on the path to starting a company.

You need to check your ego at the door and ask yourself, "Is it worth it?"

Chapter 4

Qualities of a Founder

Why care about the qualities that make up great founders? As we just discussed above, the commitment is long-term, so you want to make sure that your partners will be with you for the long haul. If their commitment is different, less than yours, you may run into real trouble when things take longer than you expect, which they always do. I (Rajat) have made this mistake countless times.

Over the years, I've picked wonderful people, but some weren't ready or wanting to be founders. Truthfully, they would have been excellent first employees rather than taking on the responsibility of being a founder. I also contributed to this by not setting the right expectations and creating a structure that didn't emphasize the qualities needed from a founder.

Without an intact founding team, at least early on, everything gets much harder. You don't have the team around you to help support your journey. Investors are curious about why your founding team is falling by the wayside, and employees and potential employees want to know if there is something wrong with the business.

The result was that several of these founders left the startups early on and went and found jobs at more stable companies where the stresses and uncertainty of building something from scratch wasn't there. In short, I put these people in the wrong role with the wrong expectations. If I would have had more discipline in selecting co-founders, in many cases, these individuals may still be at our company and we would have avoided the turmoil that comes with founders leaving the business.

It's More Than Just a Job

Now that we've covered the roles that the founding team needs to fill, we want to discuss some of the personal qualities we've consistently found in successful founders. As we said earlier, there are few people with all these characteristics, and the absence of one or more of them, aside from the combination of dedication and hard work, isn't likely to keep someone out of the running from being a founder. Still, the more qualities you see within yourself, the more likely that you'll find success.

It's important to keep in mind that being a founder is more than a job title; it's a way of life. It describes a particular type of person. Generally, people who succeed on this path have certain personality traits, characteristics, and habits, which we'll detail in this section.

Those traits include being insanely curious and passionate about what you're doing, embracing change for a new future, and with that future vision, being realistic about the opportunity and challenges you'll face. Also, knowing whether you're an introvert or extrovert is a critical part of understanding who you are as a founder. Finally, in this section, we want you to be aware of the need to embrace the paradoxical nature of day-to-day life as a founder. Making decisions in the face of conflicting data and priorities is a challenge and one that most founders struggle with.

Does this sound like you? Don't worry if it doesn't. A lot of hard work and an open mind can get you there.

Curiosity and Passion

Entrepreneurs see an opening in the market that needs to be explored well beyond the surface level. Most founders are insatiably curious about the reasons why a gap exists, why it hasn't already been filled, and what that says about their bid to solve that problem. As the business gets going, they continue to stay curious about how their company evolves. Founders ask questions like, "Why are customers purchasing, and why aren't they? Why is the business good at some things and not good at others? What causes the customer to disengage at a particular moment?"

A founder's curiosity needs to extend beyond just the company's products into how to run their business as well. Successful founders are students of the companies that have both succeeded and failed before them and quickly apply what they learn. They actively pursue contacts in their market and the entrepreneurial community to glean all the information they can to help improve their startup. It's a constant, iterative process that almost never feels like work because continuous change and improvement is what founders live for.

It's very hard to build a successful business if you aren't passionate, bordering on obsessive, about what you're doing and what you're selling. Passion is the driver that helps you—as a founder—ensure that tasks are done well. It's far too easy to do half the job or get to a point that it's "good enough." Passion for your company and your customers helps you to go the extra mile. It helps tie up loose ends; it ensures that your customer is tucked in, satisfied, and content; and it helps when you have that conversation with an employee who has incredible potential but isn't quite there yet.

When you find the passion in your business, it will help you to push harder, to push longer, to perfect more, and to deliver better. Without that curiosity and passion, the job is more difficult.

Visionary and Open-Mindedness

It is definitely easier for some people to see the big picture than it is for others. Having a clear vision of what you want to create for your customers and employees is an important characteristic to possess. But, rarely does that vision magically appear. It takes work and effort. It's relatively easy to come up with an idea to base your company on, but it takes a tremendous amount of work between founders to morph that idea into a crystal-clear vision.

Your idea is just your starting point. The founding team must have the patience and fortitude to develop a vision that a company can be built on. Many entrepreneurs equate their initial idea with a vision. This is a mistake. A vision needs to be much larger and a more complete version of the idea. Many founders find this frustrating since they just want to get going, but the ability to diligently work to create a vision alongside your other founders is an important characteristic of all successful founders.

Part of that effort requires that you can clearly define and promote your vision. This means being a good communicator and even evangelical at times. It also means you need to be open to the ideas and input of others and be willing to change and adapt your vision. If you are rigid and inflexible, your vision will ultimately suffer, as will your relationship with your co-founders and the customers who provide input to you along the way. As a founder, you need to lead and be vocal, but at the same time, you need to listen and follow.

Realistic

Despite having grand visions, great founders must also deal with reality. Managing the emotional highs and lows is difficult, but the founders who can be pragmatic and realistic about the ups and downs tend to have an easier time dealing with the daily rollercoaster ride of constant change that is a startup.

Realistic founders also can listen closely to what the market, customers, employees, and investors are saying. Many times, these groups will offer conflicting advice or messages, and at other times, the messages given aren't what they seem. Realistic founders have a knack for cutting through noise to extract the important information they can effectively use to advance their company.

Extrovert versus Introvert?

When you think of a typical founder, it's likely you picture someone who is outgoing, loud, brash, and aggressive. However, that's just a stereotype based on television shows and movies. Founders and entrepreneurs come in all shapes and sizes—from any gender, ethnicity, age, or education level. It's the complete startup team with its additive skills, talents, and traits that matters. If everyone were an extrovert, it would be hard to get anything done as a team. It's not only natural that some members of the team will be somewhat introverted; it's necessary.

There are roles in the startup team that are often assumed to be taken by extroverts; CEO, head of sales, and head of marketing spring to mind. Introverts are often perceived to take on areas, such as development, support, finance, and others. The truth isn't so cut and dried. We see introverts who are great CEOs and extroverts who are amazing development and finance leaders. In fact, we think extroverts who can act like an introvert and introverts who can be extroverted from time to time are at the core of some of the best teams.

We also believe there is another type of personality that doesn't fit completely within the scale of extroversion to introversion, and that is the influencer. It's actually less important for a founder to be extroverted than it is for them to have the ability to influence others. True leaders aren't necessarily extroverted, but they are strong influencers of others' thoughts, behaviors, and beliefs. Founders with strong influential skills often become the best leaders in startups, regardless of whether they are introverted or extroverted.

In the end, understanding the type of person you are and the types of people that are around you is very important when building your company. You want a complete startup team, so the better you understand yourself and the people around you, the better you can add the characteristics and skills the company needs to succeed.

Competitive

Entrepreneurs are competitive by nature. It's competitiveness that is usually part of the foundation of what drives them to start new companies in the first place. It's also a deep motivator that continues to stoke their internal fire when things get tough. That's not to say that the basis of competition is always with others. Sometimes, they are simply competitive with themselves, always trying to move their knowledge, careers, or lives forward at a fast pace.

While competitiveness is part of being a founder, it's something that needs to be carefully managed. If the drive to win affects behavior among the co-founders, things can get out of control. Who wants to work with a jerk who thinks they are better than everyone else, right? Being better or defeating another member of the founding team has no place in making a successful founding partnership. Instead, successful founders compete as a team and help each other grow personally and professionally to the benefit of the company.

Ability to Manage Paradoxes

As a founder, you'll find that you're consistently balancing paradoxes, i.e., situations that are self-contradictory and have no single resolution. You'll be barraged with choices without a clear path, and decisions that have to be made with little or even conflicting information. While you'll strive to make decisions that are simply black and white, almost none will fall into either category. You'll be hit with the problems of having limited tools at your disposal and being conflicted about which ones to use. And, oh yeah, the decisions and choices you make will probably be critical to the company's future.

Are we having fun yet?

There's a time to be passionate, almost dogmatic, about your vision, and then there's a time to be curious when something isn't working correctly. Maybe instead of pushing forward, you might have to step back and look into why something has stalled. There's a time to be a visionary, to know where you want to go, and then there's a time to be realistic about where you, the market, and your customers are. The reality is that maybe you need to take additional steps before you can make it to your vision. Rather than taking one giant leap, see and accept that there's a time to drive your team as a leader, and there's also a time to pull back and use a softer touch as a manager.

A founder must have the ability to be a good speaker and a good listener; be a believer in the company and its direction and be accepting of negative feedback; be a leader who drives the company forward and the manager who knows how to help a team execute on the details.

One paradox that all founders face is making decisions that involve short- and long-term trade-offs. Inevitably, founders find themselves in the position of choosing whether to take some action now or wait until a later date to do it. A simple example is delivering the first product to customers. Is the product complete enough? Is the quality high enough? Can enough units be manufactured?

It's easy to wait to make sure everything is in place and to work hard to make sure you're ahead on all counts. Yet, waiting leaves you open to more competition, and every day you wait, you spend money without making any money. A paradox. There is no one answer, and you won't know if your answer was right until it's too late to change it. Get comfortable with these, since you'll face them all the time. You'll get better at dealing with them through experience, and you'll be happy you have a startup team around you when you face them.

Habits of a Founder

By now, you should have a clearer idea of the personalities and qualities that make a successful founder. Another critical variable is the founder's basic habits. While it's normal for each founder to have different habits that work for them and their company, there's a baseline, a common core, that cuts across virtually all successful founders. You can still succeed without these habits, but your path will be more difficult.

As you read through the habits below, we suggest that if you find you're missing some, then make sure that others on the startup team have them. Or, ideally, you should start to work on developing these habits for yourself.

Ability to Prioritize

Do you know how to best use your time and how to focus on the most pressing objectives? Being able to ruthlessly prioritize tasks is immensely important—we may even go so far as to say *required*—to be successful. As a founder, you will always have a long list of personnel issues, direct responsibilities, and a myriad of things to do that will beg for your attention. But, you can never have two number-one priorities. A great skill that founders build is the ability to take a set of tasks and prioritize them. It's incredibly difficult when everything is important and needed right away, but building a constant habit of deciding what is most important is powerful.

There are many ways to think about what the most important thing to do is at any point in time. We like to always be thinking about what is going to move the business forward the most. Sometimes, that means undertaking a small task to keep a member of the team moving, or at other times, it may mean putting your head down and working on a large project that only you can do. Whatever it is, make sure you aggressively attack the concept of prioritizing what's most important to the business at all times.

This prioritization habit takes incredible discipline because it involves saying, at times, "not now" (or sometimes "not ever") to employees, customers, vendors, and investors. The benefits, though, are incredible. If you correctly prioritize your efforts, you will optimize how fast the company moves forward.

Persistence

You'll face resistance, challenges, and a seemingly insurmountable number of unexpected problems in your pursuit of starting and growing a company. Building a business is extremely hard, and you're told "no" more often than you can imagine. You'll also face obstacles again and again. Persistence is what will see you through these moments, and it's what will drive you to find the best path to a solution. Sometimes, the best path is to ask for help—and that's OK. We encourage you to seek help whenever you need it.

Other times, the best path is to let go or to find a way around or through obstacles. When you hit a barrier and the best path is to forge ahead, will you have the perseverance to push through? Will you have the determination to keep banging your head against the wall until you create a tiny crack that eventually breaks the barrier open? Do you have the strength to shake off defeats, learn from them, and keep the company evolving?

Being a founder is tough, and you'll need to draw on a well of persistence to keep going, no matter what you encounter.

Clear and Frequent Communication

Whether you're a one-man band or you have a team of people, whether you're an extrovert or an introvert, having clear and regular communication is a powerful habit to possess and develop. You'll need to clearly communicate through the written word and in conversations with your customers, teammates, vendors, investors, and others. Communication doesn't happen just once, it's an ongoing process. Successful founders have the ability to speak clearly, openly, and directly with the rest of the startup team and beyond.

Effective Execution

Execution is far more encompassing than a singular skill. But, it's worthy of mention here because the knowledge of its importance and the desire to do it correctly needs to be at the core of each individual on the startup team. The best ideas are useless without good execution. Well-executed mediocre ideas will beat poorly executed innovative ideas any day of the week.

Having an idea or dream about what the company can be one day isn't enough. You have to sit down, take action, and get the work done. You must follow through on hitting milestones to move the company forward. This means you need to break tasks down into bite-size chunks and either accomplish them yourself or, more importantly, through others on the team. Without the ability to execute, the startup won't go anywhere. It won't grow. It won't move. It won't be successful. But, with the ability to execute, paired with a clear vision, your team can be unstoppable.

Work Hard and Smart

Can you build a successful company by working from 9 to 5 and taking two-hour lunches? We suppose it's possible, but we've never seen it done. Taking a company from idea to a full-fledged operation takes hard work and lots of it.

We've all heard the idea that working smart trumps working hard. While we believe that working smart is always a good idea, we're great adherents to the idea that working smart simply opens up more hours in the day to work hard. It doesn't change the amount of time worked, just the quantity of work that's delivered in that amount of time.

No one is promoting one-hundred-hour workweeks here, but we question the chances of growing a thriving company by working only forty hours a week. Every founder needs to find their own sweet spot when it comes to the hours they put in, and, to be successful, they need to optimize those hours by working intelligently.

Sacrifices of a Founder

The idea of work–life balance, where someone might spend 50 percent of their time at the office and 50 percent of their time away from it, is a myth for a founder. Becoming a founder means that life will be unbalanced in favor of the company. Of course, it's important to carve out time and to do the right thing for family. Spending 100 percent of your mental, emotional, and physical energy on the company is unhealthy. But, founders don't have the same kind of flexibility with time that other career paths provide.

If this is your first time starting a company and you have a growing family, then it's likely you will find being a founder more difficult. As founders and parents, we often have to prioritize work over our children, spouses, families, friends, and important life events. We make these decisions daily, knowing we'll never get that time back with our loved ones.

As a founder, you'll sacrifice more than time and relationships. You'll also sacrifice money because in the beginning, you'll likely make very little of it. Then there's the stress that you'll experience. You'll feel the emotional strain and burden and the impact they have on your body more than you would if you were an employee. Research also suggests that the traits that make many entrepreneurs successful also make them more susceptible to strong feelings of depression, despair, hopelessness, worthlessness, loss of motivation, and suicidal thinking.*

And, it doesn't get easier as the company gets larger. Being responsible for a hundred people is more difficult than being responsible for three or four.

* * *

Have we scared you off from becoming a founder yet? That's not our intent, but we think it's important for any entrepreneur to know what they're getting themselves into. We love starting and building companies. This work, as challenging and frustrating as it is at times, fulfills us. It's more than a job; it's a lifestyle choice, albeit a difficult one, even when you love it.

Before you jump into being a founder, seriously consider whether you can make this your priority. Can you dedicate the required time, energy, and focus to building a company? Do you feel passionate about it? Can you handle the intense emotional swings from elation to despair? Are you willing to constantly make the effort to learn and grow?

The founding team will, and should, work harder than everyone else. The commitment to work hard is not only at the beginning, but throughout the life of the company. Of course, founders have a greater financial and emotional vested interest, so this shouldn't be a surprise.

Additionally, to be a founder is to make a long-term commitment to the company, a commitment that is open-ended.

While failed startups die relatively quickly, successful ones can take a long time to find a good financial exit. A significant part of what it means to be a founder and the commitment you must make is to embody specific roles and responsibilities, including operational and cultural leadership, vision and direction, and building a great extended team. This coupled with curiosity, passion, and pragmatism is powerful. And then, of course, you need to layer on great habits including working hard and smart, being communicative, breaking down walls through persistence, and focusing on the most important items to move the business forward.

Part II

Getting Off the Ground

Chapter 5

How Do I Know If My Idea Is Good or Not?

The first two startups I (Will) worked on were both founded on the belief that we knew the solution to a problem and that customers would see our solution, smack their palms to their foreheads, and beg us for an opportunity to pay us for it. However, it didn't work out that way, and, in fact, both companies failed.

But, by the time I was co-founding Viewlogic several years later, I saw the correlation between involving customers early in the process and the ultimate success of a startup. What I learned, in fact, was that the initial ideas we had for the company were only small kernels of the solutions that needed to be created to address the needs of the customer. There was actually no way for us to know what to do without involving the people who would use our products. It seems ridiculous to do it any other way now.

This lesson was permanently fixed in my memory when an early customer completely abandoned our product. They stopped using it and demanded their money back. We, of course, did everything to try to turn the situation around by addressing problems and offering support. Nothing worked.

After realizing that we were never going to turn the sale around, one of my co-founders basically begged the now ex-customer if we could fly across the country for a brief post-mortem meeting with them to better understand what we did wrong and how we could improve. It was brutal. The customer took us to task and didn't hold anything back. To say we learned a lot would be an understatement. One of those things is that I never wanted to get beaten up like that again.

At first, I thought this was an early-start phenomenon and that eventually, the intense level of customer interaction would fade. Over time, though, I realized that customer communication and focus was the most effective way to create success and happiness with the product and, in fact, all aspects of the business. Once I began thinking about how to market and sell the product before it was even completed, everything started to work synergistically. Everything started to become easier, including raising money.

An Idea Is Just an Idea

If you've made it to this section, you've decided you have what it takes to start a company—your motivation, habits, and qualities are, at least, all in the ballpark, or you're committed to working on them. In Part 2, we're going to talk about how to get started with building your company. We'll discuss your idea and the most important tasks to work on in making it a success, how to form your startup team, and how to create your corporate entity.

This first chapter of Part 2 will serve as an overview of what you need to explore and to prove as you start your new company, starting with your idea. We'll make the point that your idea is not, contrary to standard thinking, the cornerstone of your startup. In fact, you don't have to even have an idea when you start your company. You and your co-founders can do that as your first team project. Yeah, really.

Trust us, you won't be without ideas for long. You'll likely have an insane number of new ideas about various parts of your business as you start and build your new venture—ideas about the market, your solution, your customers, and the people you'll want to surround yourself with. You'll not only be thinking about the core of your idea, but also about how you'll get funding for it and even where you'll be located. For now, though, what we're referring to is that initial idea from which you're going to start.

It's the combination of the unsolved problem that you see in a market, and the solution you come up with to address the need created by that problem. It's the hole you're going to fill and what you will fill it with that we're talking about. Problems aren't sufficient to be the foundation of a company, even at the earliest formative stages, nor, conversely, are solutions without a real problem to be solved.

> Your idea is the combination of the unsolved problem that you see in a market and the solution you come up with to address the need created by that problem.

But first, let's get this out of the way.

We're sorry to say that it's highly unlikely you have a unique idea or will come up with one. The world is loaded with really smart and observant entrepreneurial people. Often, these people are already working on implementing an idea similar to yours and may even have funding to accelerate their progress.

The good news is, none of that really matters. Sure, if you're the one-hundredth person to have an idea to meet a need in a well-established market, it's probably not going to turn out well for you. In most cases, though, after you've refined your idea and built a highly differentiated business around it, you can still create a successful company.

You don't need a great idea. The secret is that it's not great ideas that make great companies—it's the excellent execution of a great business model that leads to success.

> It's not great ideas that make great companies—it's the excellent execution of a great business model that leads to success.

What do we mean by a business model? It's everything you do to make a successful company. It includes the market you're in to how you make potential customers aware of what you're offering to how you sell your product or service and, ultimately, to how you make money. It also includes how your company is funded and the team that you put together to make it all happen. It's this complete business model that needs to be strong and differentiated from the competition, not just the idea that starts the whole process off.

A business model is everything you do to make a successful company. It includes the market you're in to how you make potential customers aware of what you're offering to how you sell your product or service and, ultimately, to how you make money. It also includes how your company is funded and the team that you put together to make it all happen. It's this complete business model that needs to be strong and differentiated from the competition, not just the idea that starts the whole process off.

Here are a couple of well-known examples of the power of a solid business model.

Apple famously introduced its original iPod three years after the introduction of MP3 music players by a variety of other companies. By the time it came out, there were loads of good, solid, low-priced competitors, let alone an incumbent in Sony with their Walkman series of music players. Yet, as time has shown, Apple has been hugely successful in music players. (The iPhone has, of course, taken the mantel from the iPod.) It wasn't the fact that Apple had a better product idea that made them win; it was their vastly superior business model. They knew that without a platform for music distribution (aka iTunes) that created an entire music experience, their competitors were merely products without an ecosystem. That ecosystem was the part of Apple's winning business model—more important than the idea of a music player.

The companies with unique products and poor business models are not as well-known because, well, most of them have failed. But Kodak is a great example of a failed company.

The company that basically invented compact, portable photography also created digital photography. Kodak had the idea to create a digital camera and developed their first prototype in 1975. They then released their first model to the public in 1995, long before any other major player was in the market. Still, they couldn't make a success of it. Kodak's business model was all about supporting their film business, and thus, they struggled to make a successful play in digital photography. Kodak went bankrupt in 2012. Great ideas can't make it without good business models alongside of them.

So, it's best if you think of your idea as a starting point to building the business model—a first step in the journey of building your business. All you need in the beginning is an idea that's good enough and that solves a real problem. Don't worry if it's not all-encompassing at first. That will come later.

On your way to your complete business model, you'll first need to expand your idea and consider how you'll bring it to life. You'll answer questions like, "How will I turn my idea into a product? How will I get access to and excite customers? And, where will the idea lead me in the future?" You'll start to think not only about the core of your idea, but about the bigger, grander problem you're trying to solve and how your solution to it will morph over time. That vision, the future of your idea, will be what you test with early, potential customers, and ultimately, it will be the foundation of your business model.

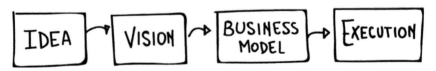

Diagram 1 The Path from Idea to Execution

Say you have an idea that the world needs cheap, disposable clothing. That's it, the core of your idea. It's your starting point.

From there, you expand it and consider how you'll develop it, get your initial prototypes created, determine who your early customers will be, and how you'll market and sell your product. You might even think about ways to manufacture it and, ultimately, make money from it. These considerations add a big factor to what happens to your idea over time. And, that's what turns your idea into a vision.

Of course, your vision needs to be tested before you move forward. Simply put, you don't have a clue if you can make disposable clothing, if anyone wants it, if you can get funding for it, or if you can even make money at it if you don't formalize it and test it first. That happens as you build your business model. The business model for your disposable clothing vision is what you execute to build your successful disposable clothing business.

As you turn your idea into a vision and then into your business model, it will morph and evolve. That is, as you can imagine, the point in formalizing the development of your business model—to make sure you've got it right. With each revision (which we refer to as an iteration), you'll make it a bit stronger, a bit better, and a bit more focused. It may even completely change as you understand your target customers and market better.

In this part of the book, we give you the framework for how to evaluate and expand your vision into a business model. As we'll discuss in more detail later, we strongly advise that you seek out guidance and feedback from other entrepreneurs, mentors, and advisors to help you make the right decisions along the way. Your startup team may be strong and well rounded, but there's nothing quite like the wisdom and knowledge of those who have done it before in making sure you're asking all the right questions.

Coming Up with Your Initial Idea

We often think of great companies as solely being founded on an idea that came to the founders in a moment of inspiration. Sometimes, it happens exactly like that, but often, great ideas come from a systematic discovery process in which the founders go out and find their idea. There's no need to wait around until an idea hits you. Go out and find the idea to base your company on right now. There are many ways of doing this, but here are three that we see frequently used:

1. Based on a personal need—yours or someone else's
2. Based on a customer need
3. Through research

Personal need. A personal need, or a passion, is when you or someone you know personally experiences a problem, either at work, home, or in some aspect of daily life, and you wish a solution existed to solve it. After doing some research, one of three things generally happen:

1. You find there are already good solutions to the problem that you didn't know existed.
2. Solutions exist, but they are inadequate, expensive, or difficult to procure.
3. Nothing exists that satisfies the need you had identified.

In the first case, you can go on and start searching for the kernel of another idea. It's almost never worth your effort to compete against established solutions without some fundamental and substantial advantage, and by substantial, we mean that your product is at least ten times better than the existing solution in terms of features, price, or availability. In the second and third cases, though, you may be inspired to create a new or improved solution.

Many businesses have been created because someone wanted something, be it a product or service, that didn't exist in the marketplace. To address that need, they came up with the idea and then built a company around it.

An example of turning a personal need into a business is Dollar Shave Club. The two founders were completely frustrated with the cost and difficulty of buying razors. After doing research, they discovered they could buy high-quality razors at a very low cost and distribute them via the web. Using catchy marketing and keeping their prices low (it's built into their name, after all), they established at least a tenfold improvement over existing solutions. They grew quickly and were acquired by Unilever in 2017 for about $1 billion.

Customer need. When you develop an idea through a customer need, it means you're in touch with a person or company that describes a problem to you or you deduce that there is a need from your interaction with them. Either they have an idea about how to address the problem that they share with you, or you come up with a solution yourself. In this instance, it isn't a personal pain point for you, but you realize it's a problem for a company or segment of the population. Often, the challenges of one company or group of people are the challenges of other people and companies as well, and potentially, it's an indication that there is a problem without a reasonable solution.

We regularly see businesses started by people who interact with a company in one capacity, say sales or consulting, only to learn about a serious challenge in another area of the company, like information technology or finance. Through these exchanges, entrepreneurs are often exposed to market opportunities and potential customers, which inspire them to conceive an idea to help solve the problem. They then will go and start a business around the solution.

When Salesforce.com was started in 1999, Mark Benioff, one of the company's founders and its CEO, was working at Oracle, the large database company. Benioff witnessed the difficulty Oracle's customers had installing new software, managing their data, and maintaining the computer systems required to run Oracle's solutions. Using this experience, he came up with the idea of supplying software as a service (now known as SaaS). In SaaS, the software runs on the supplier's servers—in this case, Salesforce's computers. Since Salesforce managed the hardware, software, and data for the customer, the customer only had to worry about their use of Salesforce's software over the internet. Benioff's work with Oracle's customers gave him insight into a new way of solving the problem, and he built a hugely successful company with that as his idea.

Through research. A third way you can generate ideas is through research. Not just the in-the-laboratory kind, but utilizing all the avenues available to you to gather information from every resource you have access to. We've seen people start businesses because they found an opportunity by reading technical journals, analyst reports, Federal Communication Commission reports, 10-K reports which the US Securities and Exchange Commission publishes annually, annual reports from companies, or virtually any other published material about companies and industries. Research can also take the form of in-person reconnaissance at conferences or trade shows to see what companies currently offer and to more generally learn about what's happening in a market.

When generating ideas through research, you don't necessarily interact with people, but rather, you use information that already exists to learn of opportunities. Unlike the first two ways to generate ideas, your thinking here is neither driven by personal need nor a specific customer desire. This doesn't mean that research is only a standalone method for coming up with ideas. You should use it to investigate the ideas you come up with through personal interactions, or those driven by the customer need that you identified as well.

A classic example of a successful company created through research is FedEx. Fred Smith, FedEx's founder, was doing research for a class in college when he came to the realization that rapidly increasing demand for consumer electronics products would create logistical nightmares for manufacturers and distributors. He recognized that the ability to get products into people's hands quickly would offer value that they would pay for. The rest, of course, is history.

Ideas are generated in many ways, so keep your eyes and ears open always. Just an informal conversation with someone in line at the coffee shop or elsewhere while going through your day-to-day routine can make you aware of new ideas and opportunities. Read everything you can—even the news can be a resource for opportunities. Attend conferences and conventions. Talk to your friends and family members. Ideas abound if you're paying attention. If you're at all entrepreneurial, you'll see opportunities everywhere.

*****

We can't emphasize enough how we feel that many in the entrepreneurial ecosystem have made too much about the value of an idea. Good ideas are great, but they're not sufficient for the success of a company. They're not nearly as important as the business model you build that'll be a roadmap for everything you do. A singular idea won't have nearly the impact that a high-quality founding team and the solid execution of a good business model will have on your startup. If you take care of those things first—make them a more important part of how you plan on building the company—then there are many ways for the team to come up with an idea or refine the idea that brought them together in the first place.

Opportunities abound, after all. There are a huge number of unmet customer and personal needs that can be addressed, and the list is always changing. New options will be available all the time. Basic research will further uncover ideas and markets that you didn't even know existed.

Don't get stuck thinking that you don't have a good-enough idea. After you get going, your initial idea will be a small part of your overall business.

Chapter 6

Vetting Your Vision

In the early 2000s, I (Rajat) had the idea to base a company on a web-based application service for small-to-medium sized businesses (SMBs). The idea was to package together all of the software that SMBs would need into one web-based portal. Think Microsoft Office, QuickBooks, contact management/lightweight CRM, and more, all in one spot that people could access via the web. Sounded like a no-brainer back in the early 2000s when there was so much complexity of implementing software.

As we began the process of researching the details, things began to unravel quickly. Not all of the customers wanted the same software. The solutions that we were including had never been hosted in the cloud at scale, not to mention that people barely knew what the cloud was at the time! The software partners we needed didn't have what is now known as SaaS business models, so they felt like we were cannibalizing their revenue and margins. And, back in the early 2000s, most SMBs didn't even use the web or internet for much business use other than email.

While I am sure that if we could have adjusted the vision in a number of ways, we could have potentially built a significant company, the chances for that particular vision working were about zero. So, luckily, we pulled the plug on the idea before we raised money and gave it a shot. We never formally founded the company. It was really tough to let go of the idea after investing so much time into it, but just think what would have happened if we would have sunk more time and money into it as well as having hired people, built the product, and more? Since that time, others have built successful companies based on similar ideas. If I had only iterated on this more, perhaps I could have built one of them.

In the end, though, I realized that this idea just wasn't going to work for me and how I was approaching the opportunity. Although painful, it was better to move on and find an idea that had a better chance. Over the years, I've had more than a few ideas die at this stage of the vetting loop, and rightfully so. It is painful when you put so much time and energy into it, but you want to be focused on ideas that have the best chances for success.

Refine, Refine, and Then Refine Some More

Once you have a nugget of an idea and have stretched it into your vision by thinking about how your product will evolve, you need to vet it. Vetting entails a thorough examination designed to refine your vision to make it stronger and better through iteration. Refining your vision takes a great deal of time and patience. The more you consider it, along with the market you're addressing, the more things will start to come together. Be patient with the process. It's a grind, but you need to go through it.

To start the vetting process, you'll need to start thinking about your ultimate business model. It's not sufficient to prove to yourself (and others) that you've discovered a problem that needs to be solved. You also need to prove that the solution you propose can be successful and that you can build a solid business around it. It's only by proving that you can build a company to back up your vision that you'll have a solid foundation for a startup.

Here's an example. You discover that many people are having trouble identifying why their electric bills seem so high. You think that a device that measures the electricity used by each appliance might be a perfect solution to their problem. You work with some smart friends on a solution to the problem by talking to potential customers and thinking through the implementation of the device you need.

As you start checking out the competition, though, you realize dozens of companies already offer solutions or have been funded to develop and sell one. You're clearly late to the market. But, while talking to potential customers, you recognize there's a similar problem with water usage. So, you pivot (a term frequently used when you modify or change your idea in a big way) and start building a business model around water consumption.

In this example, it was only by actively doing research, by going online and talking to many people, that you became aware that while your vision was good, it already had loads of competition. Checking out the market is one of the early parts of vetting your idea and vision. By following the process we outline in this chapter, you'll be able to get similar feedback and guidance at each step while you're refining your vision and business model.

Frequently, companies we work with skip the process of vetting their vision, and honestly, early in our careers, we did, too. Often, founders are so eager to get to the actual implementation and funding that they miss the value of the exercise. We get it. It's certainly not the fun part of building a company. But, unfortunately, it's hard to recover from most of the mistakes that occur when it's not followed—mistakes that tend to be deep and profound. Non-existing markets, missed competition, expensive sales channels, inability to hire the right people, customers with no budgets, lack of interested investors, and many other critical elements of building a company are all startup killers that can be avoided simply by spending time vetting your idea and business model.

We think those who have a deeper understanding of their markets, customers, competition, and the overall environment they plan to sell into will have a far greater chance of getting funding and, ultimately, succeeding as a company. Background research will help you to better understand the needs of your customers, the way to further refine your product to make their lives better, and the type of competition you'll be up against. The vetting exercise will also expose weaknesses in your vision. Sometimes, you'll come up with an idea to solve a problem, create an interesting marketing plan, and develop a strong sales plan. All of this is great. But, it may be meaningless or flawed until you can dig in to research, talk to customers and analysts, and conduct surveys or testing online to verify your beliefs. It's like being a scientist with a working hypothesis. Until you test your vision, you don't know if it will work. It isn't until you start experimenting that you can modify and change that hypothesis and, ultimately, find out if it is correct.

The groundwork you lay at this stage will be used later when you approach investors, hire people, price your offering, and actually build your product. In later chapters, we'll refer to this process frequently when we describe the best way to do these things. If you follow the process we outline here, many of these other efforts will become significantly easier.

During this process, you need to keep in mind that you'll be highly biased in your evaluation of the results at each step. This is natural since we all think our babies are the cutest. So, make sure the team is as critical as it can be along the way. Being your own toughest critic will lead to better results.

Diagram 2 is the vetting process for your vision and business model. While it includes steps similar to other startup method-ologies, we think its specific combination of actions are the keys to solid and successful business models.

Diagram 2   The Vetting Process for Your Vision and Business Model

We've talked about what a vision is. It's an extension of your idea, with both a problem and a solution, that gets you closer to how you'll eventually execute your plan. But, at this point, it's just a hypothesis—your starting point. The rest of the vetting process is about proving or disproving it. As you read through the steps, don't be surprised if you can't answer one of the questions positively. It's better to find problems now when they're easy to address than later when they're much harder. You might even discover that your original assumptions weren't valid, which might lead you to pivot. That's OK, too—better now than later. Remember, it's unlikely you'll exit this process after one iteration. For most of us, it takes many.

We're going to spend some time on the vetting process. In this chapter, we'll discuss how you get started. How you move from your vision to a solid model of a company that is fundable and has the best basis for success. Where do we begin? With your customers, of course!

Who Are Your Customers?

Seems like a basic question, right? Unfortunately, the answer isn't always so simple. Sometimes, errors in defining a target market are obvious, like when we run into entrepreneurs who describe their market as "everyone." Everyone is not the target market for anyone. More often, the errors in defining a target market are more complex, like discovering late in the process that the people who need or want your product can't afford it or that you underestimated your competitor's ability to change and adapt.

To minimize such errors, you need to clearly define your customer correctly at the beginning. The best way to do that is to go out and talk with as many prospective customers as you can. Every market is, of course, a bit different, but from our perspective, you should be thinking of talking to at least twenty to thirty potential customers to start with.

After you collect that feedback, use what you've learned to create a model of the target consumer of your product. We'd recommend you do this by creating a persona. A persona isn't an individual, but a composite of sets of problems, situations, needs, demographics, ages, backgrounds, company sizes, incomes, and geographies that are treated as if they were the characteristics of an actual prospective customer. Your persona might represent a company or a department within a company. The data you use to build one is taken from a combination of people you speak with (building a persona doesn't replace talking to potential customers), market research, and your best guess about the market, in general.

> A persona isn't an individual but a composite of sets of problems, situations, needs, demographics, ages, backgrounds, company sizes, incomes, and geographies that are treated as if they were the characteristics of an actual prospective customer.

The idea behind using a persona is to help you understand the needs of your market and to verify there are opportunities for your product to fulfill those needs.

This becomes especially clear when you enhance your persona by digging deeply to get very specific about their situation. Go beyond just who your target customer is, to why they'll buy your solution. Ask yourself why your target customers have the problem in the first place. What sorts of things do they do as a person or organization that contributes to them having that problem? What is it about them that makes other options not viable or undesirable? Why will they be willing to spend money to solve it? If they are part of an organization, what people in the organization feel the pain of the problem the most?

While it may seem counterintuitive, you should fight the urge to make the persona general in any way. You want to make it as specific as possible. Your persona should represent the smallest group of people that will be satisfied with your product, that is, small enough to tightly define your target but large enough to indicate that you have a solid business.

Why? Sometimes, just the process of tightly defining a customer makes you realize that few or even none really care about your product or even your vision. If you can't find a sufficient number of people who will buy what you're selling, you know that you need to refine your idea. If there is a reasonably sized group of people that fit the criteria, however, you know that your idea is providing real value (even if just to a small number of people). You have a group in which you may find early adopters to give you feedback and zealots who will promote your product to others.

Since we already used Dollar Shave Club as an example for how to create an idea for a startup, let's take a stab at the persona they likely built for their initial customers. The Dollar Shave Club Customer is:

- A man—while women can use the razors, of course, they are not the target of the advertising campaigns
- Living in the US—where advertising is focused
- Old enough to shave—over 18

- Young enough to respond to hip, whimsical advertising—primary target is under 40
- Budget-minded—annual income less than $150K
- Shaves with a blade (as opposed to an electric razor)—not making an effort to convert current electric users
- Shaves daily—cheap razors aren't as attractive to people who shave infrequently
- Likes the convenience of online ordering
- Likes the idea and already uses subscription delivery for many consumables
- Gets much of his product information online
- Consumes a lot of internet content and is likely to be exposed to more Dollar Shave Club advertising
- Is not primarily attracted to the latest and greatest technology in razors—cost and value are the selling points, not the number of blades or anti-friction strips

Using a persona like this, you can create a baseline for the smallest group of potential customers that will likely buy your product. This is the group that you should test your idea against. If you can find enough people who fit your persona and are prospects for your initial product, you know you're headed in the right direction.

Once you've established this baseline group, loosen one or two of your criteria in your persona and see how much you predict your market will grow. Any new customers will represent your immediate expansion opportunities beyond your core, initial customers. Perhaps that will require a more mature product or some additional features. To be successful, you'll naturally have to move beyond the small market you start with. The easier this can happen, the more potential your startup will have.

Make sure you test all your assumptions about your customer throughout this process. The best way to do this is to contact some of the people or companies on your short list—ones that helped you build your initial persona. You should think through your value proposition (detailed in the next section) before you do this, so you're not wasting anyone's time—theirs or yours. The more you know about your target customer, the better the rest of your business model will be.

Understanding the environment your target customer is currently in, including any alternatives they have to your solution, either from competitors or alternate solutions they've created themselves, is critical. If any alternatives they have are reasonable or inexpensive, you may even have trouble selling your solution to them.

> Understanding the environment your target customer is currently in, including any alternatives they have to your solution, either from competitors or alternate solutions they've created themselves, is critical.

Automotive manufacturers are superb at this. Each vehicle they decide to make has a specific persona being addressed. They consider economic, physical, and demographic preferences and even create color palettes, based on their research of their target customers. Car companies are large enough to target multiple personas with a range of vehicles, each one specifically created for a target market. As a startup, you can focus on just one.

Only when you develop a specific customer model, a persona, and can answer such questions will you know who your customer really is.

What Is Your Value Proposition?

The value proposition identifies the problem you're solving, how you solve it, and the benefits of your solution. The big assumption all new founders make is that someone, somewhere, is willing to pay for their idea. But, is that actually true? To arrive at the answer, you have to look at the entire picture. What will your customers gain when they use your product? Will it generate money for them? Will it reduce their expenses? Will it have entertainment value? Will it reduce work? You get the idea.

Take the online learning startup Skillshare as an example. Their value proposition is straightforward:

- Skillshare is an online learning community where anyone can discover, take, or even teach a class.
- Classes are taught by expert practitioners.
- There are classes for your career and for your passions.
- Learning is on demand. Take classes offline with your phone or tablet—on a plane, a subway, a park—wherever and whenever you learn best.
- Teach on Skillshare. Earn money. Share your expertise. Build your personal brand.

They address their two types of customers—those who want to learn and those who want to teach. For the former, they emphasize expertise, career advancement, and accessibility (on demand via mobile and offline), and, for the latter, the fact that experts can make money and build a brand. Their simple value proposition covers the key benefits they believe their customers are looking for and the value the customers will get by adopting Skillshare's solution.

Of course, Skillshare has quantified the value of what these benefits mean to their target customers. They've likely used this information to judge whether they are differentiated from their competition and have set the prices for their services accordingly.

Your value proposition will include everything the customer hears, sees, and experiences with respect to your offering, well beyond just the product delivered. This includes how the offering is marketed, its advertising and positioning, the packaging design, price, and even how it's sold.

We want to call out one specific instance of a problem that we feel is very important when it comes to considering your value proposition. It's a problem we run into all the time. If you're developing a product, is what you're proposing actually just a feature of a more expansive product? Or, if you're developing a service, is what you're creating substantial enough to stand on its own?

We've seen many companies iterate (which means they go through numerous versions or drafts) on their entire value proposition and business model only to realize very late that what they're building is not sufficient to solve a problem large enough that it makes enough of a difference to the customer. Their solution is simply not broad enough to warrant a customer's attention and money.

Unfortunately, this is often only discovered once the startup tries to get funding, and potential investors recognize the problem. As you can imagine, there is a lot of effort wasted only to get to the end of the process and find out you don't have a viable company. Truly understanding feedback from potential customers will make this problem clearer very early on, and it will save you from wasting time, energy, and resources that you could have spent pursuing a product that isn't viable.

There isn't just one way to create value with your product. You may have a new way of solving a problem, or perhaps your solution is better than what the customer currently uses to address their problem. Maybe your solution is cheaper than other alternatives, or you just might be able to offer better service or support. Given your target market, any one of these can create value as it's perceived by your customers.

***

Too many startups skip early planning in a rush to build product or get funding. It makes much more sense to vet your idea by answering some basic questions, as we've laid out in the vetting process. The starting point is with your customer who is the cornerstone of everything. Why will they be interested? Is there a need? What is the value of your product to them?

These are all critical questions that, when asked before you build your product and hire members of your extended team, can help you validate that you have, at the very least, a market for your idea. It's a major part of vetting your idea, but it's only the start. Most importantly, it sets you up for what may be the biggest test in the vetting process: whether your product or service addresses a real need or desire of that market.

Chapter 7

Product-Market Fit

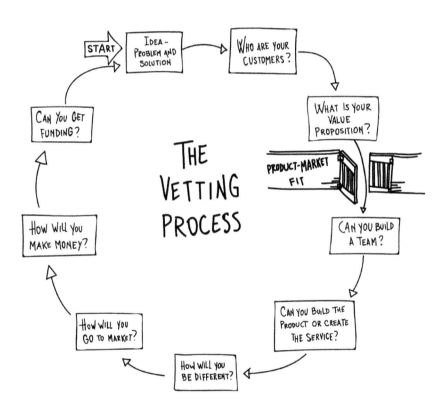

Several years ago, I (Will) was an investor and board member in Zipix. Zipix was a startup founded by a small team with a lot of business and technology experience. The company's core technology was in optimizing images and doing it in such an efficient manner that many images could be reduced in size by up to 50 percent and, more importantly, Zipix's algorithms ran fast and efficiently on any mobile device. This allowed cheaper phones to quickly process photos with less memory, a cheaper processor, and lower battery power. Who wouldn't want all that?

The company was founded with an early working prototype of the technology. So, it had the product. In determining if there was a market, the company realized that since it wasn't actually capturing the images, just processing them, we would have to partner with the providers of the photo app functionality on the device. At the time, we thought the best avenue was to work with the cell carriers (think AT&T, Verizon, Sprint, etc.). I know, right? This *sounds* ridiculous now, and it was then too.

What the company missed, myself included, was that the carriers are driven by a much different set of market criteria than the phone manufacturers. So, while we felt that Zipix was a clear win for the users of mobile devices, our customer and, therefore, our market was, in reality, the carriers.

The carriers liked the technology but wanted to control it tightly and wanted it for virtually nothing. Well, *actually* nothing. We didn't understand this at first, and by the time we realized it, we had invested too much time and money into the technology and our partnership to make it work with multiple carriers. We didn't have the capital to pivot and do things a different way.

If we had understood and vetted our product-market fit, perhaps Zipix would have turned out to be the success that we thought it would. Because we missed it, the company ultimately failed. Having a great product is a good start, but having solid product-market fit is what sets a company up for success.

The Gateway to Success: Product-Market Fit

After defining who your customers are and outlining your value proposition, you reach a critical gate in our vetting process. Is there product-market fit? Basically, the level of product-market fit is the extent to which a good market (many potential customers) is addressed with a product that meets that market's needs, wants, or desires. It's proof that both the problem *and* the solution have value to people.

And, when we say value, we mean monetary value. Will they pay for your solution to their problem? That is the ultimate test for product-market fit. Will enough potential customers described by your persona buy the solution you're offering?

One of the most high-profile lessons in product-market fit, or lack thereof, is Pets.com. Launched in 1998, Pets.com was created to sell pet food and accessories via the web, cutting out the middleman and aggressively cutting prices. Sounds like a winning strategy, right? Well, not so much at the time. As it turns out, while Pets.com assumed people wanted such a service, the market just wasn't ready for it. They had the product, but not a market interested in paying for it. No product-market fit. The company burned through over $300M in about two years and went public before it crashed. It just doesn't matter how innovative your solution is; if there is no market, you won't succeed.

The best way to test your product-market fit is to talk to actual, potential customers. Testing your concept like this takes guts, but it's the only way to learn whether you're on the right path with the right idea. Use your connections to gain access to people and offer to discount the product, give them early access to it, or provide a similar benefit in exchange for their time.

When you're not delivering a heavy sales pitch, people are often very open to sharing their time and frank opinions.

You'll want to discuss as much about the product as possible, even parts that you haven't thought a lot about yourself. You don't know what you don't know, after all, so getting the most feedback you can from others is critical to testing your offering. Remember that testing whether they will pay money in the amount you want for the solution you're offering them is a critical question.

The answer to the "How much would you pay for our solution?" question will tell you a lot about your product-market fit assumptions. The price the customers give you will almost never stand up once you're ready to sell the product, but you should be able to test whether you're in the same ballpark. For example, you might say to a target customer, "If the price was $150, would you buy this product, which I'll deliver by May 6?" For some customers, you should even go further and ask who else will have to agree to the purchase.

This is a tactic we regularly use, especially when it's early in the process of vetting an idea. By asking an excited customer about their willingness to purchase on the spot, you'll learn if there's legitimate interest in your idea and a desire to pay for it. A customer's readiness to move forward with purchasing your product sends a strong signal that you may have hit upon an idea you can build a business around. Even if they're reluctant, their reasons for not moving forward may be even more valuable than their early purchase.

Sometimes, a potential customer who has otherwise been excited about your solution may balk when the discussion of money comes up. Often, there's a gap between a person saying they like an idea and their willingness to pay for it by a set date. If this happens, test other price points and delivery dates to see how their reaction changes. Remember to remain completely open to the idea that you may have an interesting idea but not one that is worthy of the price you need to charge to be successful.

Many people will tell you that product-market fit is black or white. You either have 100 percent fit or you don't. We don't feel that way. Especially in your first loop through the vetting process, it's likely you'll find some fit, but it won't be complete. You may find that the group of potential customers that you add value to is small, or the problem you're addressing isn't big enough. This is completely normal, and because you're testing this early, you have plenty of time to fix it.

Markets are hard to change for any company and, as a startup, almost impossible. Obviously, products are easy to change before you actually build them. Rethink your value proposition to see if the persona you created will be more likely to buy a different product. Then, go out and test it again with real people. This is a loop, after all.

You should also consider the market you're targeting. Although attempting to change a market in a missionary fashion is close to impossible for an early startup, your idea might have more success in a different market completely.

Remember to be as critical as possible at this point. It's much easier to change now than to do it later. Keep in mind that product-market fit will also be one of the first things that investors look for. The more prepared you are to answer their questions and provide proof of solid product-market fit, the better off you'll be during the fundraising process.

As we said, we don't think you need to prove that there will be 100 percent adoption to move forward. There are still many steps in the vetting process. You might find that you can further refine your vision as you go through them to increase your product-market fit. You don't even need to find 100 percent adoption to ultimately exit the whole vetting process, either. As you grow and have additional resources (including funding), you'll be able to shape your product and message to address larger groups of customers. Still, you should establish a large enough group of potential customers at this point through iterating on your vision and value proposition to be able to convince yourself and others that there is a real market for what you're creating.

***

Lack of product-market fit is one of the biggest reasons that startups fail. Simply put, there has to be a large enough group of customers who both have a need and will purchase your product for the price you're asking for your company to be viable. Seems simple, right? Unfortunately, most startups don't even test for it—ever.

The time to understand product-market fit is *before* you build the product. How else will you understand the constraints that the product will be bounded by once you're selling it? If you find that during your testing for product-market fit that you can't make the product you originally dreamed of work, you should celebrate. Seriously!

You were going to find it out eventually and finding it out early makes it easy to loop back to the beginning and rework your idea before going forward. Ultimately, you'll have a better product with a much better chance of success.

Chapter 8

If You Build It, They Will Come

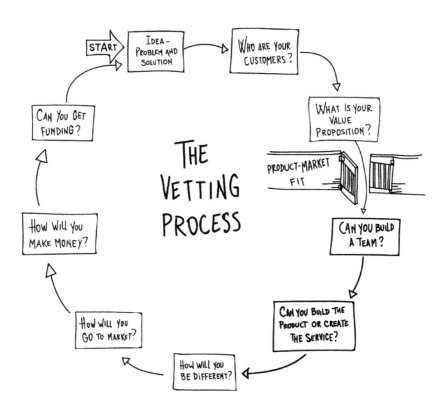

Our customers at JumpCloud kept asking us for help with updating their computer software. I (Rajat) couldn't figure out how to build this functionality along with everything else we were doing, so I decided to start a new company, called Automox, with a separate group of people.

Given that the concept was adjacent to what we were doing at JumpCloud, I really felt that we could reuse so much of the business model, go-to-market approach, and technical architecture that was already figured out. With all of the customer requests and calls we had done, we knew that there was a market need for the idea.

Once I made the decision to start the company, I also knew that I couldn't build the company myself because I was running JumpCloud. So, I searched for the right technical skillsets and hired a small team of people to help build the first prototype. We were able to get it to market, albeit lacking in a lot of functionality. That first prototype proved that we could eliminate a great deal of the technical risk in the business. And, with all of the customer conversations, we felt that the market risk was minimal.

After building that prototype, and with confidence that we could technically solve the problem, I embarked on building a team around the idea. We found a CEO and hired a number of leaders to join the team. This early team was able to take an early prototype and iterate with customer feedback in order to create a product that could be sold.

This process took over a year, but at the end of it, we knew that we had an idea that could be built and a team that was passionate about building a company around the concept.

Can You Build a Team?

Now that you've nailed the important product-market fit for your idea, we come to the next phase of the vetting loop where you determine if you can build it. And, by "it" we mean the company. *That* requires building the team and the product.

We've talked about the team before, and we'll continue to talk about it in detail in Chapter 12. However, as you consider whether your idea is worthy of building a business, you also need to consider whether you can build a team that can help you create a product and a company. A good, well-rounded team stacks the deck in your favor. It's hard to make up for it when you get this one wrong.

With respect to the business model for the specific business you're trying to build, you need to consider whether you have people who know how to lead the company and build the product you're proposing as well as the right people to market, sell, and support it.

The value of the startup team was outlined in Tracy Kidder's book *A Truck Full of Money*. In the book, Kidder outlines how Paul English, one of Kayak's (the online travel site) founders put together the key team to build the new company right at the beginning. The team included English's co-founder, who was previously a VP at Orbitz, and two others whom English had worked with previously—one with a broad view of the technology and the other a very strong operational person. English credits this team with the success of the company.

If you don't have access to the key personnel required to create the company you propose, it's likely nothing else will pass muster. Without the right people, getting funding for your startup will be particularly difficult, since it's seen as the most important factor in a company's success or failure. If, for example, your new company is going to write the next killer mobile app and no one on the team has ever done that, proving the rest of your business model becomes nearly impossible.

On the other hand, if your founding team covers almost everything you initially need, that's great. Still, take a look at this in each iteration of your vetting process. As you refine or change your idea along the way, you may find that your idea has morphed into an area where you no longer have the expertise or experience you need on the founding team. Again, that's OK, but you should look at adding any missing skills through your larger startup team as soon as possible. Make it part of your updated business model. Again, investors will focus on this, so you want to make sure you have it covered.

Can You Build the Product?

For your idea to be viable, you have to be able to build the product. To know whether this is possible, you need to answer important questions like, "Can the product be developed at the price the customer is willing to pay? Can you overcome any technical requirements that may arise? Can you adhere to all regulations and laws that apply to your product or market? Are there any relationships that you need to develop, say with a manufacturer or another company, to create your product?"

Obviously, the ability to deliver the product is tightly tied to finding a value proposition that works and building a team to deliver on it. Understanding what it is that you need to create and knowing if you have the experience or knowledge to do so goes a long way in proving to yourself and potential investors that you can deliver. As with all phases of the business model, the more data you have, the better off you'll be.

The most important rule of thumb here is to be as detailed as possible during this planning stage. If you have the right startup team, there should be enough experience within the group to make some reasonable estimates as to the effort and time required. If you're creating a software product, map out the development in as much detail as you can. If there is hardware involved, add manufacturing and production to the list.

Every product will have a different development process. Make sure you have the expertise in the startup team to reasonably model what needs to happen. One trick that we see successful startups use at this early stage is to focus their thinking on the likely bottlenecks in the process. Bottlenecks can occur, of course, in parts they already understand, but it's important to remember that bottlenecks are more likely to occur in the parts they don't understand. A completely new and unique product will likely have more unknowns than well-established ones. If you haven't developed something similar before, seek out guidance from others. Your efforts here will decrease risks substantially in the future.

Build a Prototype

If it's possible—and in most markets and with most startup products, it is—build a prototype. Try not to get sucked into loads of details, but get something working that you can show to prospective customers for feedback as soon as possible. The prototype should show off the compelling features that differentiate you from the alternatives your target customers have to solve their problem—especially versus your competition.

But beware. Don't get caught trying to design and develop your final product. Too many startups get stuck at this stage, wasting time, money, and market opportunity trying to make it perfect. Your first prototype will not be your last. As you refine your idea and your business model, it's quite likely you'll create new prototypes to validate with your market. Spending too much time on any iteration can be a killer.

A prototype is not the same as an MVP (minimum viable product).* An MVP is a minimal version of your complete product that demonstrates not only its functionality, but the entire user experience for the customer (we'll talk a lot about an MVP in Chapter 23). A prototype, on the other hand, is just a patched-together, working model of the core functionality of the product. It's merely proof that you can build the difficult parts of the product and show them to potential customers and investors.

For example, say you have a vision of a breakthrough coating for skis that reduces friction tenfold over current technologies. Your prototype may be a block of wood coated with your new material. The MVP, however, will have to be testable by potential customers and visible to your prospective investors. So, your MVP will have to at least take the form of a ski and be demonstrable in a skiing situation.

The bottom line is that building a prototype proves you can do what you say, and it's a springboard to getting feedback on your product and value proposition from your target customers.

Keep in mind that as you receive feedback from potential customers, their responses will tell you if you're getting close to delivering on your value proposition. But, if you're tempted to label the current iteration as final (a complete product) don't do it.

Ideally, you should plan to discard the prototype and apply everything you've learned as you vet your idea and business model during a new development stage. The reason for this is that the fast iteration that you've done to roll out successive products has likely created a tower of Babel that won't be sustainable over the long haul and probably isn't even a complete product. Of course, starting from scratch is insanely difficult psychologically. You'll be under huge time constraints, and you'll desperately want to move forward with what feels like a completed product. Instead, we recommend that as you pull it together and converge on the finish line with your prototype, you think about the sustainability of what you've created—what parts are solid and what needs work—and make sure you leave time to refine the weakest areas that you have.

Additionally, and we'll discuss this later in Part 4, the product you've been showing to your potential customers is not the MVP you'll want to deliver. Your MVP will include documentation, support, and integration with other solutions where necessary, along with many other items. Again, you don't need to worry about any of those items now. All you want is to give your target customers something to visualize, so you can see which areas of your product work and which ones need greater attention.

Discovering whether the product can be delivered can take a lot of work, but it demonstrates that you've thought through the process at a detailed level. You might be surprised at how many hurdles you run across when answering this question. Solving any challenges now will make building your product and company a lot easier down the road.

Sometimes, in the end, even the right team finds it impossible to build the product that fits all the constraints in the model. As we pointed out earlier in this chapter, if you come across insurmountable problems during this vision and business model vetting, or any phase, while iterating through your model, don't give up. Refine your idea and start the process again. You'll be much better off for it.

***

Most startups do the building first. Usually the product and then the team. This is almost comically backward. Not only with respect to the fact that the team should come first, but because you shouldn't be hiring your extended team or building your final product until you've determined product-market fit.

Building your first prototype will almost assuredly be more difficult than you think it will be. The more you understand the likely pitfalls you'll be subject to along the way, the more likely that you'll minimize your surprises. You won't eliminate them, but the more layers of the development onion you peel back, the more efficient your building process will be.

The most important of these is making sure you have the right team to build what you need. As we discuss many times throughout the book, the better the team, the easier everything goes. That's why asking yourself if you can build the team comes before asking yourself if you can build the product in the vetting loop.

Chapter 9

Your Market

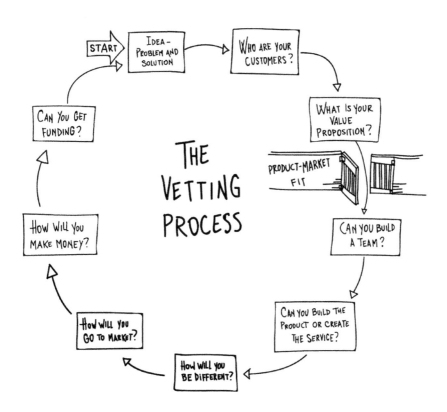

As an early investor in FitnessKeeper (the makers of the well-known Runkeeper app), I (Will) got to see the founding team turn their passion for running into one of the world's leading fitness trackers. While FitnessKeeper was relatively early to the market, they weren't the first ones to arrive. There were other running apps with established markets and a few general fitness apps that also tracked running. So, one of my first questions of the founders was: How are you going to differentiate Runkeeper?

Their answer was that the existing apps didn't offer everything that the runner needs. There was GPS tracking for sure. Both the specific running apps and the general purpose fitness apps had that. But, for example, there was no coaching or music playlist integration and these offered opportunities for their app. Their enthusiasm and what seemed like huge market potential convinced me to invest.

As the company grew, I kept asking the question about how the team would continue to differentiate the product and make it stand out from its competition. The founders never wavered—by focusing on the runner. They did that and their market share continued to grow. Even when, as a cyclist myself, I pressed for integration of specific tracking functions dedicated to cycling, they stood firm. I argued that by expanding their functionality, they could get access to a much larger market. But, they chose to stay the course and continued to put all of their energy into running.

As it turned out, they were right. It didn't take the team long to make Runkeeper the leading fitness app on mobile phones. The focus they had on their customer and their deep understanding of the needs of their market offered plenty of differentiation from other, competing products, even in what became a crowded market.

That focus-led differentiation became the core of their business and the basis for their huge success.

How Will You Be Different?

When you reach this point in the vetting loop, you've made some significant progress. You have product-market fit, and you've convinced yourself that you can build both the team and the product. The next part of testing your idea is determining how you'll be different from current solutions available to your target customer and how you'll get their attention.

Differentiating your product is a very important hurdle in creating a business that you can grow. Actually, we'd go so far as to say that differentiating your product is an absolute key to success. It's very hard to build a business if you don't have a discernible advantage. Additionally, it'll be unlikely you'll get funding or be able to sell your offering if it isn't highly differentiated.

If this makes you nervous, we have good news for you. Your advantage doesn't have to entirely come from the product you create. As we said earlier, the tendency for many founders is to focus on the uniqueness of their product, when in fact many great businesses have been built on the uniqueness of their approach to delivering a product to the customer—their whole business model. Often, we've witnessed companies with a mediocre product that have beaten a company in the marketplace with a stronger one, because the company with the mediocre product had a superior marketing campaign, sales approach, great support, or an innovative pricing model.

Use Diagram 3 to think about five major axes in which you can differentiate yourself aside from the pure uniqueness of your solution: price, quality, service, functionality, and focus. Even if there are other companies offering a solution like yours, you can still differentiate your product along one of these lines. A competitor might lead in one or two of the five areas, but it's difficult to lead in all of them. If, while discovering your value proposition you see an opening, you can excel in one of these dimensions to create the differentiation you need to succeed.

Diagram 3   The Five Major Axes of Differentiation

- Functionality: What your product does—the number and depth of features you offer.
- Service: What you provide beyond your product, including the level of support, training, and assistance you offer to your customers.
- Quality: The performance of your product with respect to errors, omissions, failures, and, ultimately, returns.
- Price: The price of your product relative to the rest of the market.
- Focus: Your focus on specific geographies, demographics, packaging, or delivery that can enhance your uniqueness.

Take Drybar, for example. Drybar is a hair-styling chain that solely offers "no cuts, no color, just blowouts." One might question whether their singular focus was differentiated enough in the crowded hair-care market to succeed. Yet, Drybar has grown to about $100 million in revenue and seventy stores in their first six years of operation. According to its founder, Alli Webb, "There's a secret sauce that is not easily duplicatable. There are a lot of copycats out there now, but they can't replicate the full Drybar experience."*

As Webb explains, consistency is key to Drybar's magic formula. A blowout looks the same whether it happens in San Francisco or Dallas. "Webb herself oversees a robust training program to ensure each stylist takes the same steps, down to the conversational pattern with clients and the direction of a brushstroke to achieve a certain look."†

Drybar differentiates itself through focus and consistency. Every salon looks high-end and similar to the others, regardless of its location. It's always comfortable, and it always delivers to the client's expectation. This is true differentiation in service.

As you consider what makes you unique, it's of course critical to take into account the competition. We repeatedly hear from new founders, "Oh, we don't have competitors." This is almost never true. Admittedly, it's challenging for inexperienced founders to conduct a rational and objective analysis osssf the competition. All startups should consider the fact there are always two incumbent competitors—companies selling alternative solutions and the status quo.

On the former, there are often companies that startups don't consider to be competitors because they aren't approaching the customer with a similar solution. Yet, they still may offer the same value proposition. Say, for an extreme example, your startup wants to offer a new printer technology that makes it easier for your target customer to get clean, sharp prints of documents. The obvious competition comes from other manufacturers of printers, but the more subtle yet real competition may come from fast-turnaround printing services that print documents offsite and deliver them quickly to your doorstep. Many founders ignore the substitute product or service. If an easier, better, or cheaper solution exists, then the customer will take it.

On the other point of competing with the status quo, change for customers often comes with difficulty. The larger the change, the more time and energy it takes people and companies to endorse it. Sometimes, it's just easier for your potential customers to do nothing or to set the acquisition of your solution as a low priority. The way things are is true competition, and the bigger the change the customer or company must make to adopt your solution to their problem, the greater the competition it creates. Inertia is always a competitor.

It's great if you're the only company supplying a solution to fill a market or customer need, but attaining that type of uniqueness is difficult. Think about everything that the customer needs—the entire business model—and you may find other differentiating opportunities.

How Will You Go-to-Market?

Go-to-market is a commonly used term that refers to all the things a company needs to do to get their product to market. A classic go-to-market plan encompasses many elements we've already discussed as part of the business model, but here, we'll use it to describe the methods you use to get your product into the customer's hands. That is, how you market, sell, and publicize it.

The goal of your go-to-market plan is to make the customer's experience great from the first moment they hear about your company and product through the time they have purchased and are using it. You should have a good feel for the best ways to approach the customer from your discussions with them about your value proposition. Use what you've learned during those discussions to help you find similar potential buyers and sell to them. Just as you did when refining your idea, you may change your strategy over time as you become better known, and the marketing and sales efforts change in efficiency.

The go-to-market plan should include who your target customer is, the best way to make them aware of your solution, the key messages that will resonate, and the method that they will use to purchase your product.

We'll be talking about sales and marketing in much more detail later in the book, but for now, here are some options to consider. In terms of marketing, you want to ask whether you will create demand through advertising, through direct contact with target customers, through references from others (like word of mouth or social media), through SEO (Search Engine Optimization) of your website, or through simply shouting from rooftops.

You also want to consider how you'll sell your product. Will you sell directly to customers (via direct, person-to-person sales or over the phone), through channels (via resellers or integrators), self-service (via the web), through retail outlets, or through some combination of these?

Dropbox, the cloud storage company, kicked off their growth to over four million users in less than two years with a great go-to-market strategy. Before they even launched their product, they started to market it to the world and built a community around it. They built their web presence and instituted a broad beta program to get early customer feedback. Then, once launched, they built virality into the product. To truly be useful, others needed to use it, too. Happy users got other people to adopt it. Combined with a product driven from customer feedback, the strategy created exponential growth. While not nearly the first product to market, Dropbox beat their competition with a better go-to-market plan that truly differentiated them in the eyes of their customers.

Understanding how you're going to reach customers and then sell your product to them is critical. Many startups find this a breaking point in their thinking about the business strategy. They can build a differentiated product, but they struggle to make potential users aware that it exists. Obviously, you need a way to get the product into the hands of your potential customers; otherwise, your startup will quickly fail. You may need to make another iteration on your business strategy if you're having a difficult time figuring out your go-to-market plan. Alternately, if you don't have specific marketing or sales expertise on your team, then you may need to grow your team or seek outside help.

***

The go-to-market portion of the vetting process helps you think more about your customers and how you will market and sell to them. As with many parts of your business, even after you exit the vetting loop, you'll likely make changes along the way to the strategies you create here. Still, it's important that you take this time, up-front, to think about how you'll differentiate and reach your customer.

Your potential investors will also ask many questions along these lines as you look for funding. After product-market fit, differentiation is a cornerstone of what investors are looking for when it comes to analyzing your likelihood of success. Understanding it and how you will reach customers makes a big part of your sales pitch to investors.

Chapter 10

Money—Getting It and Making It

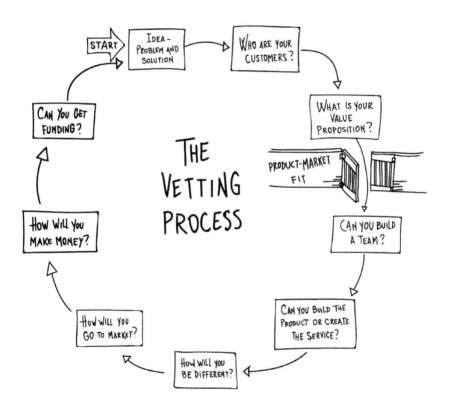

I (Will) invested in Harmonix Music Systems (the creators of epic games like *Rock Band* and *Guitar Hero* among many others) when they were just a fledgling startup out of MIT's Media Lab. It's not that I had a great vision for what they'd become.

I just liked the people and the underlying technology, which looked nothing like the future products that the company would produce.

Harmonix was one of those companies that appeared to most as an overnight success. In reality, success took over a decade to achieve. Before it became a unicorn, the company raised a lot of money through many equity offerings—that is, with the sale of shares in the company to a variety of institutional and angel investors. At times, it wasn't clear, at least to those of us investors on the periphery of the company, that the company would make it. Sometimes the capital seemed to arrive just in time to keep food on the teams' table.

Brilliantly, through multiple diving catches and many offerings, the company suffered very little dilution. The portion of the company that the founding team and the early investors had didn't decline much, as it ordinarily does through many rounds of funding. The company always communicated the value of what they were doing and earned higher valuations at each funding round.

The team accomplished this by nurturing investors along the way and taking money from partners—often referred to as strategic investments or partnerships—when it made sense. In these strategic relationships, the partner often got the rights to distribute Harmonix's products, sometimes on an exclusive basis. This increased the value to the partner and justified their investment at a higher valuation.

Such relationships also gave Harmonix a sales channel with bigger partners who had skin in the game and worked hard to make Harmonix successful. In turn, the relationship with a big-name company and subsequent sales by that company increased the valuation that Harmonix could demand in later funding rounds. Wash, rinse, repeat.

A big part of Harmonix's ultimate success came about because the company wisely used investment from multiple sources, some of which simultaneously increased their revenue and perception of success. It was a winning strategy for getting money and making money.

How Will You Make Money?

In the final portion of the vetting process, you'll analyze capital formation—how your company will get the capital it needs to be successful. Capital formation first involves raising funds to start the company, usually from outside sources. Later, the capital needed to grow and thrive comes from profitability.

When we talk about how much money you'll make, we mean much more than the revenue you'll collect from sales. We're also talking about your profit from operations: the difference between the revenue you collect and the cost to execute your entire business model. While both are important, it's obvious that profit will ultimately matter most.

Except for some slower-moving, bootstrapped startups, most startups will lose money until they gain momentum. Your costs will be higher than your revenue as you develop your product and start to deliver it to customers. There are some companies that run at a loss for a long period of time, and their investors support the loss because they feel the company is gaining critical momentum, or there are enough customers that will lead to revenue further down the road. There are even companies that continue to run at a loss as part of their strategy with the hope they will be acquired because of the size or quality of their customer base or for their technology.

Consider Amazon, which lost a tremendous amount of money in order to gain market share before it turned profitable many years after its founding. Or Uber and WeWork, which both continue to lose billions of dollars while they try to find profitable strategies and markets.

We'd urge you to initially come up with a model that brings you progressively to profitability, one where you can envision that your cash collections from revenue will pay for your efforts within a reasonable period of time. Once you become a solidly funded company, you can discuss the model going forward with your investors. If you have venture capitalists who stand behind you and encourage you to spend furiously, then that may be appropriate. It's just not wise to start off that way.

For now, you should think about whether your sale to the customer is a one-time event or whether your initial engagement will lead to more sales to that same customer. Perhaps you sell to one group in a large corporation and you expect your product or service to expand rapidly to other groups. We'll talk a lot more about selling models in Chapter 25.

Another factor to consider up front is whether you will sell your product or license it. If you sell your product, your customer owns it in perpetuity. If you license it, the customer pays for the use of the product for a specific length of time. When that time is over, they have to pay you for another license.

It's not only about how you want to do it, but what your potential customers prefer as a model. To remove obstacles to the sales process, it's best to sell your offering to the customer the way they want to buy it. Hopefully, you've determined some of this while discussing your value proposition with the customer as we mentioned earlier.

You'll be making many assumptions in this part of your business model planning. Try to gather as much information as possible to make sure your assumptions are based on real feedback from potential customers. Otherwise, it will be difficult to convince investors that you can pull off this critical part of your plan.

Can You Get Funding?

There are many factors involved with getting funding, the biggest of which is whether you have a solid business model (we'll discuss funding in detail in Part 3). Do your absolute best to make this happen because it will optimize your chances of getting funded. There are other factors, of course. The investors' perspective on whether it's the right time to fund what you're doing, and if you're the right team to build the company you propose are also huge factors. And sometimes, it depends on who you know—who can make the right connections for you, so you don't get lost in the sea of company pitches investors get daily.

While getting funding for your idea isn't a perfect test of your business model, it's a pretty good one. Venture capitalists and angels have seen a lot of business models and are great at pattern-matching, comparing your business model to that of others. While there are no universal business models, most of this pattern-matching will involve components either similar or identical to the business model we propose here. They will compare your position with respect to many of the points in this model with what they have previously seen. If your results match up with failures in their portfolio or that they have witnessed before, they will likely pass on an investment in your company. On the other hand, if your results match the pattern of successful portfolio companies, they are far more likely to be interested.

Are they looking for specific results? Sometimes, but that's not likely—at least not initially. They are more interested in the rigor you've used in building the business model. If your diligence and research can convince them there's a real market, there are solid potential customers, you have a strong value proposition, and you can execute on the product, they are far more likely to invest in you.

The best way to go about investigating whether you can get funding for your startup is to first approach experienced entrepreneurs who have previously raised multiple rounds of investment. They have, likely, spoken and presented to many of the venture capitalists (VCs) that you're interested in speaking with. Their experiences can help you test your thinking and give you a perspective for what VCs in your space or location are interested in. They've also probably learned a lot during their experiences, which can help shape your ideas and presentation.

You can then sample a few VCs that you have found in your research who are focused on the type of market and solution you offer. When you contact them, be sure to communicate that you are working on your idea and would like their input. Often, a VC or an associate at a venture capital firm will give you time and feedback so they stay on top of what's going on in the community and get a chance at investing when the time comes.

Don't be shy about asking whether your startup is something the venture capital firm would invest in. They won't commit, of course, but understanding why they would invest or not will help you form the rest of your business model.

While investors have the wisdom of having seen hundreds of companies before yours and involving potential investors as part of your business model, iteration is a good idea, but we'd recommend you don't do it too often. In our experience, as much as investors say they want to be part of your planning process, once they have a negative view of your plan or your ability to execute it, they'll often move on to look at one of the myriad of other companies that interest them. When they do this, they rarely come back with interest in your venture.

* * *

Capital formation—getting the money that a company needs to operate and grow—involves both raising money, initially, then making money, well, forever. Before you start building your enterprise, it's important to know how you will do both.

As we've discussed, iterating to understand these, as well as the other parts of the vetting loop, will be critical parts of your success. That doesn't mean they won't change as you grow and adapt, but getting a handle on these factors early will help you start your company as fast and effectively as possible.

With the completion of understanding how you will access capital, you've come full circle in the vetting process. You likely have a new or at least renewed vision, applying everything you've learned. If you don't, then you probably haven't truly tested your vision and expanded it through each stage of the process. As we said at the beginning of Chapter 6, almost no one iterates just once and many founding teams loop two or three times. The good news is you're probably converging on a greatly improved model at this point, and each subsequent iteration will become far easier.

If you've followed our approach so far, here are the results you should be seeing: You have potential customers you can talk to and get feedback from. You've thought about a refined value proposition and have a better handle on testing your product-market fit. You've already thought about funding and filling out your team, and most likely, you already have a prototype. Things will go much faster now.

But, if you've hit a place where you're stuck, where you realize there's no pathway for moving forward, you'll have to leave your idea behind and move to something else. This is to be expected and even a sign that you're doing everything right. It's time to pull the plug on your idea when you discover one or more of the following scenarios:

- If the product or service isn't resonating with customers.
- If the vision isn't compelling to outsiders.
- If you can't figure out how to bring the product to market in a cost-effective way that gives you a strong chance to make money in the long term.
- If you can't develop a revenue model that makes sense for the customer and for your company.

A key point to remember is that the worst thing you can do is to fall in love with your idea. When you go through this vetting process and iterate on your business model, you may arrive at the end only to realize that your best option is to let your idea go. Letting go of your idea can be difficult. When you pour yourself into something like a startup, it's hard to step away from the inspiration that started you down the path. Many people stay with a bad idea too long because they believe they're only one challenge away from pulling it off, while others fear they'll never come up with another idea as compelling.

In fact, it's a good thing to change, adapt, and even punt on an idea. You'll become a stronger team, you'll learn more, and your refined—or new—idea will be that much better and have an even greater chance at success.

Of course, you'll be anxious to get going and you may want to skip any further iterations. We encourage you to stick with it until you've learned what you can. So, how do you know when to exit the loop?

It's hard to come up with an objective measure of when to exit the vetting process. Still, if half of the twenty to thirty people we encouraged you to talk to are seriously interested in purchasing once you've completed everything you've proposed in your business model, that's a good indication you're ready to move on to execution.

Chapter 11
Getting Help

(Rajat) am going to make Will blush for a bit and talk about another mentor, Brad Feld. Will, Brad, and I all started working together when the two of them invested in my first company, NetGenesis.

I met Brad when he was guest lecturing a course I was taking at Sloan, the business school at MIT. I shared my idea for a new company with him, and he immediately wanted to help. Subsequently, he introduced me to Will and a number of other people in the Boston startup community.

I had been getting to know them both for several months before they decided to invest. A key reason that I wanted to take their money was not really because of the money but their expertise. I had never built a company, and both Will and Brad had experience and knew many of the pitfalls. More importantly, both Brad and Will were committed to help me grow and learn.

That commitment has now gone on for about 25 years. We've gone on to work together in many different ways (Will and I on this book!), and through it all, both of them have been supportive of me in my growth.

There's no doubt that I was fortunate to find two amazing mentors and build deep, lasting relationships that have spanned multiple decades. Thank you, Will and Brad!

Those same types of relationships are out there for each entrepreneur. They are hard to find, but there are experienced mentors who want to help entrepreneurs build their business.

Be selective, and find people that you can learn from—and make sure that you give them back something too!

Finding Mentors

Vetting your idea and building a business model can be tough. To help you think through the challenges and areas we've outlined in the previous chapters, we strongly advise that you find a mentor or two or more. The faster you can accumulate wisdom, the faster you'll turn your idea into a strong business. One of the first actions you can take when searching for a mentor is to look at the entrepreneurial ecosystem surrounding you. Many cities have specific outlets designed to help new founders grow and learn. These include mentorship groups, technology meetups, conferences, accelerators, city and state startup facilities, university-based mentorship programs, individual angel investors, and other entrepreneurs. Search online, and you'll find references for local events that'll get you started.

It really doesn't matter how you find people to help you, just that you do. Make sure that you trust them and that you enjoy being with them. That personal connection is one of the key differences between mediocre and great mentors. There are plenty of people out there, who will want to give you advice, but naturally, you want people who are invested in you as a person and your startup.

We see many founders struggle with the process of finding and retaining great mentors. While this can be an issue with the founders (lack of communication and poor listening skills destroy many would-be relationships) it's not always the founders' fault. Many people interested in helping aren't necessarily in it for the right reasons.

A red flag for you as a founder should be a mentor who seems to be accumulating advisory board positions or is pushing hard for equity to be a mentor far too early in the process of working together, usually within the first few meetings. On the other hand, as a founder, you should be sensitive to taking up too much of somebody's time without compensating them. If you like working with an advisor, figure out a way to make it worth their while, too. It doesn't take a lot, but being sensitive to it will help build a strong relationship.

Also, be aware that not all mentors and advisors are equal. There are some excellent ones and some poor ones. Often, there are people who just aren't qualified to give advice. Sometimes, they haven't done anything that gives them a reference point to offer any valid guidance. We've also found that some people who want to help are primarily in it to boost their own egos or to elevate themselves to a level in the startup community that they can use to further their own personal gains. Don't be shy about investigating what a prospective mentor has done. Ask and find out if they have experience that can be valuable to you. Consider whether they have succeeded in a way that you envision for yourself and your company. Just because they are available and may have a few gray hairs doesn't mean they can help your startup.

Although it should be self-evident to founders and mentors, we'll repeat this here: founders should be open to the advice of mentors but not in any way obligated to follow it. From our perspective, the best thing that can happen between a founder and mentor is an animated, deep discussion about a particularly important topic. Whether the advice is followed or not is secondary; it's really all about getting founders better informed about critical issues.

> The long and short of it is that founders should be open to the advice of mentors but not in any way obligated to follow it.

* * *

Talk to as many people as you can and try to recruit several advisors to help you at a deep level and who will meet with you regularly. These people have a lot to offer, and most of them are interested in sharing their hard-won knowledge with you. There is no way to grow faster than with the help of people who have been there already.

Chapter 12

Pulling the Founding Team Together

I (Rajat) made every mistake in the book when it came to building a founding team for my first company, NetGenesis. I started with five other co-founders. Yup, you read that right. There were six of us. That was a huge problem by itself, but it was compounded by the fact that none of us had started a company before.

I struggled with how to split up equity (who gets what percentage ownership of the company), get clarity on roles and responsibilities, and ultimately make decisions. Realistically, there wasn't any difference between us in a lot of ways. After all, none of us even had any formal work experience. Every member of the founding team was a smart, motivated individual, so we all had valuable contributions. As a peer, how could I tell people what they could and couldn't do?

I didn't understand what it meant to be a founder or a CEO. Primarily, I didn't do a good job on the critical task of building a team. It's important for a founding team to be aligned both personally and professionally. It takes tremendous leadership from the CEO to accomplish that, and in this case, I wasn't able to get everybody on the same page.

With all of us being equal and peers in my mind, I needed consensus to make decisions, which across six smart, opinionated founders, was difficult to come by. This impacted us on things like product strategy, hiring, and even from whom to raise money. In short, we all had differing opinions for just about everything, which meant that creating alignment was incredibly difficult.

Over time, the venture capitalists who had invested in the company realized I didn't know how to run the business, and they brought in a team of experienced executives to run it. The transition ended up ultimately working, and I learned so much that would help me in future startups. In the end, the company was able to go public and was subsequently acquired.

The Most Important Aspect of Your Startup Is the Founding Team

Often, the difference between winning and losing in the startup world can be directly traced to the founding team, which is the foundation of most successful ventures. A high-performing founding team can steer a company to success while a dysfunctional team can destroy it. Really, it's that critical. Employees, investors, customers, and other constituents all know this, too. It's why there is so much focus on the founding team.

In this chapter, as well as in Chapters 13 and 14, we'll focus on three major areas of building and operating a winning founding team. The first is picking the right people to join the team. The role of the founding team has specific requirements, and you'll want to make sure your team can cover all of them. Sometimes, you go out and find people to join your founding team, but most often, the team just comes together with the people you have around you. We'll walk you through how to handle both situations and how to optimize them for success.

Once you've set the founding team, the second major area you must address also happens to be one of the most critical and contentious conversations that you will likely have as a founder. That's how to split up the ownership in the company. This conversation rarely goes well or easily, but it's a necessary step. We'll show you how to use this difficult conversation to dig in to how each of the founders view themselves and the opportunity ahead. Yes, this conversation will challenge you and your co-founders, but it's also a valuable opportunity to set expectations with each other and ensure that you build accountability into your team right from the start.

Finally, we'll talk about optimizing how your founding team functions, including how to make the team more productive and effective. This is a topic that rarely gets talked about or gets the attention it deserves. Executive coaches know this all too well and encourage founding teams to spend time figuring out how to work well together. We'll show you how to make this happen and to get the most out of your founding team.

Building the Founding Team

Many founding teams are created as a matter of convenience. Typically, what happens is that someone has the flash of an idea and decides to start a company. Instead of taking the time to look at skill sets and personality matches, they choose people to join them who are most convenient—usually friends or co-workers. We often see new founders act impulsively as they rope in someone with specific skills to address an immediate need as the company is just starting out, or someone who other people suggest they need without really thinking about the future of the company or its long-term requirements. Unfortunately, we've done this ourselves, too.

As you can imagine, these situations rarely turn out well. Occasionally, you might get lucky, but most often, they lead to the most difficult problems you can have in a startup. Issues with the founding team are divisive, unproductive, and are an external red flag for everyone involved in or with the company.

Fortunately, most of these problems are avoidable if you understand the importance of the team aspect of the founders and you take the time to think through and be diligent about the process. Let's start by looking back at the skills and capabilities required in a founder.

Recap of the Founder Roles

As we discussed in Chapters 3 and 4, founders have specific roles that only they can play and embody in the company. These roles include leading the business, creating a strong vision from the kernel of an idea, setting the culture, and building the startup team. Here's a quick recap of those roles.

- **Leading the business.** Somebody on the founding team needs to take on the role of CEO and also be the person who drives the organization forward to execute on the vision.
- **Creating a strong vision.** The startup needs to know where it's going and why that vision of the future is compelling and interesting. The founding team needs to be able to crisply convey their vision to the extended startup team as well as external constituents.
- **Setting the culture.** The founding team is responsible for building the culture of the organization—the values and beliefs that underpin how the company operates, the decisions it makes, and the behaviors it rewards.

- **Building the startup team.** The founding team cannot build the company alone, but they are responsible for assembling a startup team that can. The additional people who expand the initial founding team should fit the mold of what the founding team values and requires in order to take the company to the next level.

Delegating any of these roles to other people in the organization can put the startup's long-term success at risk. Our advice is to cover your bases on these issues at the founding team level. Make sure the founding team has the skills to fill these roles. If they can't, you should think about expanding or changing the founding team.

> Make sure the founding team has the skills to fill all its roles. If they can't, you should think about expanding or changing the founding team.

A Word about Single-Founder Companies

Before we dive into the architecture of your founding team, we want to take an additional minute to once again dissuade you from starting a company alone.

As we discussed earlier, being a single founder of a company is tough, really tough. While success stories exist of solo entrepreneurs who have made it, we strongly advocate going the route of a founding team. You'll likely make better decisions with a diversity of opinions, get more work done faster, and have an easier time fundraising with a strong founding group. There is simply too much that needs to be done by founders and too many roles to cover for one person to do it effectively. Multiple founders create a greater margin for error for any startup. With the 90 percent failure rate we discussed earlier, wouldn't you want to increase your margin for error?

> We strongly advocate going the route of a founding team. There is simply too much that needs to be done by founders and too many roles to cover for one person to do it effectively.

In our experience, there are many investors, particularly venture capitalists and accelerators, who won't even talk with you if you're a single-founder company. Their bias comes from the fact that they have seen most of their single-founder investments go south. Not only does a team with multiple founders offer a broader set of skills that can help the startup succeed, they also have a built-in support system that makes them more resilient. Forgetting the fact that it's a bad choice practically to go it alone, you're not likely to get far down the path of building your company, since it's probably a nonstarter when it comes to financing.

If our words of caution aren't good enough for you, then take it from First Round Capital, a venture capital firm specializing in providing seed-stage funding to technology companies. First Round Capital's portfolio includes Uber, Blue Apron, and Warby Parker. The firm looked at its most successful deals in its first ten years of existence and found a number of reasons why the tech companies they invested in succeeded. One of those reasons? Multiple co-founders. "Startups with more than one founder performed 163 percent better and solo founders got seed rounds that were 25 percent lower than their peers."*

* * *

Choosing the right co-founders to build your startup is as much about talents and skill sets as it is about finding the right personality match. The relationship between co-founders is one of the special relationships you'll have in your life. It can (and likely will) also be one of the most difficult.

Building the right founding team is at least as critical as having a founding team in the first place.

Architecture of the Founding Team

The relationship between co-founders is special, but it's extraordinarily difficult to create and maintain. It's a high-stress relationship. The intense pressure of starting a new venture and then building momentum takes a toll on these relationships. Many, if not most, don't survive. On the other side, if you choose the right co-founders, then the bonds you form can last long after you've parted ways.

The co-founder relationship is a lot like a marriage. During the good times, you bond over shared successes. During the bad times, it will be emotionally taxing. Any co-founder you choose to partner with has to be someone who you can live with in this manner and who can live with you. When we say "live with," we mean it, because we guarantee that you'll spend more time with your co-founders than you will with your family. That's the nature of starting a company, becoming an entrepreneur, and doing it in tandem with other people.

Founding a company becomes a shared life experience, and the closeness you develop with your co-founders is hard to beat. If co-founders part ways—and it does happen—it's akin to experiencing a fiery, flaming divorce. A separation between co-founders also threatens the success of the company. According to Noam Wasserman, a professor at Harvard Business School who studied ten thousand founders for his book *The Founder's Dilemma*, 65 percent of high-potential startups fail because of founder conflicts.[†]

At the core of the co-founder relationship, there must be mutual trust and respect among all parties. What level of trust are we talking about here? Virtually the highest level of trust, one in which you can share your dreams and aspirations without fear. Yeah, you have my back in a foxhole kind of trust.

When you trust one another, then you can safely disagree and have open conversations. You'll need this as you debate the best course of action, timing, and a million other details that go into creating and launching a product and the actual company. Understanding the level of importance of a particular issue is also crucial. Creating contention on issues that aren't material isn't worth it in the end.

Respect is fundamental because founders need to present a united front to the rest of the company. You may disagree, and hopefully this happens behind closed doors, but you need to show the company one unified perspective and direction. Even better is when founders can debate in a healthy manner in front of their entire company. That shows tremendous strength and creates a model to dissect issues and create better outcomes for the rest of the company.

Truthfully, few relationships can withstand this level of intensity and commitment. As you look at possible co-founders, ask yourself if you'll be able to disagree with them without taking things personally. Ask yourself if you can put aside yesterday's argument to move it forward today. Ask yourself if you can put aside your anger or frustration with a co-founder to appear united in front of the startup team, your early core team, including founders, employees, and your extended advisors and board members.

Sometimes, this is profoundly difficult. Take the example of Twitter's founders, which plays out like a Hollywood movie. Some founders were never credited as such and were fired early on. The remaining three founders had various disagreements, and there was a coup where the original CEO was fired in favor of a professional CEO. Ultimately, the professional CEO was fired, and one of the original founders (different than the original founder/CEO) returned to run the company. Add in that the company became one of the most significant and influential companies in the world, and you have to wonder how hard it is for founding teams of average companies to make it.

Filling Gaps in the Founding Team

As you create your founding team, you'll want to carefully assess your ability and those of your co-founders to play the key roles that founders need to play. If you find a role that's more challenging for you to play, you may need another founder to step in and assume that role. You'll also want to evaluate how closely your views of each role align with your other founders. When founders have conflicting visions and viewpoints for what the roles should look like within the startup, that's an important sign of a lack of alignment.

Ideally, your co-founding team should fill in your weaknesses or the areas you're not interested in performing so that, together, you create a solid foundation to grow the company. For example, perhaps you don't love to be in front of people, evangelizing the vision of the business. It doesn't have to be you. It can be another member of the founding team. Or, say, for example, you aren't a great manager of people, but you're an outstanding individual contributor. The structure of the founding team should account for that. All the roles of the founding team need to be filled, but it's not required that each of the founders can do all of them.

As you reflect on your strengths and weaknesses, sometimes it isn't necessary to fill in your gaps with someone else if you're willing to work on them. When many entrepreneurs set their mind to accomplishing a task, like improving a skill, they do it. This may be you. You may find as you consider your weaknesses that you want to get better in an area. Instead of tapping someone on your founding team to fulfill that function, perhaps you commit to learning and improving. Maybe you haven't been externally facing and out in front of customers, partners, press, or analysts, but you are ready to take the next step in personal growth and learn how to become great at those facets of the business.

That's terrific, as long as you consciously work toward this goal by making the time for it. Often, when you work on a weakness, it isn't enjoyable, and you may be tempted to avoid it or put it off. Say, for example, you're somewhat introverted, but you recognize overcoming your discomfort in front of crowds is critical to becoming a great public speaker, which is an important role in making your startup successful. If you commit yourself to break through your fears and become that great public speaker, that's fantastic. But, if you can't, you need to find someone else who can fill that role.

Again, this is about being brutally honest about your strengths and weaknesses. If you question whether you'll make or have the time to work on a new skill set, then there's nothing wrong with seeking help from other sources, especially among your co-founders.

How to Find Co-founders

As you can tell, finding a co-founder for your startup is one of the most important decisions you will make when it comes to your new company. This is one of the few decisions that can truly make or break your company; that's how important it is. Finding the right co-founders can accelerate your startup enormously. You'll figure out vexing problems quicker, you'll get more work done, and you'll feed off the energy and alignment that you each have.

Our advice to you when trying to build your founding team is to slow down and choose wisely. You can avoid having to navigate through an unfortunate situation where you chose the wrong co-founder quickly just by stepping back, casting a large net, and taking your time to thoughtfully consider (a) what you and the company need in a co-founder, (b) whether you want and can closely work with that person on a daily basis, and even (c) where that person is located geographically.

> Our advice to you when trying to build your founding team is to slow down and choose wisely.

As investors and advisors to many companies, we're always worried when the founding team isn't colocated. It's one of those things that increases the chances for problems, especially with communication, team building, and decision-making. While in this book we make the assumption that founders are all at the same location, in today's global economy that may not always be true. We highly recommend having co-founders located in the same place. If you choose not to heed this advice, at least make sure you have worked closely with the co-founder, working remotely, before and that you both know each other well.

When looking for co-founders, start with current or previous co-workers and colleagues. Talk to mentors. Ask your friends. Consider the industry your company will be engaged in and go to meetup groups (events where people with common interests get together and share ideas) in your area, or attend conventions and conferences. Join industry associations, use professional social media networks such as LinkedIn or AngelList, and seek out accelerators (although these groups have a different mission, you can still find alignment with people of similar minds). In our experience, the best co-founders have been colleagues of colleagues.

In the end, it comes down to activating your network and telling people who you know and trust that you're looking to build your founding team. Share your idea and tell people about the strengths you're looking for in a co-founder and the needs of the company. If you've made an honest assessment of your weaknesses, and you know what gaps need to be filled for the company to succeed, then this list should come easily to you. When you're armed with a detailed description of your ideal co-founders, then this significantly drives your ability to activate your network for help. You'll get better leads on potential co-founders when you can say to people, "I have this idea for a company. Of the four things I need to optimize for success, I possess two of the capabilities. Now, I'm looking for one or two others who can bring in these other capabilities to round out my team."

If you plan on bringing on a co-founder you don't know, then consider working with them briefly first before you decide to go into business together. You'll want to do this carefully due to intellectual property and legal issues—you don't want to create a competitor right out of the chute—but it can be a great way to test the waters before jumping into a co-founder relationship without enough data. If you decide to test the relationship before committing, then put together the appropriate paperwork to protect yourself and your potential co-founder. At a minimum, set up a contractor relationship where it's clear that the work being done is owned by the company, and in exchange, there will be some compensation. That compensation can be in cash or even stock in the company. If you decide to pursue this path, you should quickly talk to a lawyer to create a legal agreement describing your relationship.

Co-founders versus First Hires

One mistake we've watched new entrepreneurs make, and one we've made, too, is having too few or too many co-founders. We've attended meetings as mentors and advisors where groups of nine co-founders have walked into a room. That's absurd and unnecessary. And, while there isn't a magic number, a good target for you to aim for is two to four founders per startup. Still, in founding teams with more than two people, a small subset, likely two, tend to take the lead.

It helps to understand the difference between a founder and a first hire. Just because someone is there in the beginning doesn't mean they're a founder. Conversely, a founder doesn't have to do everything to be called and viewed as a founder. Think of the founder as someone who is truly indispensable to the company's success. The company can't get built without their help. For employees, it's a job; for founders, it's a way of life.

> Think of the founder as someone who is truly indispensable to the company's success. The company can't get built without their help. For employees, it's a job; for founders, it's a way of life.

A co-founder is a peer with whom you can debate the problems and challenges in the business. Co-founders are people you believe are required for the company to succeed. If you're considering a co-founder, be prepared to make them equal in influence and impact on the organization.

Founders are generally significant owners in the company, so they should have a deeper level of commitment to the startup than first hires, while also being significant contributors. Founders know they will do whatever it takes for the startup to succeed.

The success of the idea and the company is something that will keep founders up at night and will be something that is constantly on their minds throughout the day. It's a burden they'll carry. First hires, although committed and dedicated, won't shoulder as much responsibility or feel that same level of dedication. Another way to differentiate founders versus early hires is to consider the impact on the company if a founder was lost. This is a good test because replacing a founder should be much harder, if not close to impossible.

Ideally, the founding team, as a group, will round out the weaknesses of each of the individual team members. As you separate a founder from a first hire, here's one of the questions you can ask, "Is the weakness that I'm looking to compliment fundamental to the success of the company?" For instance, if you bring someone onboard, knowing they'll be the visionary of the company, then they're likely a co-founder. But, if you're looking for someone to build your product, then it isn't a foregone conclusion that they're a founder. Also, if you're hiring someone, then by definition, they aren't a co-founder. You don't hire co-founders—you partner with them.

Co-founding with Friends, Family, or a Significant Other

The environment in a startup can be very difficult. Sure, before you have real customers and investors, the stress doesn't seem so bad. There are a lot of hours involved and demands on your time, but the sunk cost of your time and effort are the only things you're risking. When the company's fully operational, the risk feels tangible and the stress, at times, can be visceral. The strain on the founding team can be almost absurd.

Consider this if you're thinking of starting your new company with someone you really care about personally. Can your relationship stand up to the pressure and the demands of the roles you're performing? Do you want to even test that out? If you're thinking that it'll be no big deal and your relationship is plenty strong enough or that you'll always prioritize your relationship first, so it won't be a big deal, we encourage you to reevaluate.

We've seen countless personal relationships go bad when friends, family, and significant others are co-founders. In the end, the demands on founders are just too extreme for most relationships to stand up to. This is especially true when spouses are co-founders. To work like maniacs at your startup all day and then go home and try to create a life outside the startup is incredibly challenging. Think hard before you add this pressure to the load of other pressures that come up day-to-day in your new company.

***

The founding team is the most important team in the company in the earliest stages. Over time, that changes to some extent, but at the beginning, the team is relied upon for the company's success. Choosing your co-founders wisely and then working with them to build a strong and solid relationship between the founders is critical. Inevitably, there will be many difficult subjects and conversations that the founding team will need to deal with. Take time to build the relationship between you and your co-founders, and it will pay significant dividends.

Chapter 13

Equity Splits

As I (Rajat) mentioned in the last chapter, at NetGenesis we split ownership in the company equally. As you can imagine, this led to some people feeling that they were underappreciated relative to their contributions and then when two of the founders left, that their ownership was too much even with their shares being vested. Lesson learned: don't split it equally.

Of course, with my next companies we didn't split it equally, but the up-front conversations were a lot harder. It took much more time, tense discussions, and vulnerable moments to get to the other side where we had agreement and alignment on the equity splits. More than once, we've had a founder withdraw because they didn't believe that the ownership allocations were fair. Even I have walked away from projects where I didn't feel that my contributions were being valued fairly.

All in all, though, having that difficult conversation out in the open at an early stage in the company's life cycle is critical. A lingering feeling of unfairness in a founder's ownership is a recipe for disaster. Inevitably, it will lead to significant problems, and even the destruction of the company. My advice: have the conversation directly and continue it until everybody is on the same page.

Splitting the Pie

Once you've assembled your founding team, determining how to share ownership of a company is one of the most difficult conversations you'll have with your fellow founders. It's also a discussion that may happen multiple times throughout the life of a company. Often, complicating this conversation is the discussion of cash compensation and founders taking below-market salaries. The initial equity ownership conversation needs to cover these topics and create alignment in the founding team.

That's easier said than done.

Too often, we see founders choose the path of least resistance and opt for a simple solution: split the company equally. This is almost always a bad approach and frequently leads to major relationship issues down the road. It's far better for you and your co-founders to have the discussion, or debate, up front about who will get what percentage of the company and why. If you find your team heading down the path of equal ownership because it seems easier, then that may be a sign your team isn't able to discuss and hash out difficult issues—a major red flag for the future success of your company.

> Splitting the company equally is almost always a bad approach and frequently leads to major relationship issues down the road.

Founders aren't created equal. Someone always takes the lead and becomes the de facto, or elected, CEO. When founders objectively look at their team, they know deep down that some members will have a bigger impact than others on the relative success of the venture going forward. This is, of course, assuming they've done their due diligence in assessing each founder's strengths and weaknesses.

There are any number of approaches you can use to decide who gets what percentage ownership of the company. There is no right or wrong model to use, but as a team, you should agree on the one you want. Part of figuring out your model includes figuring out a structure, based on your philosophy for overall compensation to each founder, which can include equity, salary, and potential investment.

Before you figure out your structure, we advocate creating a few ground rules to help you get to a fair result. The following ground rules are some of the ones that we've used in the past and can help to give you an idea of the types of rules you should set, too.

- **Ground Rule 1. Separate the equity a founder receives for the role they play from any equity they receive because they are foregoing salary**—that is, equity they receive in exchange for taking a reduced salary. This approach creates clarity for what founders are being granted equity for. When you mix conversations, it becomes very difficult to understand what a person was given equity for and why. Separate them out, and it will make the conversation a lot easier both now and later.
- **Ground Rule 2. Consider how valuable the idea is versus the ongoing execution of the startup**—often, the idea is given too much credit as part of the equity discussion. Our view is that the idea holds relatively little value and shouldn't be credited with much, if any,

additional equity. The ability to execute your business plan, however, is worth much more.

- **Ground Rule 3. A cash investment into the company should be treated separately from founder equity**—similar to the first ground rule, if a founder puts in some cash to help the company initially, the value of the cash should be calculated separately from their value as a founder.

- **Ground Rule 4. Equity will be vested**—vesting is a process in which a person earns their equity over time. That means they must remain at the company and continue to contribute. If somebody doesn't work out, vesting is a mechanism that protects the other founders from giving somebody equity disproportionate to their contributions.

- **Ground Rule 5. Equity may be adjusted up or down based on contribution or role**—this may be more controversial and harder to implement, but founders play different roles over time, and building a startup is a long-term endeavor. If one of the founders turns into a shining star over time and adds far greater value than their anticipated contributions, it may be reasonable to reevaluate that person's equity relative to others.

After you've built some ground rules with your founders on how you will think about splitting the equity, you'll need to dive in and do it. Hopefully, these ground rules make it easier, but in general, we've found this is a difficult conversation regardless of the preparations. Keep in mind, no matter how much logic you use in splitting the equity, there is sure to be a negotiation that ensues.

One simple approach to splitting the pie is to try imagining the company four or five years in the future. Ask yourself, in this scenario, "Who from the co-founding team will have contributed the most to the company? What roles will each person be playing? How critical is that role to the success of the business?"

Another approach might be to structure the equity split around the role that each person is playing today and then figure out what that is worth relative to the other roles. Many positions in a startup have general equity ranges for the role that the person plays at an early stage. These are numbers that are widely available and can be validated through compensation surveys. You can find some compensation surveys online, but even better is to participate in one. To encourage you to do so, the resulting data is usually shared with you for free. Essentially, the idea is to pick a comparative benchmark and then allocate the appropriate amount of equity to each person to create relative ownership among the individuals.

Let's look at an example of a founding team with a CEO, VP of Engineering (VPE), lead developer, and business development person. This is a likely founding team for a technology startup. A simple model might be to give the CEO 50 percent of the equity, then the other 50 percent is split between the other three founders. The VPE gets half of the CEO's cut (25 percent). The lead developer gets two-thirds of the VPE (16.75 percent). And, the business development founder gets the remaining equity (8.25 percent). The key here is thinking about the relative value among the co-founders. Using that starting point, you can make adjustments based on standards in your specific market.

Remember, there is no perfect method to allocating equity to the co-founding team. The final decision is based on the value of each person in the context of the startup. That can be a harsh reality for some. For others who may not handle the conversation delicately, they can offend their fellow founders. More than a few companies have stalled at this stage, and many more have had founders depart because they've failed to navigate this difficult discussion.

Our best advice is to build in three fail-safes:

1. Vest every founder's equity over a long enough period of time, so each of you can see and experience each other's contributions. Four years is standard.
2. No vesting of equity should occur for a period of time to ensure that the founder doesn't leave or work out. We like to wait one year before the first shares vest, which is standard.
3. Be open to revisiting equity again, perhaps not every six months or each year, but maybe every couple of years.

There's another complicating matter with each founder's equity—salary. Many founders take little to no salary in the startup phase. That is, until the company gets a substantial investment or is generating enough profit to justify increasing salaries. The thought process is that often these founders should be compensated for what they are giving up with sweat equity.

This conversation gets complicated really fast.

Our advice is to make this conversation as mechanical as possible. Start by making the sweat equity conversation distinct and separate from the value the founder brings to the company through their skills and experience. Then make some simplifying assumptions about compensation. This, of course, depends upon how much cash you have available to pay each person. The key that you're trying to discern is who is taking a significant pay cut or not being compensated on a reasonable level relative to the other founders.

For example, if you've decided that all the founders will be paid $60,000, but one of the founders has opted to take no salary, what they have waived should be in the bucket of sweat equity, and they should be granted additional shares. Of course, a complicating factor with this strategy is how to value the shares in the first place. There are several sophisticated ways to address this, but we'd suggest that you keep it simple. Discuss what feels right among the founders, taking in everyone's thoughts on how to make the exchange. You'll find that you'll get to a reasonable answer because if the number of shares is too small, the founder foregoing his or her salary will opt to just take cash. If the number of shares is too large, the rest of the founders won't want to give up the equity. It's a balance, but if everyone is reasonable, it can be worked out fairly easily.

As a baseline, we suggest you look into what you believe will be the future value of the equity you grant, in exchange for giving up salary. When you're starting out, the value of cash is very high. If you only think of that point in time, you may value the cash too highly. By considering the value of foregoing cash compensation during the first year of the company's operation, instead of its first few months, you may get a better perspective on the real value of the exchange.

We also suggest that if somebody makes a cash contribution or investment into the company at this early stage, then you'll want to handle that similarly to people forgoing a salary. You have the same issue here, which is how to value the shares.

We'd suggest sitting down and working through what you think is fair. The same ground rules from before will apply.

Whatever path you choose, make sure the founder's investment is a separate conversation from the equity that person receives for their role as a founder, and handle it in a distinct manner with clear value parameters for the cash that is being invested. Lumping these discussions together isn't fair to the company or the founder, as you're almost sure to under- or overvalue one of the components when they are combined.

Know that whatever factors you initially settle on and agree to, the conversation about ownership will happen again over time. Equity is not a one-and-done discussion. To think that in the beginning you'll set equity and never address it again over two, three, five, eight, or ten years is impractical. People will think about it through the life of the business, and it's a more fluid, dynamic aspect of the business than people want to admit.

It's challenging because sometimes you'll set equity too low, and you'll need to revisit it to give someone more for the value they've brought and continue to bring to the company. Other times, you'll set equity too high, and you'll need to reduce it (and if you thought the first equity conversation was difficult, this one will be even more difficult). Either way, setting the tone among your founding team that the equity conversation will be revisited occasionally will set you up for success.

At the end of the discussion, everyone has to leave at peace with whatever was decided at that point in time. If things materially change, then so will the equity, but for now everybody should be good. If you can't walk away in peace, then you either have to keep the conversation going, or you have to walk away from the venture. The worst thing you can do is kick the can down the road because this issue will never go away, and it will only get harder to address as the months pass.

***

Dividing the ownership of the company up between the co-founding team is one of the hardest things many startups deal with. In fact, many new companies don't survive this process, with some teams breaking up immediately and some later with festering resentment from how the equity was divided. Some founders fear this process so much that they refuse to bring on co-founders just so they can avoid this discussion.

Don't let this fundamental step in startup building destroy your baby. Successful founding teams take this challenge head-on, putting everyone's cards on the table and working through what is a logical division of ownership. The team will be better because of the effort you apply here, and an equity split that makes sense will telegraph to investors that you have your acts together. And, always remember that you can adjust things going forward. At least to some extent.

Hopefully, the guidelines in this chapter will get you close and help the team pull together around the process. Keep in mind, as with much of your founding journey, qualified mentors and advisors can help you a lot here. But, that's not to say that just anyone can. As we discussed in Chapter 11 and earlier in the book, finding the right mentors with applicable experience is not only practically helpful, but a big emotional support as well. They can tell you what worked for them, what is commonly seen, and what has failed. You may decide to go a different route, but knowing how others have dealt with the challenge is a great baseline for making your own choice.

Chapter 14

Operating as a Founding Team

When we started Viewlogic, I (Will) was in my early twenties and a bit rough around the edges. Even though I had worked for two other startups—one my own—and a large computer company before that, I really didn't have a lot of experience working in close teams. I wasn't a particularly good communicator, and I didn't have an off switch, so I drove hard all the time. Come to think of it, I was sort of an asshole.

Of the five founders of Viewlogic, three of the team were married and had kids. As one of the singletons, I didn't have many obligations outside of the startup, so I pretty much worked around the clock. At times, I didn't understand why everyone wasn't working as many hours. The entire founding team was working incredibly hard, for sure, but when it came to 3 a.m. coding, I wondered why I was alone. At times, this attitude worked its way out of my subconscious and through my vocal cords.

While I began to understand the complexities of the situation fairly early, it wasn't until I had kids myself some years later that I really got it. It was then that I realized that my married co-founders were actually sacrificing more than I was, not less. They were exhibiting more dedication and, in fact, more effort than me to help the company succeed.

As a team, we had discussed the amount of time and energy it would take to make Viewlogic successful. And, as with most teams, we woefully underestimated every factor, including the costs to each person and their respective families. While I didn't have the context to fully understand what my co-founders had to go through, in retrospect, I wish we had spent more time on this. I think it would have helped all of us. At the very least, I might have been less of an asshole.

The Complexity of Founding Teams

It's the founders who will drive the company forward. You're the ones who will take a concept, make it a reality, and then build a company around it. Everything starts with the founding team, and if it's dysfunctional, if it doesn't work collectively, if it's misaligned on priorities or the direction of the company, and if it doesn't know how to work together, then your company will be dysfunctional, too.

It takes ongoing work and open communication with your co-founders to ensure the group remains healthy, effective, and productive. This is true even if you believe you're aligned and headed toward a common goal. Things change rapidly, and it's going to take daily check-ins, weekly get-togethers, and dedicated time as a team to make sure everyone is working to achieve the same thing. As a founder, it'll take work and attention to understand how best to manage your founding team. It also takes courage, humility, and vulnerability to make a great founding team.

In this section, we'll discuss how you can build a well-functioning team. You'll need to be clear about expectations, build alignment around the core components of the strategy, create a model for how to work through difficult issues, leverage advisors and coaches if you can, and then if you can't make it work, have a method to part ways without killing the company.

Building Alignment

Misaligned founders can be destructive to a business. Not only will the organization do different things based on differing inputs, it will create factions where some parts of the organization back one founder's vision and some back another's vision. Some of this can be unintentional with slightly differing visions and priorities, and sometimes this can be done with malice. Whatever the intention, it's one of the fastest ways to destroy an organization and kill your chances of success.

Creating alignment around a business is never easy; however, there are some ways to do it.

Personal Alignment

First, you'll want to create personal alignment on what each of you wants out of the experience by talking about each founder's personal motivations. If there are wildly differing personal agendas, it will show up later. Say that one person wants to live on a market salary while another wants to risk it all for the big payoff—if this is the case, then conflicting personal motivations may eventually cause serious friction among you and your co-founders. You don't have to each want the same things personally, but you do need to know and respect everyone's position and point of view. And, you have to make sure that you can coexist peacefully and productively if your wants are different.

Another common personal alignment issue occurs when the founders are at different stages of their lives. One founder may be married with kids and prefers to be home to have dinner and to spend quality time with the family. Another founder may be unmarried and without significant outside personal commitments, so they are focused on working around the clock. Differences in founder expectations can generate an opening for friction among the founding team, but it also represents an opportunity to figure out how to work better together.

Perhaps going home early works well for the founder with a family because they can then spend more time on the business later at night, or maybe they get into the office very early in the morning. Or, perhaps the two founders are incredibly focused and productive during their time at work, and that balances out the different schedules. Whatever it is, spend time working through and talking about each founder's personal goals and motivations. Your personal goals don't have to be identical, but they do need to be compatible.

Business Alignment

After you've created a shared understanding on the personal side, you need to tackle the business side as well. The best place to start is by addressing important issues, such as the vision, strategy, value proposition, and differentiators. These are all critical aspects of any business. An in-depth discussion will help clarify what each founder believes about the business. After you've discussed them, the team should be aligned in each of these areas.

Even with alignment on these items, there can still be misalignment on the execution of the vision and strategy.

The positive aspect is that the big-picture alignment is there, but there will be misfires on the details if it's not carried all the way through to the execution. The way to address this is to be clear on the company's, and each founder's, annual and quarterly goals. Those goals and objectives should be discussed and agreed upon by the founders and even the extended startup team. By agreeing on the details of what each person is doing, you'll create consistency from the overarching vision down to the tactical details of what people are working on daily. That's a formula for strong alignment and for getting everybody moving in the same direction.

At most companies, it's the CEO who is responsible for getting everybody moving in the same direction by creating the same shared vision and a path to execution across the company. In the early days of a startup, that responsibility falls onto the founding team. Companies with a strong shared vision can quickly move mountains because everyone is pointed in the same direction, working toward the same goal, and moving at the same cadence. If you can make this happen, it's a work of art and is something to be very proud of.

It takes tremendous effort and work to get this started and to continue the momentum and focus over the course of starting and growing your business. True alignment often means checking your egos at the door and being open and honest about where you are really at. It also takes compromise. Being steadfast on every issue isn't going to create the alignment that you and the team need. As we all know, building deep relationships isn't easy and can make us feel quite vulnerable. However, if you can succeed at gaining alignment with your co-founders, then your business will be substantially better as a result.

Setting Expectations

In the beginning, one of the best things you can do as a team is to set expectations for the division of labor, definition of responsibilities, and decision-making. Successful founders determine what the company needs, choose the people from the founding team who are best suited for each task, and acknowledge who makes decisions for specific issues. To do this, they look at each person's strengths, and they build off of those. Then they look at everyone's weaknesses and determine how to fill the gaps.

This process is all about setting expectations of who is responsible for what actions the company takes. We'd suggest rather than making this an ad hoc exercise or something that just naturally evolves that you make it an explicit conversation and write everything down. It doesn't matter how you divide responsibilities or set expectations, but it's important that everyone is in agreement with the divisions and the expectations. We've included some expectations for the various roles that a founder may play. For simplicity, we assume that different people take on different roles, but in practice, some of these roles are shared. You'll want to take time and make sure that each person's founding role is defined, too. Here's an example to help you get started.

- **Role: Leading the Business**
  - Clear overall objectives for the team and individuals.
  - Appropriate delegated decision-making authority and responsibility.
  - Clear tasking of all individuals.
- **Role: Vision for the Company**
  - Turning the initial idea into a broad vision for the company and its future.

- ○ Clear definition of company/product vision and road-map.
  - ○ Ability to understand market trends, competitive solutions, and customer needs to build a unique offering.
- **Role: Cultural Leader**
  - ○ Embody the culture as agreed upon.
  - ○ Define a clear culture, including values and principles.
  - ○ Ensure that the team follows the described culture.
- **Role: Building the Startup Team**
  - ○ Clear definition of the requirements people must meet to join the team.
  - ○ Create a process to ensure that only the right people make it onto the team.
  - ○ Consistent discussion with individuals about their jobs and careers.

These are just some ideas as you build the expectations for your founding team. We'd also suggest that you and your co-founders set expectations of what it means to be a founder in your organization. This should be handled by building consensus with the founding team about the meaning as we described previously.

There's nothing like a crisp set of expectations agreed upon by the founding team to drive the behavior and results that the group is looking for. Remember that these expectations change over time, so keep the conversation going and free-flowing among the co-founders as you continue to develop the company.

Leveraging Emotions

Founders differ in many ways, but one thing they all have to share is passion for the business. This is a good thing, because your passion to succeed and grow a business can carry you through during times of uncertainty and distress. But, strong passion can also evoke strong emotion, and strong emotions that aren't controlled can derail many co-founding teams and companies.

We've already discussed this concept in terms of the culture that you want and in terms of how a leader's feelings get magnified throughout the organization. The same is true among co-founders. It's easy to get swept away in the intense excitement or despair of a moment. Inevitably, you'll experience the highest of highs when you hit a major milestone or significant breakthrough. Just as quickly, you'll face the lowest of lows when you encounter an unexpected barrier or setback.

It's incredibly difficult to work with co-founders whose emotional states wildly change and rapidly swing from extreme-to-extreme. It's also challenging when someone is consistently negative or unrealistically positive. Either emotional state can make it difficult for the cofounding team to successfully address fundamental issues facing the company and to decide on the best course of action to drive toward a solution.

Your challenge is to find a way to be passionate without becoming overly emotional. If you can step back and regain perspective on the bigger picture—the fact that you'll face many of these up-then-down moments in a startup—then this will help you normalize your emotions faster. While you can't change the personalities of your co-founders, you can try to understand and empathize with their emotions. When you understand their emotions, then you can better manage your relationship with them and the rest of the co-founding team. Remember that as co-founders, your emotions are amplified.

Those emotions will ripple through the organization, which can cause unintended consequences.

Working Through Issues

As you can imagine, when you gather multiple people with strong passions together, it generates an intense relationship. But, no matter the intensity, you and your co-founders must be able to tackle and openly address the difficult subjects. You must be able to have conversations and discussions about things like the direction of the business, how to run it, the culture you want to establish, and the positions and types of people you want to hire. All these elements and more can lead to uncomfortable conversations, but it's well worth your effort to talk with your co-founders about the group's dynamics and how you'll communicate with each other.

Our advice is to put everything on the table early in the relationship. Ask each other how you'd like to talk about the tough stuff and try to agree upon a forum to make sure everyone is comfortable saying what they're thinking. Talk with your co-founders about what's acceptable to say and bring up in the conversations. For example, is it okay to talk to another founder about their performance on the job or the number of hours they're putting in? Is it okay to discuss the pressures you're feeling outside of work and how they affect you? The more structure you can create for these conversations, the better chance you'll have of avoiding large eruptions or having issues fester and poison the group (and the company by extension).

If you don't have the conversation early about how the team will address difficult topics, then you'll struggle, and it will likely cause more long-term damage to your relationship. There will be issues that arise, like the various roles that a founder will take on and whether you will hire a seasoned executive to run the part of the organization a founder was responsible for initially. This is usually an extremely touchy and challenging discussion for all founders, just like the conversation on equity and ownership. We promise you, these conversations, although uncomfortable, will not kill you. But, if you tiptoe around them or avoid having them early in the relationship, then we promise you that these (and every difficult topic) will rear up in many future conflicts.

While you and your team should discuss the right ground rules for your specific relationship and organization, here are four rules we have used in our companies.

- **Rule 1: Provide clear and direct communication without sugarcoating the words.** Often, in difficult conversations, there's a tendency to soften the blow, or when someone is angry, there's an inclination to make the feedback harsher than it likely needs to be. Neither of these approaches work. As we indicated earlier, founders need to be realistic, and this is a good example of needing to be balanced and real with communication.

- **Rule 2: Prove you heard the other person.** Too often, as founders, we're moving fast. That means sometimes we don't completely hear what another person is saying. In difficult conversations, that's unacceptable. Both sides need to completely hear and understand what is being communicated. The best proof that you're listening is to repeat what was just said to you in your own words, without judgment. That last part is the trick. Not only do you need to be accurate in what was just said, but it needs to be without including your bias.

- **Rule 3: Debate without making it personal.** For many founders, a company is a core part of who they are as a person, so this ground rule is sometimes difficult to stick to. Making issues personal hinders your ability to solve the problem or communicate clearly. A personal attack puts your co-founder on the defensive immediately, and it's hard to recover from that position.
- **Rule 4: Closure with next steps.** Before you leave a discussion, all the parties need to walk away with the same understanding. With difficult conversations, emotions can swirl and thoughts can drift. Many times, founders can leave a meeting with completely different perspectives on what just happened. Don't let that be the outcome of your meeting. Take time to write down what was agreed upon before you leave the room. You'll be thankful you did this later.

Difficult conversations are part of startups. So many things can go wrong, and many times, there needs to be a follow-up conversation that is even more difficult. You can make life much easier on yourself by creating ground rules on how to have those conversations. Do that early in your company's life, and it will be a lot easier for all founders.

Nurturing the Co-founder Relationship

Another way to strengthen your bonds as co-founders is to spend time together socially. Go out to lunch or dinner, or share an activity outside of work like a sport, event, or hobby. This will help you get to know each other better, and the better you know each other, the greater your chances of success. This is something you should consistently do throughout the course of running the company. This isn't reserved for those early days only. If you can consistently make sure that you spend time together and create alignment, then that will benefit the business.

One mechanism you can use to ensure that the founders are consistently getting together is to schedule quarterly off-site, founders-only meetings (as the company grows, you can extend this to your entire startup team). Do it on the weekend or at night so everyone can relax more. Part of that meeting should focus on how each of you is doing personally. If you can uncover personal issues or challenges outside of work, that may help you understand how to better work with each other.

Find an Executive Coach

A number of startup founders and CEOs use executive coaches. Once leaders outside the founding team are hired, these coaches are there to improve the performance of the founding team and the entire startup team. These coaches are like business therapists. They are there to help the team sort through personnel issues, conflicts, and stylistic problems. Executive coaches aren't right for everyone or for every issue, but they can be helpful if other avenues of communication have broken down.

Coaches are not a cheap option for young companies, but they can be very valuable. We all have our weaknesses, and those weaknesses are amplified in a startup situation. Startups are stressful and packed with pressure. Any chinks in your armor will lead to cracks under pressure, which can ultimately lead to fissures. Coaches can hit these issues head-on and help the founding team deal with them before a crisis.

For many founders, it's not just the cost that makes turning to coaches hard, it's also having the humility to be open to their feedback. Great coaches force us to examine our own behaviors, beliefs, and thoughts. Why do we do what we do? Why do we believe what we believe even in the face of contrary data or opinions? Why do we have those thoughts when there are no catalysts for them?

If, after trying our suggestions in this chapter, your founding team is struggling to work effectively together, then we encourage you to find a coach for your founding team. Take the time and spend the money to help your team work together. It's an investment that you'll be glad you made.

Parting with a Founder

Sometimes, after trying to make a co-founding relationship work, you need to let a founder go, or a founder may decide that it is time for them to move on. This is obviously a very difficult process. Founders are viewed differently than non-founders in any organization. As a result, how you handle the departure of a founder is especially important.

Culturally, everybody in the organization watches to see how the firing or departure is handled. This cuts both ways. If the person is not performing well and you don't take decisive action, then your team may feel that because they are a co-founder, they are getting special treatment by being allowed to stick around longer. If the co-founder was performing and is well respected, that is, employees don't see the problems, then a founder leaving can erode belief in the fairness of the company.

Early in the life of the company, co-founders are at the core of most of its functions. Prior to the departure, you'll want to plan for how to transfer their knowledge and also fill the role on an ongoing basis. The first part of doing that is to wrap your arms around what the co-founder is already doing. What knowledge needs to be transferred and to whom? If the co-founder had significant relationships in the industry, or with the press and analysts, how will you move those over gracefully? Once you have a complete understanding of the history, knowledge, and responsibilities that the co-founder had, then you can turn your attention to how you will cover their role in the future. You may choose to hire a new person, divide the role among existing people, promote somebody from within, or even choose not to do the work. Whatever your decision, you'll want to have the plan formulated prior to making a change.

Communication after the departure is critical. Depending upon how the separation occurred, you may have the opportunity to work with the departing founder to ensure that the message is consistent and positive for the organization, to the extent it can be. If the parting occurs on less-than-stellar terms, you may want to figure out with your legal counsel what you can say to your team about the departure. This may seem ridiculous now, but we have seen many such terminations result in lawsuits or at least, legal tit for tat.

Among founders, it's important to be as transparent as you can about the departure. With other employees, however, communication needs to be more selective. It's not a good idea to communicate personal details of any kind. It will potentially hurt the morale of the organization, it's unfair to the founder who is leaving, and it can expose you to legal problems.

Still, you need to communicate enough to assuage the natural questions that arise. Is there a problem in the company that the founder saw? Maybe it was a belief that the company won't succeed? Or, was there a power struggle at the highest senior level and this founder lost? Does it mean there is a change in direction or vision for the company? The rest of the team will want to know the answers to these questions. If you don't give them real answers, it may erode confidence in the remaining founders and the business.

Spend a fair amount of time figuring out what you can and want to say about the split, and more importantly, talk clearly about what the split means. The founder was likely central to many key initiatives in the organization. How will those be handled? You won't want to minimize the loss or sweep it under the rug. By addressing the impacts head on, it will build confidence that you have thought through the consequences and have a plan for how to deal with them.

As we stated earlier, the departure of a co-founder impacts many areas. From a legal perspective, the termination of a co-founder can be a bit tricky. Depending upon the type and amount of stock the founder owns, you'll want to understand how to handle the separation. You may be required to purchase the founder's stock. The founder may be required to purchase their stock, or the founder may own it outright. In some instances, a separation may require one partner to buy out the other. All of this can get complicated if there is no easy way to value the business, and if there is a shortage of cash to buy the shares. Your attorneys can help you think through the best way to handle a departing founder.

Here again, how you treat the founder on the way out the door will be viewed by the rest of the company. You have to assume that employees will learn about whether there was a severance package, if the founder kept their stock, or if they received any other special benefits.

Once a founder has left the company, there will inevitably be questions from outside the company as well. If the co-founder was in an externally facing role, expect lots of questions. You'll have questions from partners, investors, and other companies. During interviews with potential employees, you may even be asked why the founder departed. Know in advance what you want to say and, if possible, coordinate with the departing founder on the best communication for both the company and the founder.

You'll want to be truthful, but you don't need to fully disclose private information since it's an employee situation, which is generally confidential. If there is a legal agreement between the company and the founder that is leaving, you may already have the answer on what you can and cannot say. Most founding teams find it very hard to stay together over the long term of a company. The intensity of building a company causes breaks in the relationships between founders. If from the outset of starting a company, you understand that this is possible and you understand that founding teams may not stay together for the long term, then you can plan for the best way to handle these situations. Planning early will protect the departing founder and the company in a fair and balanced way.

* * *

Building alignment between the members of the founding team isn't a one-time event. It needs to be a continuous effort that every member of the team takes responsibility for. Sure, it's good to establish periodic meetings—weekly get-togethers where you can discuss the status of the business—but it's more important that each member of the founding group make open discussions with each other member of the team a priority.

It's so easy to let this go. Communication concerning the business, especially about what apparent disaster happened that day, always seems to be the most important thing. The problem is that it often becomes the only thing discussed between the founders. Tight-knit founding teams talk about what's going on well beyond day-to-day business. Emotions, conflicts, weaknesses, and achievement of personal and professional goals all need to be discussed regularly.

By keeping the discussions between the founding team at the forefront, the company can help make sure that it's moving forward at the fastest possible pace and that it can weather the inevitable storms that could, otherwise, damage the business.

Chapter 15

How Do I Form My Company?

When I (Will) started my first company, DataWare Logic, which, just as a reminder, failed miserably in about eighteen months (see the Introduction), I incorporated it in Pennsylvania as an S-Corp. I didn't know what vesting was; 83(b) was just a number and a letter to me, Delaware was a small state just south of where I lived, and I had no idea about the advantages of multiple classes of stock. Basically, I was ignorant and walked into a rat's nest of paperwork, issues, and changes over the short life of the company.

While, in DataWare's case, I can't blame the failure of the company on my organizational missteps, they certainly took plenty of time to deal with—time that I could have used working with customers or developing the product further. If I had tried to raise outside money, I probably would have been laughed out of any venture capitalist's office.

I never made that mistake again. In subsequent companies, I gladly sought legal assistance to get it right or as close to it as I could. Still, it took me a while to learn all the ins and outs of company formation. What I mostly learned is that it's much easier to do it correctly up front than to try to fix it later.

Creating a Legal Entity

So, you have an idea for a company, and as we outlined in Chapter 5, you've iterated on it to validate both the vision and the business model. After testing and validating, you feel that it has the potential to be a viable business. As hard as that all seemed, that was the easy part. You and your co-founders are now ready to forge ahead and engage potential customers, build the first prototype of the product, and launch the company.

But, before you get into all that fun stuff, in this chapter, we'll provide you with some of the basics about creating a formal legal entity and the nitty-gritty of what you'll want to address early. Each step in this chapter contains many options, variables, and nuances, so we strongly advise you to seek professional guidance and expertise on all these items from lawyers, financial experts, mentors, and advisors.

While we've done this ourselves many times, none of the lists below are complete. They simply point out the biggest pros and cons as we see them. The advice we give is also US-centric. Corporate administrative structures vary widely from country to country, so we only cover the basics for the US. Remember, we're not professional lawyers, accountants, or bankers; we are entrepreneurs looking at these steps as part of the path to building a great business. Also, rules, laws, and best practices change regularly, which is just another reason to access experts to guide you through officially forming your company.

Organization

So, where do you begin? The first step is to form a legal entity. You need a formal legal entity primarily to protect yourself, to potentially qualify for a tax-advantaged status, and to create a structure that allows you to share in the growth of the company with others—specifically, employees and investors. For a startup, a corporate or LLC structure is substantially better than forming a partnership or going at it as a sole proprietor, and it's necessary if you want to build anything even moderately substantial.

We run into many early startups that fit the idealistic model of a few people working in a garage, cranking away at building their product. One of the last things on their minds is what type of business structure they should operate under. This is a mistake. Even very early on, many of the structures that exist provide levels of protection, tax benefits, and a method for sharing ownership among the founders and investors that don't exist outside a legal umbrella.

Some of the dizzying array of options include Sole Proprietorships, General Partnerships, LPs (Limited Partnerships), C-Corporations, S-Corporations, and LLCs (Limited Liability Companies). There are permutations of several of these that make the list quite a bit longer, but those are outside the scope of this book.

The structures for individuals and partnerships—a Sole Proprietorship, General Partnership, and LP—can offer certain tax advantages for individuals and small groups, but they limit your flexibility as a startup. Startups usually require capital investment to accelerate progress. This investment comes from people or groups outside the founding team who invest in exchange for ownership in the company. This is virtually impossible to accomplish with structures created for individuals or partnerships.

Additionally, these structures don't limit the personal liability of the founders (the general partners in partnership parlance) nor do they allow the entity to offer Incentive Stock Options (ISOs)—an option to buy stock in the company at a low price and with favorable tax treatment, which is granted to employees to recruit, retain, or reward them (we'll talk about this in detail later).

> An Incentive Stock Option (ISO) is an option to buy stock in the company at a low price and with favorable tax treatment, which is granted to employees to recruit, retain, or reward them.

So, basically, without a way to exchange ownership for investment or to limit the liability of the founders, structures for individuals and partnerships are, essentially, nonstarters in the startup world. As mentors, advisors, and investors, we've never seen a startup adopt a structure like this and for good reason.

Instead, corporations (C and S) and LLCs offer much better options for startups. LLCs are different from corporations. Legally, you declare your company as a corporation or an LLC when you create its legal entity. Whether you are a C-Corporation or an S-Corporation is a matter of how you file your taxes. Still, all three options have many similarities and some key differences, both legally and financially. All three provide the following advantages:

- Personal liability protection for founders, investors, and employees. The entity (the C-Corp, S-Corp, or LLC) is responsible for the entity's debts, obligations, and actions. The individuals associated with the entity are not held personally responsible for them.

- Transferrable ownership/perpetual existence. Ownership can be transferred to others, owners can come and go, and the entity, by default, survives the death of one or more of its owners.
- Deductible expenses. Expenses may be deducted from the entity before income is accounted for. In a structure created for individuals and partnerships, everything passes through to your personal tax return. Any deductions depend upon the rest of your financial situation and may not be deductible at all.

These advantages are all important fundamentals in being able to create and build a startup. Specifically, the following short list provides more detail about each of the structures, why we recommend them, and why nearly all startups choose one of the entities.

LLC

The biggest reason for using an LLC structure is for its flexible tax treatment. An LLC can elect to be taxed as a partnership with profits and losses being distributed to its members and then taxed at personal tax rates, or it can be taxed as a corporation at corporate tax rates. Corporate tax rates are generally lower, but when the LLC elects to be taxed as a corporation, then the income to the principals is taxed twice—once as income to the LLC and again as income to the individual. You need to do the math to decide which works best for you if you choose the LLC route.

While a single-member LLC is relatively straightforward to establish and maintain, as the number of its members grows and the company takes on external funding, maintenance of the entity can become much more complex, especially concerning issues of taxation. But, that's not the biggest problem with using an LLC structure. That comes from the fact that most venture capitalists can only invest in corporations due to—you guessed it—potential tax issues for their limited partners. Accelerators will usually require that you be a C-Corp to even engage with you.

Unless you plan on just having a small group of employees and aren't looking for any outside funding, it's best to use a corporate structure for your company.

S-Corporation

The primary advantage of an S-Corp is its tax structure. Like one of the options for an LLC, the profits and losses for an S-Corp flow through to its shareholders. This means that any profits are taxed only at the individual level and not both at the corporate and individual levels.

That advantage comes with some fairly important disadvantages that make it a problematic structure for startups as they grow. Following are a few examples.

- Multiple classes of stock are not allowed. Having no preferred stock will make it almost impossible to attract institutional investors.
- Unlike a C-Corp, the stock of an S-Corp does not qualify for Qualified Small Business Stock (QSBS) treatment.* QSBS treatment, explained fully under C-Corp, below, potentially offers outstanding tax benefits to the company's shareholders.

- The number of shareholders is limited. An S-Corp is limited to one hundred shareholders.
- The type of shareholder is also limited. Non-US residents, aliens, and corporations are not allowed to hold shares in an S-Corp.

While an S-Corp might seem like a reasonable legal entity when you're funding your startup out of your own pocket or with money from friends and family, the mere fact that S-Corp stock doesn't qualify as QSBS should be enough to make you look elsewhere. The fact that an S-Corp doesn't allow you to issue preferred stock, which is required by institutional investors, should put the final nail in its coffin. You're going to eventually want to be a C-Corp, and it's much easier to start that way.

C-Corporation

A C-Corporation, often just called a C-Corp, offers the business structure that most startups need. This includes:

- **The ability to issue multiple classes of stock.** This is important because outside investors generally require preferred stock—stock that is set apart with the purpose of providing certain advantages and protection over the common stock of the company.
- **The option for individual shareholders of your startup to adopt Section 1202[†] of the Internal Revenue Code.** If the company's stock is a QSBS, which almost all startups qualify for, any stock held for more than five years can be excluded from the holder's federal tax—well, the

first $10 million in gains, anyway. It's not even taxed as a preference item for AMT (Alternate Minimum Tax) purposes. This can be a major financial benefit for individual stockholders in the company and only applies to C-Corps.

- **The ability to grant incentive stock options to employees.** Incentive stock options granted to employees allow each employee to defer tax on the gain until they can actually sell the stock. This is a huge benefit for employees of startups and is often required to recruit the best people in many industries. There are additional potential tax advantages for founders and employees who receive incentive stock options, including having any gain taxed as a long-term capital gain instead of as ordinary income, assuming the option is exercised and held for at least a year.

- **The opportunity to have unlimited shareholders.** S-Corps limit the number of shareholders that a company may have. With a C-Corp, there is no limit. This is important because between employees being hired and having many investors over multiple rounds of funding, the number of shareholders can grow quickly.

- **Anyone can own stock in a C-Corp.** This includes anyone residing in or outside of the United States. As a result, with a C-Corp, you give yourself the greatest number of options in terms of potential investors.

These advantages make a C-Corp almost always the logical choice for startups in the long run, and it's far easier to start out using that legal entity for building your company. For companies seeking outside investment, it is really the only choice. Being able to sell and grant equity in multiple forms is standard in today's startup world. Adopting a C-Corp structure is the only way to do that without any serious limitations. We almost never see startups that aren't C-Corps any longer.

> A C-Corp is almost always the logical choice for startups in the long run, and it's far easier to start out using that legal entity for building your company. For companies seeking outside investment, they are really the only choice.

Where Do I Incorporate?

You might be tempted to incorporate your company in your home state, thinking that it would be easier and that each state is pretty much the same for businesses, right? Wrong. There is a reason why over 50 percent of all public companies in the US are incorporated in Delaware. Delaware has made it a goal to have the most modern and efficient business environment available.

We highly recommend you incorporate in Delaware.

It's easy to incorporate in Delaware, and it's relatively cheap. You don't need to have a physical presence there, and, if you ever need it, the judicial system is practical, with judges experienced in most business matters. Most good startup lawyers are familiar and comfortable working within the Delaware law framework, even if they don't practice in Delaware. No juries are used in the Delaware Chancery Court, and decisions are issued as written opinions that can be relied upon, and, as such, there is less litigation.

Additionally, because of the popularity of Delaware for incorporation, the ecosystem of filing agents, support staff, registered agents, and other administrative assistants, procedures, and systems are efficient and accommodating.

Because of these positive aspects, as well as long histories and comfort with the legal system there, most investors want the companies they invest in to be incorporated in Delaware. If you initially incorporate somewhere else, you can move your incorporation state later, but it's time-consuming and can be expensive. Why bother? In our opinion, there just isn't any reason to incorporate anywhere else.

> In our opinion, there just isn't any reason to incorporate anywhere other than Delaware.

Getting a Lawyer

Once you get going after you've vetted your idea and business model, you should start seeking legal help to lock down the formation and structure of your company, as well as to deal with loads of other legal tasks, documents, and processes. Lawyers are knowledgeable paid advisors who are on your side. They are truly an asset to your startup.

Many new founders who we work with stress over finding a lawyer. But, getting a lawyer is much easier than you'd think. There are law firms, big and small, around the country that either specialize in startup activity or have groups that specialize in it. These lawyers understand the financial restrictions of a startup and will work with you to establish a relationship that is financially sound.

Ask around about who other startups in your area are using. The founders of these companies and your mentors and advisors will lead you to a short list of potential law firms very quickly. While there are many law firms, a small subset represents the majority of startups in any one area. Seek them out. Regardless of the size of the firm, this smaller group will be better connected, will be more up to speed on startup law, and will be more relaxed about and flexible with the relationship they create with you.

When it comes to cost, most firms will negotiate their rates for doing the initial work you need. When you speak with the firms, keep in mind that they want your business and are willing to compete for it. This is especially true if you are in a hot market or you're engaged with well-known investors. Virtually every law firm we've ever worked with has worked with us to ensure we could afford their services. Some have even taken stock in our companies in order to reduce their rates even further. They know they will be able to charge you their normally high rates later when you've become successful. There's no need to be intimidated.

Choosing a Company Name

Naming your company is harder than you think. With so many new companies being created all the time, your most obvious choices for a company name are often gone long before you even think of them. These days, with the multiple needs of trademark protection, a matching domain name, and logical social networking handles, it's more difficult than ever.

We often see that young startups have to change their name later because they realize their original name doesn't work for some reason. Trademark problems, domain name conflicts (your web address), and poor customer recognition can all lead to painful name changes down the road. Changing your name can result in the waste of all your previous marketing and selling efforts. Potentially, you'll lose expensively gained momentum. Because this isn't seen as an important step in the company formation process, many founders screw this up by picking names or logos that belong to other companies, that distract from their long-term goals, or that seem to be randomly plucked for no strategic reason other than it sounds or looks cool. When you pick a name, you're choosing something that will stick with the company for a long time—almost assuredly, the entire life of the company. This is a major part of your branding. It represents how the public and your customers view the company, what it stands for, its values, and the type of product it offers.

There's an art to naming your company, and the last thing you want to do is nonchalantly shrug your shoulders and randomly choose a name. You want to think about it carefully. Theoretically, you have an unlimited number of choices for a name. But, it has become harder to find viable ones as the number of companies being created rapidly increases every year.

1. When choosing a name, you have two basic paths: You can pick a descriptive name that explains what the company does or conveys an image of the company, like Dollar Shave Club, Instagram, or Facebook.
2. You can select something that isn't descriptive of the business but conveys other messages, like Uber or Starbucks.

Choosing a nondescriptive name that generates specific imagery as part of your marketing concept can be a safer choice. This is a smart strategy if you think your company may make a big pivot, a change in direction to some extent, or may add a new line of unrelated products or services in the future.

Although we know of successful companies with nonde-scriptive names, we still encourage founders to use a descriptive name if they can. It's harder to do, and it becomes harder every day as more people scoop up names, but it will help your marketing efforts. When you choose something that is disconnected from what you do, you have to spend a significant amount of money and time on marketing to explain what the name and the company means. Imagine not knowing that Starbucks is a coffee shop, and you'll start to understand the problem.

Either way you go, you'll want to put a reasonable amount of energy into selecting a name. During your idea-vetting process, you can ask customers what works for them and certainly run it by any mentors or advisors that you have. Consider what you are trying to convey and what people will be searching the internet for when looking to have their specific problem solved.

When you have a name, make sure you check out its avail-ability before you start investing in using it or publicizing it. It's easy to do some basic checks to see if the name is being used on the internet. Remember to check for domain names and web-pages that contain the name you're proposing. Keep in mind that a product name may be used as a domain name.

It's far better if you spend time early in the process of forming your company to strategically choose the right name. Ideally, it will be a name you can trademark and doesn't infringe on anyone else's trademarks. If you have trademark protection for your name, you have the legal footing to protect it from use by someone else in the future. Having the trademark also increases the chances (but does not guarantee) that the matching domain name and social media handles will be available.

Founder's Stock

So, you've formed your company, given it a name, and found legal counsel. Not fun, but necessary. Now, for some hard stuff including splitting up the company among the founders, setting up agreements among the team, and nailing down the nitty-gritty details of stock ownership.

In the startup world, common stock is the primary vehicle for assigning ownership of the company to founders and employees. Deciding how to allocate common stock among co-founders is one of the most important, yet challenging, early decisions you will make. We covered in detail how to decide how much stock each founder gets in Chapter 13. Here, we'll discuss how the stock is actually issued to the founders.

Early on, after you've decided on the equity split, you'll likely choose the total number of shares the company has. Then, you'll divide those shares up according to the percentages you already agreed upon that each founder will receive. The total number of shares isn't important now, although you'll want to make sure you allocate enough stock so that even lower-level employees receive a meaningful number of shares with a low percentage of ownership. Five million shares is a good number to start with. Then, someone who is granted one-tenth of one percent (0.1%) of the company will receive 5,000 shares, which is a substantial number of shares while representing a small percentage of ownership.

During the early honeymoon period when everything looks great and everyone is happy, you'll think that formal agreements aren't necessary, or you may worry that introducing formal agreements will somehow hurt your relationship with your co-founders. On the former, things will not always be great. Every company hits some roadblocks. Tensions increase, and disagreements get fractious. It will be very difficult to put a rational agreement in place at that time. It's much better to get it done while everyone is ensconced in the upside of the business.

On potentially damaging your relationship with your co-founders: get over it! You are neither the first to do this kind of thing, nor are you trying to do something punitive. It's the smart thing to do for the company, and it's not personal. Besides, in the end, when these agreements are in place, each founder is protected from any irrational decisions of others, as is the company. Everyone wins.

Founder's stock is common stock issued at a very low value upon or very soon after incorporation. The shares of stock are purchased by the founders, or they're issued to founders in exchange for their ideas, efforts, knowledge, experience, IP (Intellectual Property), or anything else the co-founders agree is valuable to the startup. Early on, the value of the company is very low, so each share has a value close to $0. This is the beauty of founder's shares. Ownership in the company is acquired at a very low dollar value and therefore represents negligible (usually zero) taxable income to the founder.

Vesting/Restricted Stock

While there are a few ways of issuing founder's stock, it's usually done with vesting restricted shares. With restricted shares, restricted or conditional ownership of all the shares being granted is given to the founder at the outset. The conditional part is that the company retains a right to repurchase some of the shares at their original cost for a predefined time if the founder does not meet their obligations. That time is referred to as the vesting period. The key obligation is that they stay with the company for the entire period of vesting.

The number of shares the company can buy back decreases over time and according to a specific schedule. Usually, this involves vesting monthly over a four-year period. That is, the company relinquishes its right to repurchase one-forty-eighth of the total grant each month for forty-eight months. After the four-year vesting period, the founder owns their shares, free and clear.

Vesting is commonly misunderstood by many founders, but it's one of the best tools to protect all interests, from the investors to the co-founders and to the company. It's a way to ensure founders stay with the company and add value over a long period because time is what it takes to generate success. But, the reality is that founding teams don't always stay together. In fact, they're likely to split. Vesting exists to protect founders, investors, and the company in this situation. If a co-founder leaves early by their own choice, or if they are fired, then the equity in the company doesn't leave with them. The founder only takes what they have earned before their departure.

Restricted shares offer a potentially large tax advantage, which is a longer holding period because ownership begins when the shares are granted rather than when they are vested. This mechanism offers better tax treatment by potentially making the shares qualify for IRS 1202 tax treatment if they have been held for at least five years or have the potential for earlier long-term capital gains treatment if held for one year or more.

We believe that using restricted stock for founders is the only way to go because of its built-in protective mechanisms for the entire founding team as well as the tax benefits that the founders can receive when you grant stock early on.

> We believe that using restricted stock for founders is the only way to go because of its built-in protective mechanisms for the entire founding team as well as the tax benefits that the founders can receive when you grant stock early on.

We'd be remiss in not mentioning a special case of vesting that frequently occurs when vesting has already started and your startup takes on an investment from a venture capitalist. Often, the VCs will ask that you re-vest some of the shares that you have already vested. In a sense, they want to turn back the clock to make sure they get some security from the extension to the restricted stock's conditions. While this is relatively standard, you should still negotiate just how far the vesting is rewound. Rewinding six months to one year is OK. Anything more than that should be avoided.

Accelerated Vesting

Another item you should discuss with your co-founders when talking about stock in the company is the acceleration of vesting. If you are vesting your ownership in the company, you have to consider what happens to any unvested shares if and when there is an acquisition. You can, of course, assume that the acquiring company will maintain the vesting schedule you have in place, but there are no guarantees. In fact, there is no guarantee that a founder will remain with the acquiring company. Many founders are not needed after a transition.

To account for this, there are often triggers put in place that cause the acceleration of vesting. The triggers are often very simple. A single trigger is one in which a single event, like the sale of the company, causes the founder's remaining stock to be vested at the time of the transaction. A double trigger is one in which two events must take place. This could be the sale of the company and the founder is either being fired without cause or has their job responsibilities substantially changed.

These are the simplest and most common versions of triggers. There are also instances in which the triggers are more complex. Keep in mind that whatever you decide up front may be renegotiated with your investors when you raise capital to fund the company.

Investors and acquirers of the company don't like single trigger acceleration. Having it in place makes it harder for the company to be acquired because the acquirer believes the founders have no economic incentive to stay with the merged entity. As a result, the acquirer must offer more incentives to the founders, which may increase the purchase price of the company (or subtract from distributions to other shareholders).

From a founder's perspective, you want a single trigger. As founders, while double triggers are much more common than single triggers, we think that a single trigger is a reasonable benefit, and you should have it as part of your vesting agreement. You've created the value that ultimately led to the acquisition, and you should get the benefit of what you earned along the way, or at least the option to choose your near-term path. If the acquirer wants you to stay, they need to incentivize you to do so.

This will almost certainly be a negotiation between the founding team and the company's investors. In this discussion, note that, practically speaking, the founder's role almost always changes, making an acquisition a double-trigger event by its nature—the sale of the company and the change in their job responsibilities. So, even if you're not able to agree with your investors on a single trigger, it may ultimately work out that way for you.

Taxes

Decisions on how you are going to distribute founder's shares are greatly driven by tax issues. We already discussed long-term capital gains and QSBS. Another option is the 83(b) election, which needs to be filed within thirty days of acquiring the shares. The 83(b) election tells the IRS that you should be taxed on all your equity now instead of when it vests. This allows you to pay a small amount of tax while the value of the stock is low, rather than paying more tax as the value increases and your shares vest. Yeah, it's complicated. As we mentioned earlier, we recommend you seek counsel from legal and financial professionals before making a final call on how you want to set things up.

Intellectual Property Agreements

When you're building a company, your first allegiance isn't to yourself, it's not to your co-founders, and it's not to your individual investors: it's to the company. This means you must protect the company and its needs, always. One of the ways you accomplish this is by having appropriate Intellectual Property (IP) agreements in place. These clearly explain that the company owns and has access and rights to all the intellectual property created by the founders, employees, and others associated with the company. In the beginning, especially, founders generate most of the intellectual property, often before IP agreements have been created. So, it's good to create and execute these agreements early.

The IP agreements you put in place should cover all intellectual property that is created—from the time a founder or an employee begins working on it until they are no longer an employee of the company. Everything created for the company should be owned by the company. There cannot be any confusion over this. All founders and employees must sign the appropriate IP agreements.

Why? Simply put, things go bad. There are disagreements, fights, and breakups. What happens if a founder who owns the core technology, lists, data, and relationships that they created as part of your founding team leaves the company? The company has to own them. IP agreements are the way you make sure that the fundamental knowledge and intellectual property of the company can't leave it and potentially destroy the business.

The most common IP agreement is a Proprietary Information and Inventions Assignment (PIIA). This is the agreement that everyone signs as soon as they join the company, whether they're an employee or a founder. It states that any of the intellectual property the individual creates related to the company is owned by the company. It also prevents people from working on something similar for another company at the same time, creating a competitor to your startup. Yeah, it happens.

When founders create intellectual property before the company is officially incorporated, then you can use what is called an IP Assignment. Generally, an IP Assignment states that you, as a co-founder, in exchange for the stock you receive, assign all relevant intellectual property to the company, including any applicable concepts, information, designs, and so forth. An IP Assignment ensures the company has complete ownership of that material from the moment it was conceived.

Investors are going to want proof that the company and not individuals own all the IP required to move the company forward before they invest. During an acquisition or an IPO, you can be sure the auditors of the acquiring company or of your public offering are going to do serious research into whether your company controls its own destiny by owning everything core to its existence. If it doesn't, acquisitions may be derailed and IPOs terminated. It's that critical.

***

While it's not unreasonable to think that the formation of the legal entity for the company is secondary to everything else a startup needs to do, it is actually a fundamental requirement and integral to the company's success. Just think of it this way, the legal structure offers protection for you and your ideas. It's also the basis for having outside investors becoming involved. It's pretty basic and important. It's also easier than you might think.

No matter what you do for stock issuances, vesting, or acceleration, remember to document everything properly and make sure all the founders agree to what you've decided as a group. As we mentioned in Chapter 12, this is not a single discussion that happens at one point in time. It's a continuous one that will come up time and time again. Time and circumstances often change people's memories of what actually happened. Having everything agreed upon and written down will help you continue to work as a fluid team, and when issues arise (which they will) down the road, the documents will contain terms that have been previously agreed upon, and they will remove any temptation by a founder to assert leverage or renegotiate terms.

You can't build anything on a weak foundation, right?

Chapter 16

Finance and Human Resources

Ah, now we're getting to the fun stuff: finance and HR at the beginning of a company. I (Rajat) kid, of course. I don't know too many founders who are dying to be booking debits and credits and filling out IRS paperwork. But, here's the thing: getting this wrong can derail a business, if not outright kill it.

I'll give you two examples from my startups, which in this case will remain nameless. Example number 1: we were about to go public and the investment bankers had just run a background check on all of our leadership team. Out pops an issue with one individual. We, as founders, had no idea of the issue and when confronted by the legal team from the investment bankers were in a panic. We were trying to get our IPO completed as quickly as we could because we were running out of cash, so this presented a very real issue to us in raising capital. How do we handle this with the public market investors, and then how do we handle this internally as well?

Example number 2: we were raising our first institutional round of capital for one of our companies. We had just given the potential investors projections and a financial model for the future of the business. Literally, the next day we found an error in the model that rendered it materially wrong. We ended up sending them a revised model, but not before they seriously questioned our abilities to execute and understand our own business. How could we send them a model that was so wrong?

In both instances, we ended up getting through the crises, but both should never have happened in the first place. With the right focus on some basic financial, legal, and HR processes, we could have found these issues before they almost derailed these companies.

Company Hygiene—The Early Required Systems

Some of the traits that make entrepreneurs great, like their willingness to take risks, their ability to deal with the unknown, and their disposition to radically think about new products and ways to do business, can hinder their interest in putting systems and processes in place. There are rarely bigger examples of this than when it comes to dealing with the company's financial, accounting, and human resources procedures.

Too often, founders adopt a blasé attitude toward these matters. They shrug their shoulders and say they'll take care of payroll by writing checks from their bank account; or they don't believe they need to keep receipts for expense reports, so they toss them in the trash; or, since they don't intend to offer health insurance benefits, they don't bother to report or file any paperwork. On every account, their assumptions are wrong. Don't join this group. The IRS and other state agencies will nail you, and you'll lose money for incorrectly reporting taxes, wages, and other employee benefits.

Just like the other items in this chapter, the sooner you adopt the proper accounting and financial practices, the better. The major financial elements that you and your co-founders will want to discuss and adopt, possibly with an accountant or financial expert, include the following categories.

Basic Bookkeeping

This is basic accounting. It includes items like expenses, customer accounts, and the revenue that is generated. You'll want to make sure you have all the proper paperwork and receipts and make sure they all get into the hands of whomever is responsible for accounting. We love founders who take risks and break new ground, but this isn't an area for you to get creative. Creative accounting means there's a big problem, and it usually doesn't end well. Accounting processes and procedures are well documented and regulated, and systems have been in place for decades, so go with something standard and widely available.

There are dozens of low-cost solutions to help you deal with finances correctly, and many of them are found online. Some examples of these are QuickBooks, Xero, MYOB, and Sage. As soon as you have more than a handful of employees, some outside investment, or revenue of any kind, we recommend that you bring on a controller or at least a bookkeeper, even part-time, to help you manage all the pieces of the financial puzzle.

Controls

Once you have money coming into the company and checks regularly going out, it's critical that you have clear and proper controls in place as to who has the authority to cash checks, make wire transfers, and pay bills. No, you're not too small to do this now. It shouldn't be a free-for-all. You should be explicit with who has the control to approve payments and to actually spend the money. Without these controls, it's very easy to get taken advantage of and to make a costly mistake.

So, think, discuss, and decide on the best course of action with your co-founders, like who will pay bills and who will approve expense reports and other expense-related matters. If you don't, then you can run into serious personal and personnel problems when this is unclear. As with most of the items in this chapter, any potential investors will require that specific controls are in place before agreeing to invest in your startup.

A simple methodology we use is to make sure the person who signs the check is different from who writes it and logs it into the accounting system. No one can sign checks to themselves, and any checks or wire transfers over even $5,000 require two founders to okay them. There are many more controls that you can implement, but those will get you started.

Expenses

In the early stages of the company, expenses will make up the majority of the accounting. This is yet another area that founders often have trouble dealing with, thinking that systems for paying expenses somehow indicates a lack of trust among the founding team. "I told you I paid for something; just pay me back," is a common, but dangerous refrain.

The key to understanding the importance of expenses is that they represent a huge portion of your early financial activity and, as such, greatly affect your legal reporting requirements and taxes. Expenses need to be itemized, because they impact your taxes and how the company records and reports its progress.

Very few accounting processes effect as many people in the company as expense reporting. It's always painful and always somewhat difficult. Make sure you explain why detailed reporting is vital to your co-founders and to new employees.

Make them part of the process and try to streamline it when you can.

Payroll

This is one of the earliest expenses you will incur, and it's also one of the most highly regulated. If you fail to pay, or incorrectly pay taxes on your payroll, the state tax department and IRS will come after you with serious penalties and fines. Don't think that they'll ignore you or give you a pass because you're small.

Although it may be tempting, don't pay people under the table or pay them without paying and reporting taxes. Once it's uncovered, you'll find yourself caught in a nasty and costly situation that will, at the very least, be a major issue when you try to get funding. There are many inexpensive options to help with payroll, and even the big names in the business offer solutions for small companies at reasonable rates. There are many internet-based providers of these services as well. A few we see being adopted today include TriNet, Gusto, Sage, Insperity, and Paychex.

Benefits

Early on, you may be able to do without a company-wide benefits package. Still, you should consider one fairly early after the creation of your startup. You'll likely need one to recruit people, and, eventually, you'll grow to the size where you'll be required to offer certain elements of one.

The primary benefits you should consider right off the bat are health insurance, vacation time, and sick time. In terms of health insurance, you may think you don't need to offer anything because your employees can either get their own or are covered under someone else's plan (read "parents or spouses"). While this may be true, you will eventually be required to offer one. In addition, many of the people you hire will be thinking of the future and what they will do after their other options have expired. Having a plan may help you recruit new employees to your startup as well. It's simply better to have one, even if it's minimal.

In terms of sick time and vacation time, your options range from offering a specific number of days to not accounting for them at all. The former allows you to specifically account for the costs of the benefit and contain possible abuse of it. The latter sends a signal to employees about work/life balance. Though, in practice, the unlimited plan is almost as limiting in a tight, newly formed startup team, where no one feels they should take any time off. Of course, you can choose most anything you want within the limitations of the laws of the state and country you're doing business in.

Keep in mind that the benefits package you choose will be bound and somewhat determined by both legal and financial/accounting constraints. It's best to discuss these with your legal and financial advisors.

Insurance

As with most of the topics in this chapter, insurance is, for the most part, a requirement. Also like most topics in this chapter, it's closely tied to everything else. Have you incorporated? Do you have payroll? Are you offering benefits? Are you filing taxes? These are all linked in various ways, and it's why getting your company going is as complicated in its own way as coming up with a viable business idea and getting that product into the market. Insurance, too, is tied to each of these tasks and is often required as part of them.

It's an unfortunate circumstance that almost every part of your business needs some level of insurance. You'll be required to carry or fund policies that include workers' compensation, disability insurance, Social Security (yes, that's insurance), and unemployment insurance. Depending on your state, the levels of insurance you need for each of these will likely be predetermined—this isn't optional.

There are plenty of other insurance policies that are optional—sort of. But, many are required to recruit investors, certain customers, and some employees. While you may think that because you're so small, adopting such things doesn't apply to you, in most cases, you'd be wrong. In fact, because you're small, your customers may want you to have even more insurance. As you grow, many activities in your company should be or will need to be insured.

When you're just starting out and before you raise any outside capital, we'd suggest getting minimal coverage in a couple of specific areas. Aside from the insurance that is mandated by the government, you should at least have some property insurance, including theft and fire coverage. The loss of computers, equipment, or even furniture can be devastating to a new startup with limited capital. You'll want to find a way of protecting your property.

As you grow larger, you'll want to add at least liability insurance, and as you take on investment capital, your investors will likely require at least a couple of additional policies. These include D&O insurance (Directors and Officer's insurance is liability insurance that specifically covers the team and the board) and, potentially, key-man life insurance, which is sometimes required by investors to hedge against something happening to one of the founders. We'd suggest working closely with your investors to determine just how much coverage you'll need. It's not cheap.

There are, of course, a myriad of other types of insurance, but from our perspective, the only other one to consider as a startup is E&O insurance (Errors and Omissions insurance). E&O insurance is a form of liability insurance that protects against claims of inadequate work or negligence. We'd suggest avoiding adopting this until your customers require it. Not surprisingly, it's also expensive.

Your customers may even demand certain levels of insurance before they do business with you. In general, our advice on this topic is to do what you need to do to cover your organization, as well as make sure that your customers feel comfortable with your coverage, but balance all this with the costs of over-insuring. Even when insurance is required, you can sign up for minimal coverage where appropriate, and the policies can be relatively inexpensive.

Again, your legal and financial advisors will help you figure out what you need for insurance. There's nothing new to invent. You just need a checklist of agreements to be signed and processes that need to be carried out. You'll be dealing with people who want to sell you their products and services, and they'll do everything they can to make your life as easy as possible.

Outsourcing

As we mentioned earlier, it may make sense to bring on a part-time bookkeeper, controller, or accountant, or perhaps you'll even want to hire an outside human resources consultant. Someone with experience will significantly improve your chances of getting all of this right on the first try, avoiding potential legal and financial mistakes. Outsourcing can make it substantially easier for you to get it all done in a timely manner. Later, when your company reaches a certain size, you'll likely bring those responsibilities in-house, often by making these part-time people full-time.

One way of dealing with the complexity and the sheer number of things you have to do is to outsource big chunks of the effort. While basic bookkeeping is difficult to export completely, insurance is normally managed by an outside provider. Much of the rest of what you need to do can be consolidated with the use of a professional employer organization (PEO). A PEO can manage your entire human resources infrastructure. They'll manage payroll, file and distribute W-2 forms, make sure your payroll-related taxes get paid, and they can oversee and track all the other employee benefits, like vacation, sick days, or paid time off. You'll, of course, need to collect data to supply to them, but they'll do everything else.

Additionally, PEOs allow small- to medium-sized companies that offer large corporate benefits by including your company in a pool with many others just like you. For example, if you have only twelve employees, it's hard to contract with insurance companies or to negotiate a health care plan that is reasonably priced. But, when you go through a PEO, it can get you access to more affordable plans. You can also contract with them to handle the human resources infrastructure for the employees working at the company.

Although it costs you money to use a PEO, it saves the company in the long run. People look at the benefits package when deciding which company to join. If you want strong talent working for you, then you have to offer a competitive package, which is difficult to do with only a few employees. A PEO allows you to offer employees better benefits than you could on your own while reducing the management load on your startup. Using a PEO allows you to focus on what you do best rather than focusing on the company's infrastructure.

We'd highly recommend the use of a PEO once your company has more than ten people. Some popular ones are ADP, TriNet, and Paychex, and although there are almost 1,000 PEOs in the US, you might find a specific one that meets your needs locally.

No matter which way you decide to do it—in-house, hiring someone part-time, hiring consulting help, or paying an external organization—just remember these actions are not optional. Not only do you need to do them for legal reasons, but they will almost assuredly prevent you from getting funding or hiring new employees if ignored.

***

We know this seems like a long list of actions that you probably think are unnecessary for your small startup right now. While there are many things to do to form your company, these are not difficult tasks. Rest assured that every founding team before you has done every single thing we've highlighted in this chapter. You may not know it, but you're surrounded by people, including fellow entrepreneurs, investors, mentors, advisors who have done all of it and can help you out. There are also legal and accounting resources and people who will be more than happy to help you through the list of things you need to do—for a fee, of course.

While you don't have to get everything in this chapter done the day you and your co-founders start brainstorming about the company you're about to create, we highly encourage you to tackle these items early on. All of them apply to the company, and most apply to each of the founders as individuals. You don't need to be a large company or have hundreds of employees to get them completed. Think of them as the practical foundation on which you're building the company.

Part III

Funding Your Startup

Chapter 17

Funding Basics

As a first-time founder, when I (Rajat) began raising money for NetGenesis, it was basically a disaster. The company was in a new, hot space—the internet—and we had exciting ideas of things to build. Unfortunately, I didn't know how to raise money for the venture.

I spent a lot of time meeting with a wide variety of investors, including angel investors, corporate investors, and venture capitalists. I didn't understand the game they were playing, so I would often say the wrong things and share information that was detrimental to me because I didn't quite know how to get through the process.

Ultimately, I was fortunate enough to be in the position of choosing between multiple term sheets from different VC firms. Of course, not realizing what was important, I chose the higher offer rather than the better fit for me and the company. At the time, I believed a higher offer (valuation and amount of money invested) was the better one, but I quickly learned that terms and conditions of a deal are as important—if not more important—than the total value to a deal. The legalese that we all dread reading and don't really understand, yup, that too is super critical when considering an offer from a VC firm. We don't want you to have this same experience, so we will detail critical legal terms here for you as well.

Ultimately, the VCs came in and made several changes, some of which were excellent and some that weren't, including replacing part of the management team. Sometimes, a better offer on face value isn't the better offer overall for the company or for the founding team.

Raising Money Is a Process

If you've just opened this book for the first time and turned right to this section, we understand. In our experience working with many startups, of the top ten items on a founder's list of things to get done, funding often occupies all ten positions.

Yes, getting funding for your startup is probably critical to its success. Still, as you'll see in this section, it doesn't stand alone. If you haven't done the legwork of vetting your idea, building a team, and getting a handle on the details about your market and product, funding is going to be extremely hard to nail down. So, if you jumped here first, go ahead and take a look through this section, but we highly encourage you to read the previous sections before you start to implement the ideas here. Trust us. Doing it that way will save loads of time and optimize your chances for success.

While the process of getting your startup funded can be difficult, the good news is that there are more people interested and engaged in funding early stage businesses than ever before. Of course, you can always use sales to bootstrap your company by funding its growth. But, there are better models that have emerged to help generate capital for fast-growing companies. It's not easy to raise money, but with the right preparation, process, and effort, you can put yourself in a great position to do so.

In this chapter, we'll walk you through the background information you'll need to raise money. In the rest of this section, we'll describe the various sources of capital, how to prepare your company to raise money, and then walk you through the process of raising capital. We'll share some lessons we've learned and the tricks we've used to increase our odds of raising money. Raising money is often a difficult and painful process—even for the best startups—but perseverance and a few tips will help you accomplish your goals.

Why Do You Even Need to Raise Money?

The reasons for raising money are foundational. You'll need money to execute your plan, including investing in building your product, hiring the right people, and optimizing your marketing efforts. All these steps take money, especially when you need to do these things in a competitive market, one where there is competition for the customer's attention, for employees, and for distribution channels. Yes, that basically means all markets. Many entrepreneurs try to take the cheap way out, and there are occasions when that can work, but often, it won't. If you invest in critical areas of your business, you'll have a chance to generate returns. If you don't, it's a lot harder and potentially impossible.

As we discussed earlier, because barriers to entry are so low these days, computers are cheap, websites are easy to build, and practically speaking, there are really no original ideas, just new takes on them, you're almost guaranteed to have a lot of competition. You should assume there is always someone right behind you looking at the same opportunities that you are, someone who is better funded and smarter, and has a bigger and potentially better team. You will need to quickly move into the market, and the only way you can do that is with money. In almost every instance, your startup will need cash quickly to compete in a meaningful way.

You and your idea are likely not unique, so you need to be more innovative than everyone else, and you need to run faster than them. We rarely see companies fail because they were over-funded, but we often run into companies that fail because they are underfunded.

When thinking about funding their startup, founders often make at least one of two critical errors:

1. They underestimate the amount of money they need.
2. They think they can fund their growth with revenue.

We have this discussion with startups all the time. These errors happen, mostly as a result of having incomplete or poor planning, and both mistakes are easily avoided with a realistic business plan.

Many founders are optimistic and perhaps even unrealistic when it comes to their business plan. Because founders are so passionate about their company, it's easy for them to overestimate how many people will want to purchase their solution and how quickly the company will grow. We get it. Highly publicized unicorns, companies that have grown to over $1 billion in value seemingly overnight, make it appear like success happens very quickly. As such, many founders think they can fund their fast growth with early cash collected from happy customers. Usually, that's a big mistake. Growth takes time. In our experience, the vast majority of major successes take close to a decade to reach a solid financial exit for the founders and investors through an acquisition or IPO. Think about our earlier references to Facebook and Uber. Facebook took nine years to go public and Uber, ten. They were built over a long period of time with tremendous effort.

We don't want to dissuade you from trying to generate as much revenue as you can early on. And, there are successful companies that have funded themselves with revenue. Doing that usually stunts the company's growth and leads to a lot of risk. We just think bootstrapping doesn't generate enough capital to put your company on the trajectory you want or need. Startups often need to invest heavily in their initial solution and have long lead times between when a product is built and when it's ready for sale. In the early stages, these startups almost never get their product to market fast enough to generate revenue from customers. These startups need to get outside capital for the business.

If you are building a high-growth startup—a business with a significant opportunity to be scalable and continuously grow—then we strongly advise that after you've done the planning we discussed in the previous section, you raise money and charge toward your goals as fast as you can.

If you are building a high-growth startup—a business with a significant opportunity to be scalable and continuously grow—then we strongly advise that you raise money and charge toward your goals as fast as you can.

What It Means to Raise Money

While we almost always advocate that you raise money for your startup, we don't ever take lightly the obligations and responsibilities that raising money entails. In many ways, it's a bit of a sacred pact in the entrepreneurial world. Your side of the pact includes putting your investors alongside of you, making them ostensibly an equal partner in your baby. You commit to being a thoughtful steward of their funds, and you work hard to create a success for both you and your new partner.

On the other side, an investor's part of the pact is to be helpful, supportive, and "do no harm." We are using the term *investor* here loosely to represent any person or firm that is providing money or even services to your startup in exchange for some type of ownership in the business. These are not legal obligations (there are many of those that we'll discuss later), but rather, they're a view into how the startup community functions and, in our opinion, how they should function concerning investments.

As a founder, if you decide to raise money, you should expect your business to change. You should want it to change. You have a (hopefully) wonderful new financial partner or partners to help you build your business. You'll want to run the business more methodically, sharing your objectives and plans, including financial metrics, strategy, and overall performance, with your new partners. Ideally, you'll also regularly get together with your investors to talk about the business and learn from them and they from you. As part of the investment, you'll also have several legal obligations with respect to the investment, including sharing of key information, approval of certain transactions, and how returns are distributed to your investors.

We'd definitely advise that you spend time with other founders who have raised money in similar ways. Get their feedback and advice. Discuss how their businesses changed for the better (or worse) by having certain types of investors involved. There are pitfalls with all investors, for sure. As you seek out information, you'll probably hear some horror stories about investment relationships that went bad. Keep in mind that while you should learn from these, they are in the minority. Few companies fail because of their investors per se.

Glossary of Terms

Before we dive into how to raise money for your startup, we want to define a few terms and ideas that we'll be talking about. There is lingua franca when you raise money, and it is better for you to know it before you step into discussions with investors. This is one of those topics where educating yourself as much as possible before you engage with investors is helpful. While you may be learning on the job, you'll probably not want to appear like you're still working on the most rudimentary concepts in front of investors. We're here to help.

Equity

Equity is another word for ownership in the company. Equity can refer to different classes of stock, including stock options. It is generally used in the context of how much ownership a person or entity has, that is, the amount of the company they own. The term is also used to denote a specific type of financing. An equity round is one in which ownership of the company is sold in exchange for cash, usually through the sale of stock.

Capitalization Table

Cap table, for short, is a spreadsheet of all the people and entities that own a part of the company. Every type of equity is listed along with the number of shares, what it cost to purchase those shares, and what ownership percentage that person or entity has in the business. Cap tables can become incredibly complex as the number of rounds and investors increases. Your cap table determines how proceeds are distributed upon an exit of the company.

Convertible Note

While the convertible note is a debt instrument, it is almost always just a path to a future equity investment. With a convertible note, the investor exchanges cash for a note from the company. The note, generally, states that the company will repay the debt or will convert the debt to equity in the company at a future date. The intent is that this conversion will take place. Usually, the conversion happens at the next equity round that the company closes, and the terms of the note usually provide a discount to the equity round and/or a cap on what the valuation of the company (what the company is worth) will be at that time.

Convertible notes have become popular as the primary form of early investment in the tech investment sector because money can be raised without the founders and investors agreeing on a current valuation. Basically, it kicks the can down the road. The convertible note converts into equity at the valuation chosen during the next equity round.

Liquidation

When a company has an exit, one in which the founders and investors (unfortunately, sometimes only the investors—see liquidation preference below) receive a return on their investment, it comes in the form of cash or sometimes stock in the acquiring company. This cash or stock is exchanged proportionately for stock owned in the company exiting. The exit itself is referred to as the liquidation event. The total value of the cash or stock is called the liquidation amount, and the order in which the exchange happens is called the liquidation preference. Those with greater liquidation preference get their money first. If the liquidation amount is low, some founders and/or investors may not receive anything.

Common Stock

This is the base type of ownership in a corporation. The common stock of a company is, as its name implies, generally the most common form of stock in any company. It is usually the type of stock given to founders. Options for common stock, that is, the option to buy shares of common stock at a low price, are usually what are granted to employees. Common stock is generally the last in line to receive proceeds from the liquidation of the company if there is debt or preferred stock involved.

Preferred Stock

A class of stock that has some preferences over the common stock is called preferred stock. Preferred stock can have any number of advantages over the common stock, but in financing rounds, the key ones that investors will focus on are liquidation preference over the common stock and anti-dilution rights—the right not to have their ownership reduced through dilution in subsequent financing rounds.

Stock Options

An agreement to purchase stock in the startup at a certain price is called a stock option. Stock options generally vest over a period of time and are used to incentivize employees. Stock options are ideal for granting to employees because they can be exercised when the employee chooses, assuming the options have vested. As such, employees don't have an out-of-pocket expense for the underlying stock until they want it. Often, they delay the exercise until there is a liquidity event and can exercise and sell at the same time.

A key negotiating point for both founders and investors is the size of the stock option pool, or the amount of equity that is reserved to be granted to key employees who will join the startup. While this can get complicated, investors will often want the reserved option pool (usually 10 to 20 percent of the company) to be allocated prior to their investing. That way, the dilution created by the allocation of the pool will only affect the founders. You'll want this pool to be allocated as part of the funding round so everyone is diluted equally by the formation of the pool.

Valuation

Valuation is a term used to describe how much your company is worth. In the context of a financing round, you will hear investors and others say, *pre-money valuation* and *post-money valuation*. These terms essentially refer to the value of the company before money is invested (pre) and after money has been invested (post). For example, if your company has a pre-money valuation of $4 million and you raise $2 million, then your post-money valuation will be $6 million. The infusion of $2 million into a company already worth $4 million results in a company now worth $6 million.

Dilution

Dilution is the amount that the pre-investment ownership is decreased once an investment has been completed. Every time you take on an investment, your amount of ownership in the company is diluted since new shares need to be created to exchange for a new investment, the total number of shares increases, and therefore, your proportion decreases. In the previous example in valuation, the existing owners have been diluted by 33 percent ($2 million/$6 million). Founders will want to pay attention to the dilution that they experience over time. It is important to raise money, but dilution is the factor that impacts your personal ownership. Don't be afraid of it. As we'll discuss, a small piece of a big pie is usually much more valuable than a big piece of a small pie.

Term Sheet

The high-level set of legal terms that an investor will deliver to you when they are ready to make an investment is known as the term sheet. This set of terms outlines the investor's proposal to the company and is then subsequently used as the outline for the final legal documents. Note that term sheets are generally non-binding, so don't assume if you have been given a term sheet that you are guaranteed an investment.

Due Diligence

Due diligence is the process by which a potential investor inspects the company to ensure they know what they are investing in. Due diligence encompasses just about every area of the company, but investors will often pay particular attention to your legal documents, contracts, founder/employee agreements, and other major documents and filings. You can expect due diligence on your product, technology, competitive advantage, and even members of the founding team.

Lead Investor

The investor who leads the effort to invest in a company is known as the lead investor. This person or firm will generally negotiate the terms of the investment round with the company and also leads the effort on due diligence. The lead investor will also often take the point position on the legal documents and review. They may become a board member of the company as well. Securing a lead investor, if possible, is a significant step in the financing process, and this person or firm is also often very helpful with finding other potential investors.

Seed Round

Generally, the first financing round for a startup is known as the seed round. Usually, companies raise a small amount of money during this round that can help them get off the ground. The money is often used to build the first version of a product, hire a few employees, and bring an early version of the solution to market. Note that there are many stages of a seed round now including pre-seed (before a seed round) and seed-prime (sometimes referred to as seed round 2), which are extensions of the initial seed round. The average seed round for a startup now is $2.2m, three times what it was only a decade ago.*

Series A

Series A is usually the first significant funding round for a startup. Companies seek Series A funding when they are ready to start selling a solution to the market on a much larger scale. At the Series A level, the company is likely still investing heavily in enhancing and deepening the company's solution, and they're searching for that group of customers that will purchase their solution on a larger scale. Almost assuredly, companies looking for their Series A financing are still losing money.

Series B

At the Series B funding stage, the startup is typically transitioning to start scaling its sales efforts and beginning to grow at a much more significant rate. Usually, the startup's business model has begun to coalesce, and it is moving toward critical mass and maybe even profitability.

***

While self-funding can work for a limited number of startups, the vast majority of new enterprises will need to raise money to grow fast and to scale. There are certainly various ways to go about raising capital, of course, but there is a well-worn path that most startups before you have carved. Using that path, at least as your starting point, can help you optimize your chances for successfully raising money and getting your company on the right track.

Keep in mind that the entrepreneurial ecosystem has its own language. Knowing that language doesn't make it any easier to succeed, but it does help a lot when communicating with people outside your company. This is especially true with investors who seem to live and die by the vocabulary of their vocation. Not knowing what they mean can be, well, embarrassing and, even worse, can send a signal that you're not quite ready for prime time.

Chapter 18

Sources of Capital

The majority of companies that get outside funding get their capital from a combination of angel (people who invest for themselves) and institutional (people who invest for others) investors. But, as an investor, I (Will) run across companies that have to find innovative funding mechanisms from time to time. Deciding whether to engage with these companies can be a difficult call. Obviously, not being able to get interest from angels and institutions is a red flag, after all. But sometimes, unconventional funding mechanisms are ideal for a new venture.

First, you need capital. If you can't get it from angels or VCs, you simply have to find another way to get it. Now, I wouldn't recommend you sell your soul for money, or for any other reason, but it might turn out that getting your capital from other channels is the only way you can get it. If that's the case, why wouldn't you try something a bit different? It's not only that alternate means might be your only source of funding, but they might just be faster or easier for you than beating on the standard methods for a long time.

Another thing to consider is that going a different route might help you in marketing and overall visibility. If you can kill two birds with one stone, why not go for it?

There are a handful of investments I've made recently that successfully found alternate funding methods. Some were standalone—the unconventional method was the only source of funding—and some were in combination with more traditional funding. Here are some examples.

- Kuvee—Crowdfunding via Indiegogo. Kuvee, a startup that built a wine decanter and an innovative wine distribution channel rolled out their initial product via crowdfunding. The company also had angel investors, had money from an accelerator and had involved an institutional investor. Still, the opportunity to raise some early cash and get the associated marketing from their crowdfunding campaign was compelling.
- LovePop—Shark Tank. Yeah, this one is unusual. LovePop is a startup that designs, manufactures, and distributes 3D popup greeting cards. They applied to and were accepted by the show and got money from one of the "sharks." While the valuation wasn't great, they got a reasonable amount of startup capital and, more importantly, got loads of visibility as they kicked off their company. LovePop also had money from an accelerator, angels, and a VC.
- Airfox—ICO (Initial Coin Offering). Airfox, which offers an array of financial services to emerging markets, successfully executed one of the first ICOs. The ICO not only raised cash for the company, but the tokens created are fundamental to the way the company operates. This synergy made the ICO a solid choice at the time. This is much harder to do now. Airfox also had money from an accelerator and angels.

- Petnet—Strategic Investment. Petnet makes an auto-mated pet feeder and collects data about a pet's eating habits. They also sell pet food based on the data they collect. The company took money from Petco Animal Supply Stores as a strategic investor in an early round. Strategics often invest to gain some level of control over the product or company. They also are less sensitive to val-uation. Both were the case at Petnet that took the money alongside some institutional and angel investment.

As an investor in these companies, I scrutinized each of the alternate investments and in each case, felt they were a good way to go. Overall, I've been happily surprised by the marketing and visibility impact of many of them. But they can come at some cost that initially concerned me. Sometimes the old-fashioned way is the easiest way, as long as it's available to you.

Loads of Options

You have a number of options for raising capital. While the list below isn't exhaustive, it should provide you with a broad set of choices for funding sources to think about and discuss with your founding team.

Some of the options below are exclusive of one another. Others can be used together or in sequence. A few, however, are standalone and need to be focused on individually. For example, if you fund your company through debt, it will be dif-ficult to get an individual or venture capital investor involved until you've paid off all the debt; early stage investors don't want their money used to pay off previous notes. They want their investment to go toward moving the business forward.

As you consider what funding sources are best for your company, think ahead about the long-term goals you have for your startup. If you plan to sell the company, merge with a larger entity, or take the company public, you can start with almost any source of capital. If, however, you plan to run your company for a very long time and keep it independent, several funding sources that involve an actual investment in exchange for ownership may not be available to you. Investors are in it to get back a premium on their investment, after all, not to keep it locked inside the company.

Like we've said before and will continue to emphasize throughout the book, there is no best option in the list below—just what's right for your startup. Each funding source has its pros and cons. The best thing you can do is to explore each of the options and then figure out what's right for your company, or what you and your co-founding team prefer.

Bear in mind that sometimes the best option is the only one that's available to you.

Bootstrapping

- **Pros:** There's no dilution, and you maintain full control over the business.
- **Cons:** It's difficult to grow fast, and you don't get experienced support tied to the business.

Some companies initially opt to forego raising money from outside investors or to take on debt. Instead, these companies prefer to bootstrap—generating the fuel they need from the sales of their products to customers. We see this approach with small companies just starting out, where two or three people are in a garage or basement with the early concepts of an idea. The idea hasn't been fleshed out, and they can't demonstrate a broad value proposition to garner attention from outside investors just yet.

They opt to sell their product to show traction and generate cash to keep them afloat. Often, this is because they can offer their product as a service or heavily customize it on a consulting basis. If your offering is a service, you might be able to sell a subset of your final offering or a customized version that meets the needs of a smaller set of customers. This is, of course, not scalable, but it can provide some initial cash for the business.

There are other reasons why you may choose to bootstrap. Perhaps you don't feel your company is a venture-funded business, which means you don't believe you can return many multiples of the money you take from investors. Or, maybe you have been fortunate to find customers during the vetting of your idea, and you don't need external money right away. Or, perhaps you have enough cash personally to cover your early expenses.

Whatever the reason, bootstrapping your business can be a viable way to grow your startup. If you can get money from customers without giving up a portion of your company or incurring debt, then that's great. But, just remember, even if you bootstrap the business, you are still raising money, just through different means.

Bootstrapping isn't without its limits. Rarely does it result in generating the fuel that founders need to build and sell their first product. If you need a huge influx of cash and quickly, then it's unlikely that bootstrapping will help you.

If you decide to bootstrap, just be prepared that you'll risk letting competitors into your space because of potentially slow, underfunded growth.

Friends and Family

- **Pros**: These are supportive investors, and that means (usually) a quick, low overhead process that's minimally invasive to the operations of the business.
- **Cons**: Generally, they can invest only small amounts of money with large relationship risks. You'll likely lose out on experienced support and advice.

Friends and family is a broad term to denote anyone around you who invests because of a personal relationship. This path can be an easy one that's available to you immediately. Most likely, these people are already supportive of you. They know you, so when they invest, they're betting on you, your work ethic, and who you are as a person as opposed to investing in the business. The amount of money you'll raise through this channel will vary. We've seen founders raise hundreds of thousands of dollars, and sometimes more, depending on the age and experience of your inner circle and their financial standing, but more often, it's tens of thousands.

If you choose to pursue this path, just know it's risky. You want to be completely sure that you have strong relationships with the people who will invest. With 90 percent of startups failing, there's a high probability that you'll lose their money. Can your relationships withstand this outcome? Do your friends and family have disposable money, or will the stress of getting their money back damage your relationships?

For some people, and in some instances, it's fine, and this is a great option to raise money. For other people, it isn't. We've seen too many relationships destroyed over lost investments. So, before choosing this path, we strongly advise you to carefully consider the bonds of your relationships and whether they're worth jeopardizing. It's also worth having candid conversations with these investors about the realistic chances for success, so they understand what they're getting into.

Accelerators/Incubators

- **Pros**: Access to mentors and experienced advisors, which may ultimately lead to a stronger overall company and the next, larger financing round.
- **Cons**: Minimal dollars are invested for a large portion of the company. Location may also be an issue, depending upon the program.

Accelerators and incubators (which we are just calling accelerators) have emerged as an excellent source for capital and, perhaps more importantly, for advice and connections. While accelerators vary in their focus, exact program, amount of money they provide, and several other parameters, the general process is roughly the same. You'll apply to join their program. Then, you'll go through a rigorous process to ensure you're a fit for their program and whether their program is a fit for you.

If selected, you'll generally receive a fixed sum of money for a fixed amount of equity in your company. In exchange for that, you'll be part of their program or class of startups. The accelerator will then work with you to start building your company. Usually, the program will have a number of experts in a variety of areas, and you'll be able to tap these individuals to get help and support.

If you choose this path, just know that you aren't choosing it to raise a large sum of money.

While the program will likely offer you the chance to raise more money in the future through strategic connections that these organizations provide, the real value of accelerators is that they offer select entrepreneurs a short window of time (usually three to six months) to converge at a location and soak up mentorship and guidance from other entrepreneurs, investors, and executives. This can help to accelerate the growth of a company, and it increases the likelihood that the company can raise additional capital. Often, there are serious investors connected with these programs, who work with companies directly from the first day they arrive at the accelerator.

Of course, if you're in the early stages of the company and you're depending on your product or service, then the small amount of initial money can be quite significant. Just know that there is a cost to joining these programs, which is giving up a significant amount of equity at a low valuation.

Techstars, for example, a leading accelerator we're involved with as mentors and investors, offers startups in its program $20,000 in exchange for 6 percent of the company in common stock; a $100,000 convertible note to be converted to equity in the next round; and mentorship and office space for three months. Techstars estimates that companies raise about $2.0 million in outside capital, on average, after they go through the program.*

The accelerator, Bolt, that we're also involved with, has a different model. They are a combination of the classic accelerator, offering facilities, mentoring, and product development help, and a new generation of venture capital. Instead of giving a fixed amount of money to companies, they participate or lead the company's first round of funding. So, when a company joins Bolt, it does so as it completes its first equity round. Bolt's area of expertise is hardware-driven technology startups, and they bring to bear a number of experts in the field. Bolt often works with the company for an extended period of time, recognizing that it may take a bit longer to deliver a hardware-centric product to market.

Accelerators are a particularly popular choice for startups. The percentage of companies raising money in a Series A round (usually the first major investment round that a startup takes) that started in an accelerator has been increasing for several years. Recent reports state that about one-third of all the companies who get Series A financing have been through an accelerator.[†]

Angel Investors

- **Pros**: Founders find (potentially) smart, experienced investors and access to enough money to get started in a significant way. The due diligence and investment process is usually fairly light.
- **Cons**: There may not be follow-on capital available, and angels sometimes like to have a lead investor in place before they invest.

An angel investor is an individual who invests in early stage startups. Usually, angels are nonprofessional investors who invest their own money. Typically, an angel is an entrepreneur, executive, or retiree who is open to investing before institutional money (venture capital) is invested in a startup. However, angels often invest side-by-side with venture capitalists in early rounds, too.

Angel investors have historically been the group that high-tech startups have tapped for their first or second influx of capital.

While there may be many reasons that angels invest in startups, generally their interest extends beyond the financial return. Angels are often people who want to give back to the startup community by giving a new generation of entrepreneurs a chance. They may also be interested in helping the company and mentoring a founding team during their development. In other cases, the angel may be interested in the market the company addresses and has some experience to bring to bear.

For many of these reasons, angels are generally willing to take on bigger, earlier risks than venture capitalists. Of course, angels are in a good position to reap the rewards for that increased risk with a lower valuation. Angels often also have fewer legal and operational demands and, generally, won't demand a board seat. Their investment is passive, for the most part, but some angels may provide advice and counsel for founders who want it.

Although getting angels to invest is often easier than say, venture capitalists, the one downside is that you rarely get huge sums of money from them. Typically, in the high-tech space, individual angel investors invest between $10,000 and $100,000 into a startup with the median being about $25,000. If you need to raise $500,000, you'll want to find one or two investors who can put in a large proportion of that and then round out the rest with smaller checks from other angels. The end result is that you may need many investors to fill out your entire round.

It can be a challenge to manage a large number of small investors. It's often difficult to get many angels to move to closure since each one is looking out for their own best interests. Without someone taking the lead on doing the due diligence and the creation of a term sheet, the funding process can drag on.

But, for many startups and over many years, angel investors have been a critical part of the startup community, and they continue to play a crucial role in funding many new, innovative companies. They could be an excellent source of capital for your startup.

Angel Funds

- **Pros**: Potential access to a large number of angel investors with a single point of contact.
- **Cons**: The process of getting broad support by the individual angels who make up the angel funds can take a long time. The amount of money available from the funds can vary widely.

While most angels invest as individuals, some angel investors band together into angel groups or funds to invest in various startups. By gathering numerous investors into one fund, angel funds can pool more capital and leverage a group of investors for deal flow, due diligence, and legal review.

Generally, an angel fund looks like one investment entity to the startup, but it represents money from a number of angels. Even if, legally, the angel fund isn't just one investment entity, angel funds can tap their network of potential investors to pool together a larger investment. This funding source may work better for startups looking to raise a larger amount of capital in the early stages since most angel funds invest in early stage startups.

Using an angel fund can be a win-win for founders and angel investors. Ideally, as a founder, you can avoid having separate meetings with dozens of angels. Instead, you can make your presentation, or pitch, a few times to key investors in the group. Once you've convinced them your company is worth investing in, they'll take their recommendation to the group. Angel investors benefit from the group by seeing deals that they would otherwise not have seen.

The downside of angel groups is that they are often disjointed and run without a strong, centralized decision-making process. It's difficult for the founder to ascertain how much money they'll get from the fund. Often, it takes a long time to get enough angels involved with an investment.

If you're interested in this vehicle, then it's best to research different angel funds to find the best fit for your startup. Angel funds cover anything from specific geographic locations to particular industries.

In our experience, most of the companies we work with that have tried to get funding through angel funds became frustrated with the process, gave up, and found other avenues for investment. While your mileage may vary, we'd suggest you use angel groups as a backup resource rather than a primary one.

AngelList

> - **Pros**: Access to a larger amount of capital that usually entails a light funding process, similar to angel investors.
> - **Cons**: May not offer access to follow-on financing from the Angel-List syndicate and may not have experienced support for the business.

A unique type of investment platform that has gained a great deal of interest and following is AngelList. AngelList was created in 2010 as an online clearinghouse or match-making service that pairs angels with startups looking for investments. While AngelList still fills this role, AngelList's model has morphed over the last few years. It now also functions as a group of angel funds or seed funds. Individual and small groups of angels do research and propose funds that other angel investors can join. Founders can research these syndicates online and contact the lead investor to see if they have interest in their company and want to sponsor an investment.[‡] The AngelList syndicate will then share the deal with their private investors and other angels in their network. Because of AngelList's scale, this investment option can look a lot like a large angel round or even a small VC round.

We work with several companies who have successfully raised investment capital through AngelList syndicates. The process worked well, although it's too early to know how this will appear to investors when these companies seek further investment in future rounds.

Venture Capital

- **Pros**: Professional investors with significant experience and generally deep pockets can support the company for long periods of time.
- **Cons**: The VC's goal is to make money, so you give up some control and potentially significant equity to gain their support.

Think of venture capital firms as professional investors. They exist to return money to their investors by investing in great startups and helping those startups succeed. Generally, a venture capital firm and its general partners (the individuals who invest and support their investments) are experts in particular markets. The venture capitalists leverage their expertise to get investors, such as endowment funds, pensions, family offices, high-net worth individuals, and others, for their VC fund. Once the VC firm has capital to invest, the firm searches for startups that match their investment criteria. As you would expect, professional investors have a high bar for who and what they invest in. They see thousands of companies a year and often will only invest in a handful.

Venture capital often makes sense for startups that are expecting to grow fast and need significant amounts of capital over the life of their business.

But, taking VC money isn't a decision you should make lightly or nonchalantly.

When you accept venture capital, it's more than just the money; it's picking up a long-term, serious relationship with someone and their firm. More than likely, they'll have a seat on your board, and they'll want to know the ins and outs of your business until your company has an exit—a liquidation event that returns multiples of their invested capital. As we tell many founders, taking VC money is like getting married—with no option for divorce. They will always be on your cap table and, likely, involved in your business with more control than you'd think.

For startups, venture capital can be a great vehicle to access significant amounts of money, but not all venture capital firms are created equal. There are venture firms for just about every major area of business. If there is a significant opportunity to create companies, you can bet that there is a VC firm that specializes in that area. And, that's a good thing. VCs can bring tremendous domain experience, connections, and credibility to a startup.

There is also another side to VC money that, as an entrepreneur, you need to understand. While technically a VC's fiduciary responsibility is to your startup, ultimately, they are paid by their limited partners, the investors in their fund. Their exclusive job is to generate high returns for their investors. Your startup, among many others, is the sole vehicle for them to create those returns. Unfortunately, doing the right thing for your company and for their fund sometimes differs, and this can create problems, particularly along the lines of timing of liquidity or the need for certain valuations.

Additionally, the wrong VC firm or partner working on your startup can be destructive. If the VC firm or partner feels like your business isn't headed in the right direction, they won't hesitate to step up their level of involvement and even advocate (or outright demand) significant changes, including bringing in new management, letting founders go, changing the strategy of the business, or even changing economics of their investment.

Your VC's first and primary concern is to deliver great returns to their investors, and they'll do whatever they can to see that happen.

All that being said, if you are fortunate enough to get it, a venture capital investment is an excellent avenue to help grow your company. Many of the VCs that we've worked with have been excellent. They've cared deeply about the founders they have worked with and the businesses they have funded. They have been true partners and integral to the company's success.

Small-Cap Venture Capital Funds

- **Pros**: Professional investors who often move fast, are focused on early stage companies, and are well connected to help pull a round together.
- **Cons**: May not be able to make follow-on investments and continue to support the company financially over the long term due to fund size.

One type of VC is known as a small-cap VC. This is a venture capital fund that is on the smaller side, say, less than $75M of capital to be invested. Generally, these funds have a small number of partners and associates and, because they don't have capital to invest in huge Series B investments (or beyond), tend to invest in earlier stage companies—in their seed or Series A rounds.

Sometimes, these funds invest alone, but often, they invest alongside angels to complete a good-sized seed round. Their processes are usually faster and less cumbersome than that of larger VCs.

Government or Commercial Grants

> - **Pros**: Credibility. Potentially less expensive cash (may not be dilutive at all).
> - **Cons**: Highly competitive and can be at the whim of changing sentiment and markets. Government grants may not be available with administration changes. Generally, grants occur one-time with little, if any, long-term support.

Grants can be an alternate method of generating some capital for your organization. You will often see grants for companies solving basic science or technology problems in the commercial sector. You can also seek US government grants from a wide variety of sources, including the Defense Advanced Research Projects Agency (DARPA) and the branches of the military, Health and Human Services, Department of Energy, and many more.

There is also a popular US government grant for small businesses called the Small Business Innovative Research grant (SBIR). You submit a proposal that shows your company fits a set of predefined requirements, including the development of a new and relatively unique concept in return for potential funding. The grants are readily available and are small (initially up to $150,000). And, did we mention that they're grants? You don't have to pay the money back or give up any equity to get them. They are a great way to get started, especially if you're working on something that one of the funding government agencies is interested in.**

In our experience, these grants are less aimed at startups and more at small businesses. Your startup, though, may qualify, and a grant may be an excellent source of capital.

Similarly, commercial grants are also available. Often, large commercial entities or nonprofits may provide grants for innovative research or capabilities that are important to them. An example of this is the XPRIZE, where a number of donors come together to sponsor a competition for technology that will benefit mankind. The most famous of which is the Ansari XPRIZE that gave $10 million to the team that could fly a ship 100 kilometers into space twice within two weeks. Of course, not every grant needs to be as extreme in every sense; there may be grants from companies or nonprofits that would be an excellent fit for your startup and industry.

If you go down this path, you should make sure you understand that grants can often require a longer lead time, especially if the government is involved. While most grants are sensitive to intellectual property (IP) issues, it is something you will need to verify. You'll want to make sure you own the IP you create under the grant solely, and if you don't, that the situation won't hamper your future efforts.

Startup Competitions

- **Pros**: Significant visibility, and they generally don't require that you give up any equity for the money.
- **Cons**: Highly competitive and usually offer only small amounts of money.

Startup competitions have grown in popularity over the years, with more city, state, university, and privately funded competitions that encourage entrepreneurial activity. Many competitions are sector specific, too. For example, there are competitions focused on finding the best alternative energy company, where the winner gets $50,000. In Massachusetts, there's a competition called Mass Challenge. This is a state-run competition that's actually an accelerator. At the end of the acceleration period, the best companies receive substantial grants. In total, the Mass Challenge gives out $1 million a year to deserving companies.

Many schools and universities also hold competitions. MIT has a famous startup competition, and many schools have followed suit. For those founders willing to look into competitions, there's real money available. The catch with many of these competitions is that you need to launch your company at their event or somehow be tied to it (which makes doing multiple competitions difficult). These competitions are looking to show the world that the best startups are connected to them, and that drives more sponsorship and investment dollars to them.

Customers and Partners

- **Pros**: Investments from these are less dilutive and brings credibility to the company. The customer or partner can also give significant feedback and insight into the market.
- **Cons**: There may be IP issues, and company direction may be compromised in favor of the customer or partner. The customer or partner may not really care about the outcome of the startup.

Your customers can be an excellent source of capital. If you have a valuable product and one that may be in high demand, your customers may advance you money to go build the solution. Or, perhaps your customers or a company that wants to partner with you may be interested in investing in your company.

We see this in the business-to-business realm, where a customer or a group of customers desperately need the product you're building. In this case, they may be willing to commit a large sum of money up front to help you build it. It's like a pre-sale of the product. Sometimes, in this scenario, your customer may also want to invest in the company or receive some equity in exchange for their early commitment. Sometimes, when customers make a purchase commitment or invest at this early stage, they do it as a strategic move. They can learn about a new category, product, or critical area that they are interested in.

The downside of having a customer as an investor or one major early customer is that they can take you down a path that isn't what the rest of the market wants. You'll want to be careful that you don't sacrifice your long-term opportunity for short-term money.

You should note that this opportunity isn't just available early in the company's life. There are opportunities to use customers as a funding source or product development partner at many points throughout the life of a company. You'll want to be very careful about intellectual property ownership, but customers can be an excellent source of capital, information, and validation.

If you decide to take an investment from a customer or partner, often referred to as a strategic investment, it can be a cheaper alternative than the other sources (i.e., you give up less of your company for the money). The reason for this is because often the customer isn't just driven by a financial return, and, in fact, the financial return may not actually be all that important to them. But, you do need to prepare for what you'll hand over in exchange for that investment or early purchase. In these types of deals, sometimes a startup will give up revenue, a piece of the market, exclusivity on a partnership, or advanced access to their solution.

Perhaps the most significant right that corporate investors will ask for is a "right of first refusal" on a sale of the company to a competitor or other party. They'll want to leave their options open to be able to swoop in at the last moment to buy your startup instead of allowing you to sell to somebody else. This can be a significant issue and one that should be carefully thought through with your legal advisors. It's possible other potential acquirers may never even engage with you when someone else holds a right of first refusal. You want to avoid this situation if you possibly can.

Crowdfunding

- **Pros**: Minimally dilutive and often can test the validity of a solution in the market.
- **Cons**: Receive very little ongoing support for the company financially or otherwise.

There are two forms of crowdfunding: (1) reward-based crowdfunding, and (2) equity-based crowdfunding. In reward-based crowdfunding, large groups of customers finance the product development by pre-buying the product. In equity-based crowdfunding, large groups of people each invest a small amount of money that, when pooled, can act as a seed round for the company.

Rewards-based crowdfunding platforms such as Kickstarter and Indiegogo are becoming more popular. It's a way for people everywhere to encourage development of products, services, and creative projects. For founders, it is a great source of capital without having to give up any equity. There are other benefits, too, such as being able to see whether your target market is interested in purchasing your offering.

Equity-based crowdfunding platforms like CircleUp or AngelList (see above) band a large number of small investors together without any (or minimal) direct contact from the company. When using these platforms, you could potentially have one hundred investors who commit only $1,000 each. New US Securities laws are making crowdfunding easier, too. The laws around crowdfunding are changing rapidly, so we suggest that you speak with a lawyer if you go down this path to make sure you're on the right side of the law.

The downside—if you can say it is a negative—is that effectively you are incurring debt. You are obligated (at minimum, ethically) to deliver on your pre-orders via these crowdfunding platforms.

Debt

- **Pros**: Less dilutive.
- **Cons**: Significant risks if the startup can't pay back the loan.

Taking on debt is an option if you can get it. For startups, debt is a high-risk gamble for both the company and the investor. Startups usually haven't fully implemented their business model, so there isn't a predictable revenue stream coming in that can be used to pay back the debt. Even still, there are often lenders out there, who are willing to give startups debt, particularly when it comes alongside capital from other sources.

We'll talk about a couple of different types of debt, but our strong advice is that you should not take on debt unless you have a very clear sense of how you will pay it back.

Unlike a convertible note, which allows the debt to be converted into equity, the debt that we are talking about here needs to be paid back to the lender with interest. There is often a specific timeline, and if the startup is delinquent paying back its loan, there can be significant consequences, including shifting ownership of the company and its intellectual property to the lender. Debt is a high-risk gamble for a startup.

All of this being said, there are specific banks that like to lend to startups, but only in certain situations. These banks will lend to venture-backed startups where they have close relationships with the investors. While the investors, VCs in particular, aren't guaranteeing the loan, there is an unwritten agreement between the bank and the VC that if the startup cannot raise more money, then the VC will help make sure the bank is paid back before the company liquidates or runs out of money. It's a gamble for the bank, but we've seen that the relationship between the VC and the bank is an important one for both sides. As a result, both sides respect this unwritten agreement.

If a startup can gain some predictability in its revenue stream and has a model where there is consistency in cash flow, then there are often specific investors who will provide debt to these types of companies. In this case, the lender will want to be able to exert significant control in the case where the startup fails to pay them back. The legal documents will allow the lender to do this. Lenders of this type will know that they can adjust the business to run on its cash flow until they have their return. Of course, the founders and management team may not agree, but they may not have a choice in the matter. This is yet another reason why debt is a scary path of capital for a young company to pursue.

Before you take on debt, think hard about the potential downside scenarios. Unlike the other types of investors, lenders of debt, in particular, aren't in the business of losing their money.

* * *

As you think about what funding sources will fit your company best, spend a little time considering how the sources you choose will reflect on you. In current investing parlance, this is called signaling. Signaling happens when some event takes place with respect to your current investors that influences potential future investors to either invest or not. While most VCs deny signaling takes place, we can assure you that it does. Is it the most important factor when you are looking for money? No, but it is a factor.

Obviously, this is only important if you actually have funding choices. If you do and you're closing your seed round with money from a particular source, pause and think about what future investors will think of the choice you made. If you choose debt, for example, it will be difficult for you to get equity funding if you haven't paid the debt off. If you close your seed round with fifty different angel investments, some institutional investors may question whether they want to be part of such a complex cap table. A subtler signal takes place when you choose a high-end VC in your seed round that then

	Amount of Money	Stage of Company	Preferred Rounds	Support/ Help	Legal Overhead
Bootstrapping	$	Early	Pre-Seed	N/A	N/A
Friends & Family	$	Early	Pre-Seed	*	*
Accelerators & Incubators	$	Early	Pre-Seed	****	***
Angel Investors/ Angel Funds	$$	Early	Seed	**	***
Venture Capital	$$$$	Any	Seed Onwards	****	***
Government & Commercial Grants	$$	Any	Any	*	**
Startup Competitions	$	Early	Pre-seed	*	*
Customer/Partner	$$	Any	Any	**	***
Debt	$$	Any	Any	*	***

Diagram 4   An Overview of Possible Investment Models
This chart is designed to help you categorize and think about which investment model is best for you. Feel free to extend this table to add the criteria that is important to you.

decides not to invest more in a subsequent round. This is a red flag for other investors. They wonder what your first investors know that they don't, and, often, they will simply pass as a result.

You shouldn't spend too much time on this, especially if you don't have many choices for investment on the table. We always tell companies we work with that money from virtually any source is better than no money. But, that doesn't mean founders should take the first money available to them. Like any consumer, founders should shop around for the best source of capital, given their needs and the availability of money.

Knowing the basics of the fundraising process is critical to the success of your startup. Making a mistake with the wrong type of capital or partner can stunt the growth of a company—if not kill it. The good news is that the market is efficient and generally steers founders to the best type of capital for their business. Hopefully, this chapter will save you valuable time and get you to the right answer quickly. The more you can educate yourself on who the players are, the best path for raising money, and fair economics for your round, the better off you'll be.

Chapter 19

Prerequisites for Funding

I (Will) didn't have a clue that it was going to take us a full year to get funding for Viewlogic. As founders, we knocked on the doors of every investor we could find, usually getting turned away with negative feedback about the size of the market or the inexperience of the founding team.

Did we panic at times? Hell, yes! In fact, looking back, it's not clear to me why we never gave up. We deeply believed we had a good idea, and we all thought our team was excellent. We also had enough positive feedback from people in the industry to keep us believing that we would eventually get money. Or, maybe that was just naiveté and ignorance. Yeah, come to think if it, it was probably just that.

While all the rejection was painful, it forced us to focus our energy on making sure the business model was as tight as possible. We increased our efforts on talking with potential customers, on identifying our go-to-market strategy, on understanding our development challenges, and on understanding the minimum amount of money we needed to start with.

In the end, the maturity of our plan and the team, as a result of our many iterations of the business model, came through. We found two VCs who backed us in our seed round. They didn't give us much money, and the valuation was very low.

Mostly, we didn't care. We had some level of validation of the idea and the team, and we were able to get off and running. It certainly wasn't the easiest or shortest path, but it made both the company and the team better, while making it possible to get the critical funding we needed to kick things off.

Getting Capital

Now that you have a foundation in fundraising, let's walk through the process of making it happen. No, you aren't quite ready to go talk to investors yet. There's a significant amount of prep work, which needs to take place in the early stages of any financing process.

This chapter walks you through all the work you need to do to get your act together. The good news is that if you have been doing the work from the earlier chapters, this won't be so bad. You'll just need to assemble everything in a way that's more investor focused. Make no mistake about it, you are preparing to sell your idea, team, and new startup to potential investors. And, for that, you need to present your refined and vetted idea, all the data you've collected, and your deep understanding of your target market in a way that investors will understand and clamor to be a part of.

We can't emphasize enough that laying the groundwork we have talked about in previous chapters is critical to having a shot at raising money. Rarely do we see new founders succeed without putting in the level of effort required to deeply understand their potential customers, market, competition, and product fit. Even if you put in the long and dedicated hours of work, there's no guarantee of success. Raising money is a difficult process with a high failure rate. Do your best to stack the odds in your favor and optimize your chances for a great outcome.

Before You Raise Money

Before you race to set up meetings with potential investors, it's wise to pause to consider whether you can even raise money and what you need to do if you can. Investors are surrounded by startups lobbying for their money. Without a doubt, you'll face stiff competition for investors' attention and dollars.

For this chapter, we'll use the term *investor* loosely. For example, an individual participating through Kickstarter in your startup isn't generally referred to as an investor (they are called backers), but we think that referring to investors as anyone who puts money into companies at any stage and via any method will simplify the discussion in this chapter. So, we include all investment sources from the previous chapter in the investor bucket. Just remember that the process for getting capital from each of the potential sources may be slightly different. We'll outline what you should know for each investment source and give you tips for optimizing them.

You want to be strategic about your approach with all types of investors. While it's different for every company and sector, investors typically follow a similar cadence and approach before they hand out cash. While successful, experienced founders may be able to take shortcuts in raising capital, we always advise that you shouldn't skip any steps, even if you can. The work you put in during the investment process is invaluable as is the feedback you'll garner as you talk to potential investors.

In this chapter, we'll also outline the steps you should take prior to running your investment process. There's usually an order of operations that founders need to take to prepare to raise money. It starts with nailing down your strategy and building your financial model. Once you have everything prepared, you'll be able to determine the amount of money you want to raise. From there, you can decide both how and from whom you should raise money. Then, finally, with all those prerequisites completed, you'll create a pitch deck or presentation that you'll give to potential investors. We'll walk you through what that looks like, too.

Ultimately, raising money is a systematic process of packaging your company in a way that crystallizes the opportunity for your potential investors. But, there is a side benefit from all the work: you'll likely also improve your business model along the way.

Nail Your Strategy and Business Model

At this point, you probably won't be surprised when we say that your first piece of homework is to nail your strategy and business model. All the work you've done in the previous chapters to iterate on your idea and build a coherent business plan is what you'll put to use here. Much of what we'll suggest echoes what we said in our discussion of the vetting process, but there's one stark difference. The lens that you'll use for all your work is that of your potential investor. The work we recommended you do earlier in vetting your idea had more to do with your internal research, but now you need to recut those same concepts with an external investor viewpoint. It's encapsulating your entire company into an easy to digest and coherent story.

Yes, this is as big as you think it is.

Since this is a big topic, we'll walk you through all the areas to consider. Of course, you should start at a high level and outline the market opportunity and why the opportunity exists for your startup. Ask yourself what pain points or problems your startup is solving and why are they are incredibly valuable to solve. You'll want to be able to clearly articulate who has the problem that your startup will address, and what these people—your potential customers and market—are doing to currently solve the problem. You'll want to look at your competitors, what substitutes exist, and how you'll help solve the problem more effectively. Sound familiar so far? It should.

Once you've outlined what problem you're solving and for whom, you'll want to discuss how you'll build your solution. Be concise. What special ingredients do you need? Is there a certain material or skill set required to build your solution? If so, how will you obtain that? Next, you'll outline how you'll tap into the market of people looking for your solution. What's the easiest, most cost-effective way to reach them and convince them to purchase your solution?

Once you have these answers—most of which you developed when exploring your idea with potential customers—you're ready to think through your business model. Ask yourself, "What am I charging for my product, and is it a one-time or recurring fee? Do I have the opportunity to increase my sales to my customer by selling them more of my solution or perhaps building additional solutions?" All these answers will factor into your business model. You'll also want to think through the cost to produce your solution and how much it costs to acquire a customer.

Here are the questions you need to answer in an easy-to-digest form:

- What is the market opportunity?
- What are the pain points you're addressing, i.e., why will people buy what you're selling?
- What are your potential customers doing to address this pain/problem today?
- What does the competition look like? What are the potential substitutes?
- How will you build your product? What skills or components are needed?
- How will you differentiate your startup from the status quo and the competition?
- How will you market and sell your product?

Putting all these answers together into a coherent strategy is your first step. Ideally, you'll also pull together specific actions and milestones associated with your strategy so you have a roadmap for execution. These milestones are critical because they're often the inflection points for your company, the points when your company significantly increases in value. For example, when you release your solution to the market, there is generally a big step up in value. Another key milestone in valuation is when you have found enough customers to validate your hypothesis that your solution meets a critical need in the market. That is, you've established product-market fit as we discussed in Chapter 7.

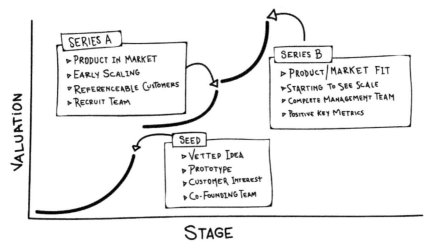

SERIES A
▷ PRODUCT IN MARKET
▷ EARLY SCALING
▷ REFERENCEABLE CUSTOMERS
▷ RECRUIT TEAM

SERIES B
▷ PRODUCT/MARKET FIT
▷ STARTING TO SEE SCALE
▷ COMPLETE MANAGEMENT TEAM
▷ POSITIVE KEY METRICS

SEED
▷ VETTED IDEA
▷ PROTOTYPE
▷ CUSTOMER INTEREST
▷ CO-FOUNDING TEAM

VALUATION

STAGE

Diagram 5   S-Curve Discontinuity

It is important to outline key milestones since these will be the points you'll want to fund your startup to, from major milestone to major milestone. That is, at any point, you'll want to raise enough money to carry you safely to the next major uptick in the value of your business. This will allow you to optimize your valuation, the amount of equity you keep, dilution, and capital at the same time. In this way, you'll raise the right amount of money to show significant progress as well as raise it at the highest value points you can. By outlining your roadmap to success, your potential investors will be pleased to see how you'll execute on your strategy as well as what your strategy is.

Generally, high-tech startups raise money every one to two years. In each round, raising about five times what they raised in the prior round. In the early stages, a decent rule of thumb is to assume your valuation will be about three to four times the amount that you are raising. These statistics confirm how founders fund themselves from major milestone to major milestone and use those inflection points to increase the value of their startup.*

Finally, here's another thing for you to consider as part of your strategy: How will you return an investor's money with a significant multiple? Or, said another way, what's the exit strategy for your startup? Are you planning to ultimately sell it or take it public? How long do you think it will take? Any serious investor knows this is just conjecture, but what they're looking for is your thought process. What does it take to get your business to a place where it can exit, and if it will be acquired, who are the potential buyers? When it does exit, how are you calculating the value of the business? What are the fundamentals that drive that value? The more you can use industry norms for your assumptions, the more likely your model is believable. Of course, the potential investor will have their own models and thoughts, and you can bet that they will be calculating what returns they can generate from an investment in your business.

In fact, the exercise of working on your business model is how your potential investors understand your ability to think through problems and solve them. They know your model will change and adjust over time, but how you analyze and think about the problem gives them significant insight into your ability to build a successful business in the face of uncertainty and shifting conditions.

Build the Financial Model

Your next step in the preparation process is to build a financial model. Everybody knows that your early financial models will undoubtedly be wrong. There is too much that can and does change over time, especially at the beginning. What your potential investors are looking for are the underlying assumptions in your model. How many people will it take to build your solution? What does it cost to acquire a customer and support them after they've purchased it? Do you have any material costs or infrastructure costs that are embedded in your solution? How do those costs scale? On the revenue side, how much will you be charging customers and how fast are you planning to grow?

You should be able to build an accurate financial model on the expense side, at least for the short term. The revenue side will likely be where you're off—and potentially off by a lot. Try not to get hung up on this, but focus on coming up with reasonable assumptions, like the core drivers of your business, and then work to validate those assumptions with your team.

Your financial model will give you a strong sense for how much money you'll need to raise. Of course, you'll want to stress test your model. What happens if your revenue is delayed by six months? Or, what if it takes many more people to build or service your solution? Remember, you're looking to fund your startup for your next major milestone(s). You'll want to add a reasonable amount of buffer for things that can and do go wrong. Following this approach, you'll raise closer to the right amount of money for your startup. You really don't want to run out of money before you hit your key milestones. Most investors will want to know what you are raising money for, so it's always good to be able to categorize what the investment will go toward. Some big buckets to think about are product development, sales and marketing, materials, machinery, and infrastructure.

You'll also be asked to provide pro forma financials, that is, your projections. Feel free to provide a reasonably high-level profit/loss (P/L) statement, cash flow statement, and balance sheet. Your potential investors will likely focus more closely on your P/L and cash flow statement. A good thing to add to these standard financial statements is a set of key metrics that help show how the critical parts of your business are performing. Occasionally, you'll be asked for the entire model, so you should be prepared to share that as well. Although in the early stages you aren't looking for GAAP (Generally Accepted Accounting Principles) level financial statements, you'll need to have some basic accounting and finance knowledge to pull the model off. If you don't have that, there are plenty of third-party resources, including many financial models online, that can help.

A well-thought-out financial model is an important step in the fundraising process. Take the time to do it right, and you'll better understand how your business works while increasing your odds of finding an investor.

Decide How Much Money You Want to Raise

As we said in the beginning of this chapter, many founders struggle with pinpointing how much money they need to raise. Having a realistic financial model is a must. Not only does it tell you if you need to raise money, but it helps you figure out how much you're going to need to cover expenses.

The amount of money you'll need will vary, depending on how fast you want to get into the market and the specific needs of the business. Even if your idea is a service-oriented business, you still need money for key activities like marketing, sales, and hiring personnel, so you can get to market quickly and have access to as many customers as possible.

We'll admit that selecting the right amount is tough. But, to give you an idea about the ballpark you'll be in, of those that exit, the majority of tech startups (58 percent of them) raise less than $10M in total prior to an exit.[†] You don't want to set your target too high, and raising too little is, potentially, even a worse option. Asking for too much money may raise eyebrows from investors because it may indicate that you don't understand your underlying business well. Of course, raising too much money from a founder's perspective may require that you give up too much of the company at a low valuation. Raising too little, on the other hand, will restrict what you can do and force you to go back to investors for additional funding sooner than you want. That could be incredibly expensive and could lead to stalling your business as you're spending your time and energy on fundraising instead of running your day-to-day operations.

Often, there is another dynamic at play, which is how much of the company you, as founders, are willing to give up. After figuring out how much money you need, you may learn that you will have to give up too much of your company to get it. Here's an example. Say, after doing all your modeling, you think you need $1 million to get to your next major milestone, one that will create a big step-up in valuation. While talking to investors about it, you find that they value your startup at $2 million pre-money. That means you will trade one-third of the ownership in your company ($2 million pre-money + $1 million invested = $3 million post-money valuation; $1 million / $3 million = 33 percent or one-third of the company) for $1 million in capital. Keep in mind, that's just your first round of investment. There are almost always several more.

While it's difficult to predict the future, you need to take it into consideration when thinking about dilution. As you see in the following chart, based on the data we've collected on the hundreds of companies we've worked with, your ownership will likely decrease fairly substantially with each round.

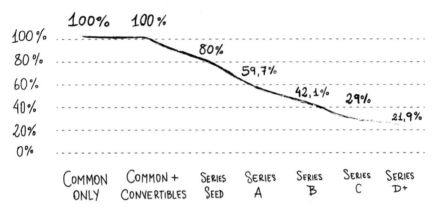

Diagram 6 Founder Dilution by Stage.

Is the money worth it? You get to decide, but in our experience, having money to execute your plan quickly is critical. If you think you can move quickly without that capital, then perhaps you can make it to that next major milestone using one of the other funding sources we described in the previous chapter. In general, we find that founders get too caught up in optimization at this level. While you don't want to trade away the store by giving up too much ownership, you should be more focused on making the company hugely successful, rather than on optimizing your slice of the pie. A bigger pie is more important for all shareholders than the size of any piece.

> While you don't want to trade away the store by giving up too much ownership, you should be more focused on making the company hugely successful, rather than on optimizing your slice of the pie. A bigger pie is more important for all shareholders than the size of any piece.

While only you and your co-founders can decide on what is right for you, we've always advocated for taking more money than you think you need. Money is the fuel you need to grow your company. The more fuel you have, the faster you can develop your startup. The faster you develop, the sooner you can get into the market ahead of your competition. It's that simple. When you're reluctant or unwilling to give your startup the funding it needs (within reason, of course), then you're holding it back.

There's another part of this, too. You may think your financial model is conservative, but in our experience, no financial model at this stage ever qualifies as conservative when looked at retrospectively. Almost assuredly, you'll need more money than you think you'll need. Things will run more slowly than you project, hiring will be more difficult and more expensive, and customers won't buy your solution as fast or for as much as you'd like. You're optimistic, and it's hard to account for that. As such, your estimates are likely to be short of what you'll need.

One other piece of advice at this stage: focus. The earliest part of the journey to build a company needs to be maniacally focused. Go after your key milestones, but don't try to do too many things at once. If you're building your solution, focus on the process of building your solution and validating the need for it. Spending time figuring out an efficient sales process, for example, is something that can be done later. This is critical because you'll most likely be short on resources, and you won't want to raise too much money because of the cost of that capital. Focusing on the most critical aspects of what you need to accomplish will optimize the benefit of the investment you take.

Choose Your Source of Capital

Once you know how much you need to raise, then you'll also have a better idea of the right source of capital. Like everything else that we've spoken about, there are some rules of thumb to follow, but clearly many exceptions. You also may mix and match some funding sources as most aren't mutually exclusive.

In our experience, your choice(s) will ultimately depend on some of the following factors:

- **Experience level of the founding team**. Is your founding team experienced in building companies or perhaps in the space that you are targeting? Obviously, the more experienced your team, the more options you have in raising money.
- **Stage of the company**. Are you looking to raise money on just an idea, or do you have a solution in the market? Or, perhaps you have customers already. As you build your business, your funding options will change.
- **Area of focus**. The area of focus for your business will impact the sources of capital available to you. Higher return areas such as high tech often have more interested investors, but that doesn't mean you won't find excellent options for other markets.
- **Amount of money needed**. The more money you need, the more limited your options become. Setting your sights on smaller amounts of capital will often greatly expand your options. Keep in mind that as your business evolves, you may also have to consider different sources of capital.

When just starting your company, most investment options are available to you, but we'd probably lean toward looking at friends and family, accelerators, angels, angel funds, small-cap VCs, and customers as the best options at first. Grants and competitions are also a good source of capital early on, but you're often limited to their timing and funding levels. As your business grows and you need larger amounts of capital, VC money is usually the best source. If you need to raise a significant amount of money out of the gate and you have a big opportunity that you're chasing, VCs may be highly interested in your business.

Specifically, a very common path we see startups taking these days is to first get some friends and family money, if it's available. That money is used for incidental costs as the team doesn't take a salary and each of the founders is working from their homes. Startups then apply to an accelerator and leverage connections there to get access to angel investors, angel funds, and small-cap VCs who can fund the seed round of the company. A combination of these sources enables the startup to raise more money without having to find forty or fifty individual investors. Later, as growth and expansion milestones are reached, VCs are added to the mix.

Alternatively, companies that don't take the accelerator path can start off by accessing grants and competitions in combination with friends and family money in order to reach those milestones that make the company attractive to angels and VCs.

As the amount of money founders seek to raise increases, we often will see a mix of angel investors, angel funds, and small-cap VCs coming together to invest in a company.

Many startups we work with turn to angel investors as a huge resource. As we've talked about earlier, these investors not only bring investment dollars, but also advice and mentorship. There are almost always angel investors in your local community, and these individuals usually are actively looking to invest in and advise new founders. It is, however, difficult to complete investment rounds much over $500K with angels alone. In our experience, because the median investment from an angel is about $25K, you need to find many investors to fill out your round. Additionally, angels don't typically lead an investment, which can make it difficult for the founder, as we discussed earlier.

If you can't find an angel who will lead, here's our suggestion: talk to your most active potential investors and agree on a valuation and terms that seem fair to both sides. You should then create the term sheet with your legal advisors and circulate it to your potential investors. Ask those active investors if you can start saying that they will invest in the company if you can cross a minimum threshold of investment. This allows you to put pressure on other investors by saying you have existing commitments if they are willing to invest as well.

There's a little bit of an iterative game you need to play to get angels to commit. But, once you have their commitment, you can then go to the rest of your potential investors and start to wrap up your round. In this way, you're taking the role of the lead investor to some extent. Many angels have no problem with this approach. In fact, it makes their lives easier and makes the path to an investment simpler for everyone.

When you need to raise even larger sums of money, angel funds can be a way to get big pieces of your investment quickly. If you can tap the right person in the angel network—someone who is well respected and one that the other angels will follow—you may be able to have a much larger investment than just one angel can provide. This does come at a cost; angel funds can be difficult to work with because no one person makes a decision about an investment. While you deal with the angel fund as an entity, you still must convince each angel that you're worthy of their investment. As we mentioned earlier, we see angel funds as a lower percentage play. While you have to touch more people, individual angels are likely to be your primary investment opportunity at this early stage.

A resource we see more often in rounds over $500K is a small-cap VC. Small-cap VCs primarily invest in seed rounds of companies, although they often reserve capital for future investments in companies as well. They invest alongside angels and work well with larger VCs. While small-cap VCs conduct more due diligence and take a little bit longer to close than angels, they generally invest a good deal more than individual angels while also offering a lot of help to the founders along the way.

We like the model of filling your seed round with a combination of angels and small-cap VCs. Angels bring money and advice, and small-cap VCs bring larger chunks of money with deeper pockets and the possibility of participating in follow-on investments.

Getting the first investor to commit is always the hardest part. Once you have that person in the boat, so to speak, they are generally very helpful in talking with other potential investors. They will often let you use their name and will contact other investors for you. As more investors get involved and are motivated to help you succeed, the committed investors will recruit others to your round, which often will help tip the scales and start the ball rolling on closing your round.

When you need bigger chunks of money, VCs are your only real option. To get money from VCs, you first have to reach several big milestones—including customers, market position, a qualified team, and sometimes actual revenue growth. VCs aren't just looking for a good idea. They want to see multiple data points suggesting a successful trajectory. You can mix VCs with angels and small-cap VCs, but keep in mind that there is a pecking order. Some VCs don't like a large number of angels in an investment. At other times, there are VC firms that just don't get along. Homework here is your friend. Talk to other founders who have dealt with the VC you're interested in to see if they have any restrictions when it comes to other investors.

As you think about which VCs to contact, do some research on what each firm focuses on; they all have some level of specialization. The focus can be on a sector of the market, the stage of the startup, a geographic region, or another area. You'll often hear terms like *early stage, late stage, seed fund, growth fund,* and others to help classify a fund. You'll want to do your homework on which funds are a good match for your startup based on your stage—the amount of money you want to raise, your geographic location, and area of focus.

Something else we feel strongly about with respect to VCs is that while many firms will tell you they want you to come to them early and are happy to work through an idea with you, this is most often not in your best interest. Venture capitalists see hundreds of new companies per year. They have a pattern-matching process that helps them separate companies they are interested in from those they are not. When you fail to clear their hurdles once, it is unlikely they will take a serious look at your company again. Therefore, you should only approach VCs when you have all your ducks in a row.

Debt is a source that we'd almost always say to leave for later. Debt needs to be paid back, while equity, customer purchases, or grants don't usually need to be paid back. Until you have a steady source of cash coming in, we'd say you should be highly skeptical of taking on debt. The one exception to this is something we'll discuss later, which is a convertible note that essentially starts as debt but really is an equity instrument.

Of course, once you start talking to potential investors, you may need to adjust your approach. You may need to raise more money, or maybe you'll need to lower the amount. Perhaps you'll have to switch from targeting VC funds, for example, to angels or vice versa. Or, you might want to alter your milestones or change your expense structure. Once you start the process, you can decide what to do.

	= PROS =	= CONS =
BOOTSTRAPPING	NO DILUTION RETAIN CONTROL	LIMITED MONEY LACK OF SUPPORT / ADVICE
FRIENDS & FAMILY	QUICK, GENERALLY EASY SOURCE NON-INTRUSIVE	SMALL AMOUNT OF MONEY PERSONAL RELATIONSHIP RISK
ACCELERATORS & INCUBATORS	EXPERTISE / SUPPORT POTENTIAL PATH TO MORE MONEY	SMALL AMOUNT OF MONEY EXPENSIVE
ANGEL INVESTORS ANGEL FUNDS	POTENTIAL EXPERTISE USUALLY LIGHT PROCESS, QUICK	LIMITED AMOUNT OF MONEY LACK OF FOLLOW-ON SUPPORT
VENTURE CAPITAL	PROFESSIONAL INVESTORS LARGE AMOUNTS OF CAPITAL	SHARED CONTROL EXPENSIVE
GOVERNMENT & COMMERCIAL GRANTS	CREDIBILITY LESS DILUTIVE	TIMING IP ISSUES
STARTUP COMPETITIONS	CREDIBILITY MAY NOT GIVE UP ANY OWNERSHIP	SMALL AMOUNTS OF MONEY TIMING
CUSTOMER / PARTNER	LESS DILUTIVE ADDS CREDIBILITY	MAY BE CAPTIVE TO CUSTOMER / PARTNER IP ISSUES
DEBT	RETAIN OWNERSHIP USUALLY LESS EXPENSIVE	PAYBACK RISK COMPANY CONTROL IS DOWNSIDE SCENARIO

Diagram 7   Pros and Cons of Various Investment Models
This table will help you think about some of the high-level benefits and drawbacks of the various investment sources we discussed in the last chapter. As we have said before, the more prepared you are, the easier it is to adjust as you gain more knowledge and feedback.

Build Your Presentation

The culmination of your homework is the investor presentation. This is the pitch deck or investor deck, as it is often called. You'll either send it to your potential investor or you'll present it to them when you meet. Generally, the investor deck is the first formal external step in the investment process.

The deck is roughly ten to twenty slides, created with presentation software like PowerPoint or Keynote, although it's generally delivered in PDF form. It helps to tell the story of your business and why it's interesting in ways we outlined above. The goal with the deck is to convince investors that your company is the one to invest their money in. But, you should note that the presentation is very rarely enough—it's often just the first step in a deliberate process.

With fierce competition from numerous startups for money, you want your deck to stand out from the pack. Many founders don't realize they rarely present their decks to investors. Most often, you send it to them via email first, and then they'll decide if they want to meet with you. Or, they'll look at it prior to a prescheduled meeting. You often won't be able to walk them through it for the first time or give them additional information, so your deck has to be visually appealing and easily understandable.

Your deck will need to explain everything that we've discussed in this chapter. Some of the highlights include what you're planning to do, how much money you're seeking to raise, why you're raising that amount of money, how you will use the money, what it will produce, and the type of return that investors will receive. These are the types of key variables that investors look for when deciding on what startups to invest their money in.

There are some tried-and-true approaches that we like to encourage founders to think about with their investor presentation. Your deck should tell a story. It should be logical and flow well. It should be compelling and captivating to the reader. The reader should walk away, having learned something new and unique.

Diagram 8   Typical Investment Slide Deck

The design of your deck and the imagery that you use can convey significant information about your company. Charts, graphics, and images can often show something about your startup rather than just using words to tell your story. Many founders often don't put a lot of thought into the titles of their slides, but they can be used to your advantage. You can broadcast the framework of your story with just the headlines. And, finally, we like to include a validating quote or logo from a customer or industry luminary on just about every slide. The goal with this is to give potential investors subtle messages that build credibility.

Most investment decks have roughly the same content regardless of the market or industry. Virtually all successful decks will have the information that we've outlined in this chapter. The variance between them will likely be in flow and style. There's no right answer on that, so do what feels like the best to you. Tell your story in the most compelling way possible.

* * *

The most important thing to remember about the funding process is that it is a direct reflection of your business model. Remember all that work you did in the vetting loop? The more you did there, the more solid your business model is and the less you'll have to do to prepare for funding. That's one of the reasons we pointed out that the time you spend vetting your idea will accelerate everything that comes after it.

There are many channels for getting funding for your company. Knowing the best one for the stage you're in will make the process of finding the best investors much more efficient and give you a better chance at success with closing the deal. The decision of who to approach and of how much you should ask for will rest on several factors: the experience of your team, the maturity of the market, the completeness of your business model, and the type of investors you choose to present to. Finding the right mix of those factors will help you optimize your chances for funding success.

Of course, part of that process is the deck you'll send to potential investors. Often, it's the gateway to further discussions and the potential involvement of the investor. We say *send* because you probably won't have a chance to present the material face-to-face. It needs to be concise and complete, and to reflect the great business model you've already built for the company.

And, remember, dilution of your ownership in your startup is inevitable and is always a tough pill to swallow. We urge you not to focus on this too much. You should, of course, try to minimize your dilution if you can, but keep in mind that building a bigger company faster will allow you to keep more ownership and maximize the value of that ownership over the life of your startup.

Preparation will likely be the difference between success and failure in your investment process. But, even if you aren't successful in your first pass at raising money, the work you've done to prepare for a financing round is invaluable. You're making your business better by analyzing it, working on how everything fits together, and more deeply understanding the model. Take your time and do it right. You'll be happy you did.

Chapter 20

Running Your Fundraising Process

Even though I (Rajat) have learned a lot since my first very difficult fundraising process, raising money is never easy. There's no doubt that getting funding for your startup can be challenging, even with the right people, idea, and results. My company StillSecure was a prime example.

My co-founder and I were repeat co-founders with previous successes under our belts. We had previously raised VC money, and our idea was in a big category. Yet, even with those attributes on our side, we still had been rejected by numerous venture firms. Sometimes, the concern was whether we could compete against the large incumbents in our space. Other times, it was that the company was too small or growing too slowly. Still others had concerns about where the company was located (Boulder, Colorado) and whether we could recruit enough high-quality talent. Regardless of the reasons, we were rejected by some investors in each of our rounds.

The silver lining of the story was that our first investment partner, Mobius Venture Capital, had supported the company from inception despite the lack of interest from other investors. The moral of the StillSecure story has been that even with many of the right characteristics in your startup, you may still face the prospect of struggling to raise money.

Chances of Getting Funded

When it comes to raising money for your startup, we have good news and bad news for you. First, the good news: there is more money to be invested in startups than ever before.

Now, the bad news: there are also more companies vying for that money than ever before. What's it going to take to get investors to say yes to investing in your startup?

The answer is simple, but challenging in practice. You need to stand out from the crowd. The homework you've done in the previous chapters prepared you to talk to investors. Now, you need to run a great investment process. Just like your diligently created business model, it's imperative that your fundraising process is well thought out, too, and perhaps even more importantly, crisply executed.

The stories of meeting with an investor over lunch, writing your business plan on a napkin, and then getting a commitment for an investment on the spot is one of those fantasies about startups we discussed earlier. Simply put, it's a gross oversimplification of the methodical process that actually takes place. You will undergo a thorough vetting by a potential investor to ensure that making an investment is in their best interest. A well-run and thought-through fundraising process can significantly increase your odds of getting an investment.

In this chapter, we'll walk you through how to run your investment process like a pro, and we'll show you how to give your startup the best chance to raise the money you want to accelerate your business. While we won't cover the process of raising money from all the sources of capital available to you, we'll talk about the primary ones that most startups use—accelerators, angel investors, and venture capitalists, both large and small-cap. As you read this chapter, keep in mind that when we talk about "investors," we're talking about any of these types of investors.

Who Do You Target?

In today's investment environment, there is a potential investor for just about every style of business. Specialization has become more critical from an investor perspective. There are just too many markets, moving too fast for an investor to be an expert in each one. Investors will often focus on areas in which they feel most comfortable and may have some competitive advantage over other investors, for example, in a particular sector, area, company stage, or location.

This information is also incredibly valuable to you as a founder. You want to find potential investors who can not only provide you with money, but who can also help you with the business. Hopefully, they'll be able to provide you with advice based on their experience in your market or with the type of business model you have. Or, maybe they have a deep network of contacts that you can tap into, which will help you with your product, go-to-market plan, or customers.

Ideally, you'll do your homework and find the best potential investors for your startup ahead of time, including what companies they've previously invested in, their investment interests, their networks, and who they trust. More investors than ever are out in the public eye, sharing their knowledge and approach to the markets that they're interested in. Many have blogs, are present at conferences, do interviews, or are otherwise known in the market as being an expert in a particular area. Your job is to find the group of potential investors who will be most likely to help and invest in your startup.

When trying to find the right investors, start by finding people that fit with the stage that the company is in. Especially for companies that are just starting, finding investors who understand and want to invest early is critical. Early stage investors are usually a little bit of a different breed. They're willing to take bigger risks before the company has achieved many of its milestones.

Another potential cut on your investor choices is based on the domain of the business and the business model of the company. Ideally, you'll find the intersection of potential investors that like the stage you're in as well as the market and business model.

> Ideally, you want to identify the intersection of potential investors that like the stage you're in as well as the market and business model.

The work you will do here will be tedious, but it'll pay off. This is a detailed research task in which you'll try to gather as much information as you can about potential investors. You'll want to be laser-focused for your potential investor choices. As the investment process goes on, you'll naturally expand your list. In fact, many investors who you'll speak to will end up introducing you to others they think are a fit as well (or an even better fit than they are). The good news is you'll be starting with a group of targets that, hopefully, will be naturally interested in your business, making it easier to get an audience and move on to the next steps.

Another word of advice on your potential investment targets: check if they have invested in your competitors. Most accelerators, angel investors, and venture capital firms don't like to make competitive investments. That's generally a good thing, so you'll be able to cross off people who have invested in your competition, making it easier to focus on who you should target.

It's always exciting to take your presentation and financial model for a spin with many potential investors right away, but resist the urge. Do your homework first to find the best potential investors up front.

Getting to Your Targets

Like everyone today, investors have limited availability. They can't possibly meet with everyone vying for their money, but they're always on the hunt for the next great investment. The best introductions to potential investors come from tapping into your network for references instead of through cold calls, which investors sometimes see as a sign of desperation.

Often, someone will suggest to a founder that they should meet with a specific investor, and that person will offer to make the introduction. As a founder, this is your opening and can be a powerful lead. But, that's only if the investor values the person who's making the introduction. If the person making the connection is excited about your company, the prospects for the business, and the investor values their insight, then this can make a huge difference in getting a meeting. If the person making the introduction is neutral on your company or the investor is lukewarm toward them, then that may kill your chances of getting a meeting.

It's a cliché, but it's who you know, not what you know, that counts at the beginning. If you're still building a network, then you have to get scrappy. You have to scramble and do some door-to-door selling. You have to utilize your existing connections and expand your network quickly. You have to ask your friends, ask friends of your friends, family members, and friends of your family members. You have to find links online, use LinkedIn to make new connections, or hop on AngelList to find names of investors.

This is when accelerators can help. They have vast networks and exist, in part, to help new founders make stronger connections in the field, so they can build and expand their networks of trusted contacts, mentors, and advisors. Of course, that only helps once you're in an accelerator. Fortunately, you probably know somebody who has already been in an accelerator program. Tap them to help in your search for possible investors.

Once you know how you'll get to your potential investor, help the person who is willing to make the introduction for you. Write the email for them that they'll send, or provide them with a brief overview of your company explaining why the potential investor should care. (Tip: Make sure your content is tailored to the potential investor.) If someone is willing to make an introduction, you should make it as easy on them as possible and arm them with the best information for why the introduction makes sense for the potential investor.

Don't be shy about passing your investment deck along in the introductory email. We watch as many entrepreneurs squander opportunities with potential investors because they don't supply enough information when they get the chance. Remember to share your complete idea in the deck. It's the execution of your idea that makes it unique.

And, don't expect a potential investor to sign an NDA before you tell them what you're working on. They'll just move on to the next founding team that isn't creating barriers. Your investors aren't in the business to steal your ideas. If they did, they wouldn't survive long. Your paranoia here will just hurt you in the end.

Getting to your target and securing a meeting is one of the most difficult steps in the process. Often, it'll take as much work to get an introduction to the right investor as it will to convince them that your startup is worthy of an investment. But the effort can pay off; you may just find the perfect investor(s) for your company.

Accelerators

Of the funding sources we're discussing in this chapter, accelerators are a bit unique. As we mentioned in Chapter 18, roughly one-third of all high-tech startups that go on to raise a Series A round are using accelerators as a growth source. So, it's a reasonable assumption that an accelerator may end up near the top of your list of potential investment partners. But, while they almost all offer funding through a small seed investment for preferred stock, a convertible note, or a purchase of common stock, their real advantage as an investment vehicle is that they can quickly help a company mature and provide an inside track to angels and VCs for a bigger round of investment capital.

Which Accelerator?

There are hundreds of accelerator programs around the world.* Techstars, Y Combinator, and SOSV are among the largest with true worldwide exposure. As with any investor, the more specific a match you can find with a specific accelerator with what you are doing and where you're building your company, the more likely you'll get the help and money you need to get going. We'd say that between domain expertise and location, the former is more important. If you can find an accelerator that specializes in your market or product area, that will be where you'll get the most leverage from the program.

There are no rules about which accelerators you apply to or their location. In fact, if location is particularly important to you and accelerators in that area are not focused on the markets you're targeting, don't let that stop you. You shouldn't be shy about getting in touch with the general manager of the accelerators in your target area to see if they may be interested in working with you. While it's better to have a good match of skills and contacts, much of the help (and money) you'll get from an accelerator is not market specific. It's better to be in one than miss out on the perfect one.

Applying to an Accelerator

Just as with any investor, an inside track will help you get into the program you want. Don't just sit on the sidelines, filling out the requisite application forms. Seek out companies that have been in previous programs, the management team at the accelerator, and even people who were previously rejected. The more you know, the better. Additionally, most accelerators pride themselves on their graduates—the companies that have been through the accelerator already. The founders of companies in this category may be able to introduce you to key people inside the accelerator, and they might be in a position to recommend you for a future session.

Keep in mind, as much as there is competition to get into accelerators—many get thousands of applicants—the accelerators are competing to get the best companies as well. They want your startup to be part of their accelerator. So, there is no reason you shouldn't apply to multiple accelerators at the same time in order to increase your odds.

As we've talked about earlier, most accelerators will want there to be a team of co-founders already formed or part of a team. They'll also want at least a subset of that team to reside at the accelerator during the program. So, if you're thinking of applying to accelerators that are in a remote location, then you should be willing to move to that location for the duration of the program.

One last thing to recognize is that accelerators are investment funds, too. With the exception of a handful of publicly run or government-oriented programs, accelerators have limited partners and are in business to make money, just like VCs. How does this affect you? Accelerators are actually looking for the same type of company that angels and VCs are looking for: companies that will have an exit or an IPO that will provide them with a tangible, and hopefully significant, return on their investment. While many accelerators promote an altruistic desire to help startups in general, virtually all of them have the same basic requirements that other equity investors have.

Getting Investment Capital—Angels and VCs

If you've identified angels, an angel group, or a large or small-cap VC as possible investment targets, then just know that getting a direct investment from any of them is a bit more complicated than starting with an accelerator. There are more steps involved, and the process is certainly less definitive. With accelerators, you do your legwork, fill out an application, get an interview, and either get accepted or not. You might do this for a handful of accelerators. With the sheer number of angels and VCs around, though, you'll have to repeat your process of reaching out to them often, and you'll need to customize it for each audience.

Much of the preparation you need to do is the same for angels and VCs. You need to have your business model nailed down and your financial model well thought through. The further down the path you are in proving each of these models, the more likely you'll get interest from investors. That's not to say you can't get any interest for an idea without validated models, but with so many startups around these days, investors are looking for more tangible results, if possible.

Angels will generally invest earlier in the development of the company than VCs. Since they're investing their own money and have no limited partners, their decision-making process is simpler, and they usually do less due diligence than institutional investors. That said, angel investments are not always fast. As we discussed earlier, angels often want someone to lead the round, someone to be responsible for doing due diligence and negotiating reasonable terms for the investment. It may take time to find that person or entity to take the lead. Angels also tend to be the most valuation sensitive of these funding sources. While they're not all looking for bargains, they want as much upside as possible for the risk they're taking.

Large VCs—those with large funds—invest substantially larger chunks of capital than angels and generally have a fairly regimented investment process that involves introductions, reviews of information, initial meetings, some due diligence, partner meetings, more due diligence, term sheets, paperwork, and so forth. They are making a major decision to invest other people's money. There are many people involved in the decision, and they make that decision using a fairly regular pattern.

Small-cap VCs—those with smaller funds—are a little like angels and a little like their larger brethren. They certainly have an investment process they use with startups, and they're investing other people's money, too. But, since they're investing in smaller chunks, they can move faster. They also can take a few more risks and invest at an earlier stage of a company. Like angels, they're generally more valuation sensitive than a larger VC, but again, this is in line with the higher level of risk they take.

We've outlined some of the specific steps you need to take with these investment partners. While many of these high-level steps are the same regardless of whether you're approaching an angel, or a large/small-cap VC, some of the details are different. We'll point those out along the way.

***

Knowing where to start your fundraising journey is difficult. We find that many startups get frozen in their tracks, trying to figure out where to start. The best place to get going is to figure out who to raise money from, what type of investor will best fit your needs. You may, in fact, have to expand well beyond that to find an investor, but focusing will help you get started and work your way through the complex space.

Don't be surprised if the process takes more time and effort than you ever thought it would. It will. Period. Almost no one ever says, "Well, that went better and faster than I thought it would." Almost everyone is disappointed with the outcome of their fundraising efforts. Often, that's because they weren't able to raise the funds they need and sometimes because they didn't get the terms they wanted for the investment. Be prepared.

Chapter 21

Your First Investor Meeting

Even having done investor meetings for many years, I (Rajat) still make mistakes. One meeting was particularly painful. Our existing investors had introduced me to an investor whom they felt was quite interested. I setup a conference call as there would be multiple partners on the phone.

When I got on the phone, I proceeded to jump right in and walk through the business. The investors were seemingly engaged and asked a lot of questions that were all over the place, which made for a chaotic meeting. At the end of the meeting, I asked them what they thought, and the answer was, "It would have been a better meeting if you had a presentation deck and we had walked through that." Sunk.

I didn't do enough homework to know that this investor was more formal and structured in their approach. Further, even if I hadn't done that homework, I should have asked at the beginning of the session whether they wanted me to walk through a presentation or they preferred an informal discussion.

With only a few chances and a small investor community, mistakes like these can torpedo a fundraising process quickly. This investor passed on our opportunity, and likely they will never invest in one of my companies because of this first impression. There are so many amazing opportunities that they see every day, so why would they invest in somebody who didn't have their act together?

This particular example irked my existing investors, as well, who had put their reputation on the line to make the introduction. So, I ended up cratering a potential new investor relationship and added strain to an existing one. Not a great way to start a financing process.

The First One May Be the Most Important One

We'll assume you've landed your first meeting after working your networks and conducting thorough research to reach the best possible investors—congratulations! Without trying to make you too nervous, this meeting with the investor is critical. If you're meeting with a venture capitalist or an associate at a VC firm, then you're probably not meeting with all the partners; it's just a one-on-one meeting. If it's an angel group or fund, you're likely meeting with one angel. Your goal with this first meeting isn't to get a commitment but, rather, to generate a lot of interest and curiosity in your startup. You want the potential investor to walk away excited enough that they want to dig in and learn more.

Like with most meetings, the first impression is important. This is your opportunity to show the investor your passion for the business, your knowledge about running the business, your plan for growing it, and your organizational skills. They'll, of course, also want to know if you're thoughtful about your solution and the company you're creating. Note that we are specifically talking about your startup. Investors aren't expecting you to be an expert at business in general. The more insight you can provide to them about your business, the better. So, be specific.

They want to see that you have studied your particular market and know it better than anybody else.

When you're dealing with experienced investors, they're not only looking for the grand-slam, home-run deals that will give them massive returns. They're looking for easy-to-spot red flags. They've done many deals and likely have worked with hundreds of founders, so they look for patterns of challenges and signs that your startup will fail. There is no doubt that their history is biased, but if you know that (if you've done extensive research, then you may have learned what startups they've invested in, which ones have succeeded, and which ones have failed), then you'll be able to use it to your advantage. Investors aren't always rational, so if you can play to their experience and emotion around a market space or type of deal, that's to your benefit.

These elements—and some intangible ones, like their view of you as an individual—factor in to whether you get a second meeting or whether the potential investor is willing to go back and do their homework on you and your startup. But, if you slip up on any of these items, if you seem dull and lifeless, if you're scattered and unprepared, then you'll miss your chance. It's hard, nearly impossible in fact, to get a second meeting if you make critical mistakes.

Most investors will decide within the first few minutes, perhaps unconsciously, if your company is a potential match for them. They'll use their pattern-matching techniques of having seen hundreds or thousands of companies up close to see whether your organization matches their patterns for success. Usually, these snap judgments are then tested over a period of time. Your goal is to have the potential investor envision themselves as investors in your company and then start to validate their decision through the due diligence process. You don't want to be in the position where a potential investor is interested in your startup but is looking for reasons not to do the deal.

Your first meeting with a potential investor is a chance to set the table for an investment. All the homework you've done is in preparation for this moment. Put your best foot forward and execute on a great first meeting, which will put you in an excellent position to generate an investment.

Partner Meetings

If your first meeting is successful, the potential investor will go off and start investigating your startup. If you're meeting with a VC, you may have follow-on meetings, they may call customers, or they may have you meet with people in their network. If their continued interest in your company yields positive results, you'll likely be asked to meet with their entire partnership.

When that happens, again, you need to be extremely well prepared, not only on the ins and outs of your company, but also on the partners around the table. You'll want the investor you met with one-on-one to give you background on each of their teammates. You'll want to know things like who in the room is in favor of the deal, who isn't, what issue will likely arise, and who will likely bring it up, who's the decision maker, which people hold more weight or power, and what are peoples' biases. As much information as you can gain is helpful and will enable you to prepare for the meeting.

For example, a VC's approach to pattern-matching is about mitigating risk. They know they're playing a risky game with other people's money. They know their success only comes from returning significantly more money to their investors than what they've received. That usually comes from one or two breakout hits in their portfolio. So, they're trying to emulate models or styles of companies they think can be hugely successful. Pattern-matching against those huge successes helps them weed out deals they don't believe will make a dent in their returns. Knowing the patterns this particular VC's partners will look for will help you to better prepare for the meeting. Your sponsoring partner, the one you met with first, will help to educate you on potential pattern-matching biases.

But, beyond knowing what to watch for, you'll want to show the potential investors your conviction and passion for your business. They need to see your enthusiasm to believe that you and your company will be a major success. This is easy for experienced entrepreneurs. They've often successfully raised money in the past, and venture capitalists believe history foretells the future. But, when you're new and just beginning this journey, you can't play the experience card, so your belief in the opportunity ispowerful.

While belief and passion are important, they're also not enough. You'll need to be on point with the story of your company. All the key factors we've been discussing previously will be rigorously tested. Your business model, the market, your competitive differentiation, your team, and anything else that might be relevant to your business will be questioned, sometimes aggressively. If you've prepared, you'll have a chance to make a great impression. In fact, we've seen founding teams get together with other founding teams and spend time practicing their pitch and subsequent question-and-answer session to make sure they're well prepared.

Your goal is to put the VC firm in a position in which they're being driven by their greed to make money and also a fear that they'll miss out on investing in your company if they don't act soon. A great presentation can accomplish that.

The partner meeting is a critical step in the investment process for raising venture capital. The potential investor is trying to get support from their colleagues to make the investment. That support is necessary for the venture capitalist and is important for you as a founder. You want the support of the entire firm and their extended networks. A knock-it-out-of-the-park partner meeting will put you on your way.

Term Sheet

When an investor decides to lead an investment in your company, they'll usually give you a term sheet. This is their proposal for an investment with their specific terms and conditions. Usually, these are the terms that you'll set for the entire round and for all the participating investors.

As we've talked about a couple of times, in early-stage companies, many investors are willing to invest, but aren't always willing to lead the investment. This means they aren't willing to negotiate the terms and do the formal due diligence work. They'll usually say to you, "I'll follow, but I won't lead." These potential investors are valuable to you, but you'll need to find that one lead investor who will issue a term sheet or at least work with you on negotiating the key terms of the round. As we mentioned before, don't be discouraged if you can't get somebody to lead.

For many friends and family rounds or seed deals, the investors do not generate term sheets. Instead, the founders work with the potential investors to create the term sheet themselves. This is just fine as long as your potential investors agree to invest on those terms.

The term sheet itself is a legal document that outlines the broad terms of the investment. While we would like to say that most investors use a common, boilerplate term sheet with the standards for the industry, that isn't true. Some common model term sheets are available from the NVCA (National Venture Capital Association), Techstars, and Foundry Group among many others. While many investors will use one of these as a foundation for their term sheet, each investment firm and lawyer has their own approach. If you're fortunate enough to have multiple term sheets from different investors, you'll want to carefully compare the terms and investors.

We'll review some of the key terms that we've found to matter most and that you should pay attention to. This is a good introduction and start to what you can expect with a term sheet; however, you'll want to work closely with your attorney. Also, there is an excellent book we recommend if you want to know the ins and outs of the term sheet and the legal process. It is called *Venture Deals* and is authored by our close friends, Brad Feld and Jason Mendelson, partners at the venture capital firm Foundry Group.

Term sheets can get quite complicated, but they're fairly straightforward once you get past the jargon and focus on the fundamental points. These points include:

- **Structure of the investment.** The term sheet will outline the structure of the investment—basically whether the investment will be done as a convertible note, preferred series of stock, or some other structure.
- **Company assumptions.** There will be some documentation about what your investors are expecting about your

company, like where it is incorporated, who is involved, stock outstanding, and other basic information.

- **Valuation and amount of investment.** This section details at what price and how much will be invested in the startup. Note that you'll want to make sure you understand what's included in the valuation and how it is being generated. For example, is the investor asking for you to add more stock options to your option pool before the deal, reducing their effective valuation?
- **Governance structure.** This is how your company will be governed. This includes who will be on the board, what decisions the management team can make, and what decisions require board involvement.
- **Liquidation process.** If the company is sold or shut down, any proceeds that remain after paying off creditors need to be distributed. The term sheet will outline how that will happen and in what order they are paid.
- **Future fundraising.** A key term in which investors will document is who is allowed to invest in future rounds and what their rights are. Often called pro rata rights, these are important for institutional investors (and savvy angels) who want to continue to support the company and maintain their ownership.
- **Information.** How and what information will be shared is also documented in the term sheet. Investors want to know what is going on with their investment.

The term sheet will ultimately be turned into the final, legal documents, so spending time on negotiating the document to accurately reflect your deal is important. Negotiating at the term sheet stage is less expensive than doing it during the drafting of final documents. Of course, you'll want to balance how much you negotiate in general. There are a number of terms that end up being reasonably standard as you see from the model term sheets, and investors won't want to negotiate those terms. In fact, they may think negatively of you if you try negotiating those terms. You'll want to work closely with your legal team to know what is negotiable and what you'll want to stay away from.

Valuation and Dilution

We would be remiss if we didn't further discuss the potential cost to you of raising money. The more money you raise at a given valuation, the more your ownership will be diluted.

In Chapter 17, we discussed important terms, and we used an example to showcase valuation and dilution. Returning to that example, let's pretend that you raised $2 million from an investor for your startup that was valued at $4 million before the investment. In order to get that investment, you had to sell 33 percent of the company. This is the amount of dilution that you take. If your personal ownership in the company was 30 percent prior to the financing, then you will own 20 percent afterward, since you had to give up a third of your ownership stake in exchange for the $2 million investment.

There is a balance that you'll need to strike between the amount of money you want to raise and the dilution you're willing to take. There's natural tension here for virtually all startups. If you focus on dilution too much, then you might not raise enough money. But, if you focus too much on getting the money you need, then you may realize down the road that your ownership in the business has been diluted away. Early on, it's difficult to generate a valuation so high that you can raise as much money as you want for little dilution or cost. So, you'll want to talk with your co-founders about what's the right balance.

Our broad suggestion is to focus on building a larger company rather than on your percentage ownership of it. Owning a smaller piece of something large can be much more lucrative than owning a larger piece of something small.

We also advocate running a model that shows how your ownership decreases over time. You can project how many rounds of financing you'll need and then build scenarios for the dollar amounts and potential valuations at each round. While your model will undoubtedly be wrong, it will give you a sense of how much of the company you'll own over time.

Earlier, we shared data on the percentage of the company founders and employees will own over time. In the following chart, we show the typical dilution experienced by the same group at each round of funding. To calculate how much your ownership decreases, multiply your percentage ownership with the average dilution during each round in the chart below.

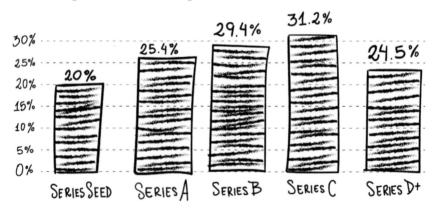

Diagram 9   Employee Dilution by Stage.

If you can, carefully consider what the money you raise will help you do in each round and how much it will increase the overall value of your startup. This will help you see if investing in the business and building something large will result in more value to you than retaining larger ownership in a smaller business.

Choosing the Right Partner

Selecting an investment partner is like bringing on a co-founder or very early employee—it's that level of relationship. In fact, it's tighter because you can't fire investors. Although they aren't active on a day-to-day basis, they will likely be involved in the direction of the company and, at a minimum, interested in what's happening with their investment. So, finding the right financial partner for you and your company is just as important as finding the right co-founders.

Nowhere is this more true than in the level and length of engagement you'll have with some of your investors. Angels are always a resource to you, but it's unlikely they'll be active investors or actively engaged over the long haul. Small-cap VCs tend to be less involved with the companies they invest in, but for different reasons. Their firms tend to be smaller and do many deals. As such, they just don't have the bandwidth to spend a lot of time with you and likely won't even ask for a board seat. VCs, on the other hand, are generally with you for the life of the business—at least until there is an exit. Not only that, they'll likely also require a board seat and demand frequent communication about the state of the business. They'll conceptually be shoulder-to-shoulder with you for the entire time you're building the company.

It's tempting to say yes to the easiest source (or the first one), the one who's willing to write a fast check. But, picking the financial partner who you want to work with over the long term is more important than cashing a check for an extra 10 or 20 percent on the valuation of your company or with somebody that decides to invest quickly.

While investors are like co-founders, there's still a huge difference between the two. If someone is investing in your company, they expect something in return. Even if you choose crowdfunding, those backers expect you to supply them with the promised product or service. You aren't given money for free or without any expectations. There's always something in return.

Hopefully, you'll have your choice of investors, and if that's the case, then you'll have to choose the best investment partner for your startup. We've found several factors that help make that decision easier.

Relationship

The beginning of any investor relationship is the easy part. Everything should be roses, but eventually, and it happens to every company, you'll hit hard times. You'll face contentious issues. Can you envision sharing bad news with your investor and having them roll up their sleeves to support and help you? You should. If you have the type of investor who you believe can and will truly work with you in an open and honest way, then that's a great sign you've found a potential financial partner. You'll want to ask yourself: "Have I enjoyed working with the investor and have they enjoyed working with me? How is the dialogue? Is it open and free-flowing or stilted and closed?"

Expertise

If you're looking for an investor who can provide more than financial capital (and you should be!), then their expertise in your field is an important consideration. Will your potential investor be able to help you with specific problems and challenges that you will face? Do they have a network of people to draw upon? If your investor can't completely comprehend what you do, then the next question you should ask is, "Are they willing to study and learn my business?"

There will always be some areas that are so new that very few people will have deep experience or expertise in them. That's okay if your investment partner is willing to dig in and learn. If they aren't, then you should consider looking elsewhere. The key factor here is if they're only focused on pattern matching and not interested in learning the details and specifics of your business.

Fund Size/Follow-On Investments

If you think you'll need more money in the future, as most startups do, then you'll want to consider the fund size and follow-on investment opportunities. Some investors have the capacity to invest in future funding rounds; others may not. Traditionally, those who can go another round are venture capitalists, although some angels and seed-stage funds will continue to invest in your company over time. Usually, grants, competitions, crowdfunding deals, and others are more one-time events, and you should know that when taking their money.

The reason you want to consider this factor is that it's possible your company won't grow as quickly as you envisioned, or it will miss the milestones you intended to meet with this particular funding round. In the upside case, your company may be growing so fast that it's outstripping your ability to fund that growth. As a result, you'll need more money, and you may or may not be in a position (or have the time in the upside case) to raise money from other outside investors as easily. Do your investors have the wherewithal to bridge (financially tiding you over) you to that inflection point?

No investor will guarantee you a future follow-on round, but many will openly discuss the process they go through when considering this scenario. In a fundraising round where you have some choice, this is a very important characteristic of the investment partner that you choose.

Terms of the Deal

Obviously, the terms that the investor is offering matter as well. Generally, we've argued for the position that having a cleaner deal is more important than valuation, but every situation is different. When we say a clean deal, we're talking about the terms the investor is proposing. Of interest are liquidation preference, board representation, and anti-dilution. You may end up having to trade off valuation for the terms you want or vice versa. If you have multiple term sheets, you'll have the benefit of being able to negotiate from a position of strength, which likely means you may be able to increase the valuation or amount of money you raise. Or, you'll get the terms you were looking for.

Reference Check Your Potential Investor

Your investors will do background checks on you. They will reach out to everybody they know who might have an opinion about you. Expect this and expect that they will uncover a great deal of your past professional life (and sometimes even your personal life, too). If they're doing this to you, there is no reason you shouldn't do the same to them. Search for their past investments, build a strong set of questions, and go sit down with the people who your investors have done business with in the past. Talk to the founders and management teams about how the investor behaved and how they added value. Ask if they were engaged and supportive of the founders. Find out if they were detached and aloof.

Also, it's important to know that your backchannel checking will get back to your potential investor. You can use that to your advantage by saying you are in a highly competitive financing process and are looking for the best financial partner. Tell them you're actively considering working with them and are searching for detailed feedback on how they work with their investments and also how to best work with them. In addition to speaking with their successful portfolio companies, it's important to also talk to companies where the investments didn't work out or where the investors let the founders or CEO go. How did the investors behave in difficult situations? That's an important counterbalance to the situation when everything is going perfectly well.

* * *

Be careful about which investors you select. Don't just say yes to the firm that offers you the most money or highest valuation. Consider their experience in your industry and market, their experience operating companies, and their ability to be a thoughtful and helpful partner in helping you build a successful company. Find a fair deal that balances the stage of your company and the amount of the company you are giving up. A thoughtful, considerate deliberation of which partner is the best fit for your organization can make all the difference in the world for your fledgling startup.

Due Diligence

As you're considering potential investors, they, too, are in a due diligence process with you from the moment they connect with you until you both sign a contract or part ways. Every interaction is a chance for them to judge you and your startup, so you should be putting your best foot forward throughout the process. Know that even casual interactions or quick emails between the two of you are being judged.

In addition to this ongoing due diligence process, there will be a formal review of your documents, contracts, and company performance data. Some investors may even hand you a formal list of data they are seeking, but even if they don't, they will likely request that you provide a great deal of information to them. The goal is for the investor to validate the claims that you have made and to ensure there aren't any legal red flags.

You want to disclose everything. We can't stress this enough: you don't want to hide anything from your new partner. Tell them the truth and err on the side of giving them even more than they ask you for and anything that can impact their perspective on the business. You're starting a relationship, one that will last for years, and if you hide something or there was some issue or problem you failed to disclose, this could seriously affect the relationship. And, it should. It doesn't happen often, but it also could get you into legal trouble, too.

Having some less-than-flattering history in your company's background isn't a deal killer. If you're open and honest early, you may be able to overcome these issues. In any event, you'll want to be strategic with how you present the information that's requested. Sometimes, data presented in isolation doesn't provide the whole story. Your job is to provide the whole story and position the due diligence in the best light for your organization while doing so honestly.

Closing the Round

Usually, simultaneous with the due diligence process, you'll be closing the financing round. This entails taking the term sheet and having your attorney create the necessary documents. There can be a number of agreements that need to be created and governmental filings to be made. A qualified lawyer will help you through the process.

The legal documents are the last major step between you and the investment. Know that many potential investments have been scuttled at this late stage. Arguments over key points (or even not-so-key points) can create a stalemate that you can't get through. Only you, your co-founders, and legal counsel can ultimately decide what you will or won't accept. In general, at this stage, if you've done your homework on your potential investment partner, you should be able to get through closing the round. We wouldn't treat this step in the process as a mere formality, but rather, you should be deliberate and focused on getting to closure.

If you get the right lawyer, they'll steer you in the right direction, especially as you're finalizing investment deals. It's easy for founders to lose control during the investment process when lawyers get involved. Generally, they're driven by the number of hours they work. If you're worried about their cost, most will allow you to place a cap on either the number of hours they work or the total of what you'll pay for their services. You may have to haggle with them over it, but once they agree to it, they'll live with it. We'd suggest that both sides, you and the investors, cap your legal fees. That way no one is fighting over things that don't matter simply to create fees. Investors don't want you wasting your money on legal fees, either, so generally, there is a term in the term sheet specifying a cap on legal fees. We suggest you use that to your advantage to keep costs under control while focusing on the end goal—closing the round.

Ultimately, you want to deeply understand the big issues between you and your investors, and let the lawyers argue those points. You can nitpick anything in the legal world. But, some things (maybe most things) aren't worth fighting over, so you're better off letting those go. Keep in mind that your lawyer works for you. They give you advice, and you make the decisions. Often, lawyers think it works the other way around.

Many founders abdicate all legal talk to their lawyer, which is a mistake. You don't have to become a lawyer and understand all the nuances, but you should have a basic understanding of what's being discussed and decided.

Many resources exist to help you, so use them. Earlier, we suggested the book *Venture Deals*. In addition to that book, there are countless resources available online. Study them and understand the issues, so you can know what the right course of action is in your situation. If your lawyer drives everything, then you may not like the outcome in terms of time and cost. You also may end up damaging your relationship with your investors. Stay in control.

* * *

Unfortunately, most companies won't have a lot of choices when it comes to their investment partner. After analyzing their opportunities and doing the work of talking to many individuals and institutions, the most likely scenario is that you'll have a very small number of options.

Still, if you are fortunate enough to have several funding sources courting you, are deciding between investors with various terms, or weighing whether you should join an accelerator prior to doing a formal round, knowing how to evaluate your apples-to-oranges options is critical.

Keep in mind that you can get help and advice from many outside sources including other founders and your lawyer. And, always remember that the relationship you establish with your investors is a cornerstone of the company. They will likely be with you for the entire time you're building your startup. As such, it's important that you evaluate the choice of investor in the context of a long-term relationship, not just for how much money they'll give you or the valuation you get.

Chapter 22

What Happens after You're Finished with Fundraising?

We'd all like to think that when a startup goes out to seek capital, they encounter a long line of people anxious to invest. This is a fantasy, of course. Many startups fail to get any traction in the investment community at all. Others fail to raise enough capital and end up on the fundraising treadmill, always spending their time raising money.

As an investor, I (Will) see this all the time and in some ways, prefer to see companies completely fail at raising any capital than not raising enough. Why? Because when a startup is continuously in fundraising mode, the founders' attention stays on capital formation instead of on hiring the best people, developing the product, and focusing on the market. It's hard enough for new companies when the founding team can spend all their time on developing a success. Doing it with one arm tied behind their back is almost impossible.

Even a bigger problem with the never-ending fundraising scenario is that the company never has enough capital to move fast. They can't hire enough people, invest in marketing programs, or utilize outside resources to help. Time is almost always a startup's biggest competitor. Not having enough capital makes time a mortal enemy.

Concrete Sensors, a construction tech company where I am a board member, has a product that revolutionizes the construction industry. But since that market has been slow to adopt new technologies, many investors stay away. Unfortunately, this has caused the founding team to spend a lot of time in constant fundraising mode and, with less capital, to move more slowly than they could to attack their market.

They are not unique. For many startups, fundraising never ends. It's a continuous process that absorbs a tremendous amount of time and attention.

You've Got Capital. Now What?

Congratulations, you've raised some money to put your startup into overdrive. Now what? Well, that's what the rest of the book is for! We'll walk you through how you start to build and expand your company. You now have the fuel you need to get your business to the next level. It's important to use that fuel wisely and appropriately to help your business grow.

We also have a few words of advice now that you've raised money. We believe that it's critical to start off on the right foot with your new investors. Work hard at building a relationship with them post-deal. Many will be open to helping you and giving you advice if you are open to it. We often hear that founders are afraid that their investors will start to meddle or be overbearing. While we've met some of these types of people, we believe that founders can dramatically reduce the chances of this occurring by being proactive. Reaching out and involving your investors before they ask questions is a great way to set the tone of your relationship with them and avoid an awkward, overbearing relationship.

Immediately after you close your financing, we'd encourage you to welcome your new investors with a letter that outlines how you'll be communicating with them regularly and consistently. They can't help you if they don't know what's going on, and they're highly motivated to help. Also, encourage them to reach out to you if that doesn't work for them, or if they'd like more frequent updates or conversations. Depending upon the number of investors you have and whether you want to work with them more closely, you may also reach out to some of them to start a regular cadence for dialogue outside of your normal updates.

Our general default has been that we send all investors quarterly updates via email or a formal letter. These updates are detailed enough for investors to understand the progress of the business, but are simply presentations of data you already have—no one wants you spending time on reports instead of the business. We'll also set up calls twice a quarter for more active investors. For those investors who are on our board of directors, we'll likely speak with them every week or two. We'll also publish financials to the board and major investors on a monthly basis and provide audited financials to the entire investor base annually. If an investor still feels left out, we'll move them to the next level of communication, but we've rarely had investors who want to be involved become disappointed by our setting expectations on our communication cadence. Ultimately, investors know that your job is to grow the business. Spending time with them takes away from that ultimate goal.

Whatever process you decide upon, we encourage you to use the closing of the financing as an opportunity to build a strong, consistent relationship with your investors. Your goal should be to set up a process that will work for you and them over the long term. Your investors are now a core part of your business, and there's no reason you shouldn't take advantage of their support.

Failed Investment Process

What happens when an investment process doesn't go your way? Of course, this outcome can be extremely disappointing and demoralizing for you. The amount of effort it takes to run a fundraising process can be extraordinary, so when it doesn't come together, it is natural for you to be dejected.

If this happens to you, all is not lost, but there are a few things you'll need to evaluate and reconcile. If you've done all the right things to raise money, like properly vetting your idea, understanding your market, building a strong co-founding team, instituting a favorable revenue model, creating a realistic financial model, and targeting the right investors, and you're still unable to raise money, then there's probably a fundamental reason why. Maybe you don't have the right CEO or the right mix of co-founders or the product doesn't fit the market. Or, maybe investors just don't see the opportunity in the same way you do or don't yet have the same conviction, perhaps because you don't have enough traction with the business yet.

If you've done all the right things to raise money, like properly vetting your idea, understanding your market, building a strong co-founding team, instituting a favorable revenue model, creating a realistic financial model, and targeting the right investors, and you're still unable to raise money, then there's probably a fundamental reason why.

While we wouldn't say the funding system is infallible, rarely have we come across a company that was turned away when it did everything right or when it had an interesting idea with the potential for serious returns and a good cofounding team. This is an efficient market with a lot of greed built in, and the founders and companies that have the greatest chances of success will invariably get funded.

If you find yourself in this predicament, then the best you can do is to look at the areas where you may be weak and try to get stronger. Don't be shy, and don't let your ego get in the way. When someone turns you down, go ask why. Go back to the basics we discussed earlier in the book and see if there's a place that needs more work.

Or, maybe it's time to pull the plug on this idea and the company and start again. That's OK, too.

Alternatives to Raising Money

If you decide to keep going after a failed investment process—and there are many examples of ultimately successful companies that were once turned away by investors—then you'll need to decide how to generate the money you need to keep you marching toward your goals.

The first thing to do is reset your plan with the new information you have. You won't be able to fund yourself for a long time with losses. You'll need to have a model that helps you sustain yourself on the income you're receiving. That likely means you'll only be able to invest in a small number of things.

The best place to start is to figure out how you'll sustain yourself via revenue. If you have a solution that your customers truly want and need, you may be able to talk to them about advance orders, up-front payments, large commitments, referrals, and any number of ideas that can generate cash for you. You may also want to explore how your solution can be converted into a recurring revenue stream so that you receive a steady income each month. If you have strong relationships with your customers, they'll often work with you to figure out how to help keep you afloat. Also, recognize that they may need to find a backup solution to their problem in case you aren't around anymore, so talking to your customers about your cash situation isn't risk free.

While you're trying to sustain yourself with a revenue stream, you should look at other sources of more accessible growth capital—accelerators, SBIR grants, competitions, and crowdfunding can all be tried, even if you've already tried them.

We've seen several companies that have had trouble getting investors interested early on go the crowdfunding or grant route. They use that money to get to the next milestone and then find they have renewed interest from angels and VCs.

Remember that a no from many investors isn't necessarily a no forever. Many companies have been turned down and then subsequently raised money even from the same investors who originally turned them down. Of course, you'll need to show a lot of progress or have pivoted into a new line of business more interesting to them. Sometimes, investors have a difficult time coming back to something they've already turned down, but it's definitely possible and it happens. One famous firm, Bessemer Venture Partners, even publishes the deals that it turned down that went on to become runaway successes. If there ever was motivation that you can still be successful even if you have been rejected for an investment, this list is it. It includes Apple, FedEx, and Google, to name a few of the many immensely successful companies they turned down.*

As we said earlier, analyze why you didn't get funded and then go address those issues. Explore the roles and responsibilities of the founding team, and make adjustments if appropriate. Even better, go out there and generate some success by getting customers for your solution who will help show investors that they made a mistake by not funding you earlier.

* * *

One of the most difficult tasks of any founding team is to ensure that the company is funded. There are many ways to make that happen, but to build a successful business, you'll need to have a well-thought-out financing strategy.

For startups, we've always advocated raising money because the window of opportunity is usually short. Get together with your founding team, decide what's right for you, and go get the capital you need to grow your company quickly. Then, you'll be ready to move on to building your product or service.

Still, not being able to raise capital isn't necessarily the end. Take what you've learned during the funding process and see if you can adapt your idea to deal with the concerns that kept you from getting funding. Process them through the vetting loop. There may be some straightforward adaptations you can make that makes it easier to get money for your renewed idea and plan.

Part IV

Running Your Company

Chapter 23

How Do I Build and Deliver a Great Product?

At Silerity, we had a bleeding-edge, high-priced automation product that was targeted at the biggest electronics companies in the world. I (Will) knew that big products with expensive price tags required loads of support, training, documentation, and of course, product completeness; and those factors drove our product development plan. We did well on most of this challenge, but we made several big mistakes delivering our complete offering.

After we developed a proof of concept of the technology—our prototype—we convinced Intel to work with us to refine the underlying technology and the overall product. This required a huge investment on our part. One of the founders was at Intel all the time. Taking advantage of their guidance, we rolled out our first MVP, then several subsequent iterations, making sure that they met Intel's needs. Of course, we considered what other potential customers needed along the way as well.

As the early product was deployed, we realized we had underestimated the support load. The complexity of the product led to dissatisfaction among the users. Our documentation was poor to nonexistent, and this cost the company dearly. To patch the hole, another founder had to be on-site at the customer's location to make sure things ran smoothly. Obviously, this situation didn't scale.

Eventually, we got it all straightened out. It took many more iterations of the MVP to improve the overall user experience and the hiring of a dedicated documentation person to reduce the amount of hand-holding required. In the end, we were successful because of our focus on customers and iteration, but things would have been easier if we had done a little more work on the complete offering earlier.

The Product Is Just Part of What You're Selling

In the first part of the book, we broke down what it takes to be a founder so that you can do a gut check on whether it's the right path for you. In the second part of the book, we showed you how to develop a concept for a product and how to lay the right foundation to build a successful, fundable company. In the third section, we outlined how to get funding for your new company. Now, in the fourth and final section, we'll discuss how you bring your concept to life and get your product into the hands of the people who want it the most.

If you've gotten this far, you're likely looking past your first round of funding and are ready to deliver a great product to your customers.

We'll kick things off in this chapter by discussing how to create your product. This involves expanding the business model you've developed in two dimensions. The first is to take your original product implementation—the one you developed a prototype for earlier in the business modeling process—and grow it into a full product, also known as your "offering." This includes turning your prototype into a solid, final, and stable product that people will pay for, but it also consists of creating everything else required to make it a complete offering, including how you'll provide support, deliver documentation, and handle customer feedback.

> Your complete offering includes turning your prototype into a solid, final, and stable product that people will pay for, as well as everything else your customers need: support, documentation, and a way for them to give you feedback.

The second dimension for expanding your original business model includes projecting how your product will evolve in the coming months and years. This is your roadmap. It serves as an overview for how and approximately when you'll add features. While you'd like to deliver everything you can at once, that's impractical. You'll almost assuredly be constrained by limited resources, and you'll need to get the most important differentiating product features to market and into your customer's hands as quickly as possible. To do this, you'll need to incorporate feedback from your customers and consider what you can deliver now and what will have to wait for a later date. The timing may be determined by the urgency to deliver specific product functionality in order to collect revenue or by the need for customers to have a certain set of features before other features you are planning.

Every product type will have varying development methodologies and specific processes that work best for your particular product and market. Rest assured, we won't try to cover all of them. Instead, we'll describe an overall approach to product development that is relatively universal.

The core of this approach is a continuation of what you did to create your initial business model and your first prototype product: using iteration and customer feedback. By listening to what your prospective customers have to say and quickly addressing those comments, suggestions, and feedback, you can converge on a solid and complete-enough version of the offering that your customers will be interested in paying for. The difference now in this chapter is that you're iterating and evolving your business model with all the components of your offering, including your product, of course, but also the other components necessary to support the product and customer.

It's important to note that at this stage, your goal is less about selling a product and more about satisfying a customer. While you'll want to start maximizing revenue right away, this shouldn't be done at the expense of broad customer satisfaction. Early in the life of your company, you need your customers for much more than the revenue they deliver. They are actually an integral part of your offering's creation. Their engagement and feedback are vital to you having a successful initial product launch. They'll help you fine-tune your offering so more customers will adopt it, and they may even become part of your marketing efforts as you expand your customer base. Your customers' success with your products and their happiness with how they've been treated is a vital part of having a successful offering that gets broadly adopted.

Think about Amazon. While their revenues have grown over time, from the beginning, they've run the company with almost no profit. Part of their strategy has always been to be the market leader in price. As such, they've done everything possible to keep prices low, even at the expense of profit.

Growing their customer base has always been their highest priority, and it's one of the reasons they've been successful.

In the sections that follow, we'll first outline the creation of your offering—your product, plus all the support pieces necessary for making your customers successful with it. We'll then discuss how to think about rolling out future offerings, expanding on what you deliver initially, and how to keep your early customers happy while expanding the pool of potential customers.

Initial Product

At the core of your offering is your product. Likely, it's what your customer sees most often and what they interact with more than any other elements of your offering. For the most part, it's what they're actually buying. If you're like most startups, the product was the focus of your original idea, and while vetting your vision, you probably spent much of your energy building prototypes of it while converging on your complete business model.

Considering the perceived importance of fleshing out a great product, it's easy to understand having an intense focus on building a perfect product. But, be aware that you could spend years doing that. You could deliver every product feature you think your customers want and hire a huge staff to handle development, support, and customer feedback. But, by the time you reach perfection, you'll have run out of money, and competitors will be so far ahead of you that it's almost foolhardy to continue with your company. There are always people, companies, and ideas pursuing the customers you are targeting. Take too long, and they'll beat you at your own game.

As a result, time is almost never on your side. So, instead of seeking to create a perfect and complete product, it's better to be the first company to deliver an MVP that will likely win customers' hearts, minds, and wallets. Of course, being first means you'll also have more time to iterate and engage with customers to get the product closer to what they want.

> Instead of seeking to create a perfect and complete product, it's better to be the first company to deliver an MVP that will likely win customers' hearts, minds, and wallets.

As we discussed in Chapter 8, an MVP is a minimal version of your product that gives your customers the opportunity to see what you can deliver and how it can improve their lives. It is not a final product by any means, but it's also not entirely incomplete. At once, it meets your customers' current needs and wants while demonstrating what you'll deliver in a more complete form in the future.

The idea behind an MVP is that it's a solid first step toward your vision that meets some of the customers' key needs while providing a great feedback mechanism for you. It's a platform for gathering information about how the customer uses the product and gives you a clear indication of how you can improve it and where you've missed the boat. It tests your assumptions and even your vision.

You'll probably recognize that creating an MVP is a similar process to the one you used in developing a prototype solution while vetting your vision. It is, but this time, the process is a little more formal. You're now narrowing down to a complete product that you'll sell. The MVP has to be more refined, and it has to create a base that you can build on quickly and soundly. For an MVP to work, your customers must see a logical progression from what you initially deliver to what they ultimately want. It's also critical that the MVP be usable as soon as it's in your customer's hands. It's not a proof of concept. Even the earliest iterations of the product need to address their needs.

Diagram 10　A Visual Representation of MVP Development.

An MVP is no good if you don't plan on actively seeking feedback from customers and building new versions of your product to meet their needs and address the concerns they voice. It's critical that you listen well and quickly develop an updated version of your offering that shows not only what new features you can add, but how well you listened to what the customers had to say.

Successful, fast-moving companies use an iterative process of listening to feedback, adopting ideas and suggestions, and getting updates into customers' hands quickly. You'll be amazed at how much you'll learn along the way. If you are truly addressing the needs of your customers and showing that you have a unique way of doing it, they will gladly give you solid feedback that you can use to improve the product—and ultimately, their experience. Their desire to use your product and give continual feedback only increases as you deliver on their suggestions.

Using this approach, you'll not only get your product to market faster, but because you'll have something to sell to customers early, you'll optimize revenue generation, too. Early revenue can, potentially, mitigate the need for extensive and expensive early fundraising while your valuation is still low. This is a win-win scenario. You have the chance to build a better product while optimizing revenue and reducing the need to raise capital.

As we've said before, you should take all the money you need to grow as fast as possible because it's unlikely that revenue alone, at this early stage, can provide the fuel you need to grow rapidly. But, if you can get the revenue wheels churning and reduce the amount of capital you raise for just a short period, you may be able to get better terms from investors. Investors love to see that you have real revenue and a product in your customers' hands. It validates your concept and reduces their investment risk.

Of course, there's a tension between bringing the product to market quickly with a less-than-fully-featured solution versus taking the extra time to polish and develop it. We've seen companies zip ahead only to discover they made many wrong choices. Some mistakes are inevitable and okay if you're moving fast, with many leading to great learning experiences for you. Some incorrect choices, however, are painful to change and correct and may slow you down significantly. We've also seen companies slow down because they're afraid to make a mistake, so they wait to perfect their product before showing it to customers for the first time. This only leaves them behind their competition. Just as racing ahead can cause problems, in some instances, the pursuit of perfection can kill great ideas because they never make it to the market or miss their market window.

> Just as racing ahead can cause problems, in some instances, the pursuit of perfection can kill great ideas because they never make it to the market or miss their market window.

Take the crowdfunded smart credit card company, Plastc. Like several other smart card startups over the last few years, Plastc set out to offer a single electronic credit card that incorporated all of a customer's credit, club, and discount cards into one credit-card-sized device. They collected $9M for 80,000 pre-orders of the product. Unfortunately, they kept refining the product to add more features instead of shipping it once its core features were ready to go. In the meantime, the market changed. Magnetic stripes gave way to chip readers, and mobile phone-based electronic payments became widely adopted. In their zeal to get everything right, they lost their momentum and let the market pass them by.

Whether you should go to market quickly or wait for further development depends on a number of factors specific to your business and situation. It depends on your customer target, how desperate they are for the product, how unique your offering is, and the price point of your offering. It also depends on the type of product that you're selling. If you're selling a product to consumers that threatens irreparable damage or harm if it breaks or doesn't work properly, then taking more time to perfect it not only makes financial and legal sense, but it's the right thing to do. Similarly, if you have a product that is difficult to change, fix, or add new functionality to or it has long development cycles, then you should make sure that your MVP is a more complete version of what you intend to offer.

When thinking about how much development to put into your MVP, you should also consider the channel you are selling through (we'll talk more about distribution channels in Chapter 27). If, for example, you're selling through a retail channel where inventory is involved, or if there will be a delay getting the product into the hands of the ultimate customer, you may also need to spend more time making sure your offering has everything it needs to hold up for a longer period of time. This is especially true if you have no way of updating the product once it gets into the customers' hands, as with software or internet-connected hardware products.

If, however, you're developing something that can be easily updated online via the internet, over Bluetooth from another connected device, or even via a new download from a website, you should feel comfortable introducing it in a way that demonstrates its key features without being complete.

None of your decisions on how fast you need to get to market should change the iterative approach that we've discussed or going to market with an MVP. With a long or short product development cycle, delivering an MVP and iterating with your customers to refine it is the best way to go.

Even if you have a complex product that involves the manufacturing of physical components or long-term research, then you should still use an MVP approach. You should hand-build your first generation of products whenever you can so that customers can use them prior to committing to full-blown manufacturing. If it's time in the lab you need, then bring customers in to see what you're doing and demonstrate how you're solving their problems in a controlled environment. Stay as close to your customer as possible and iterate quickly and often. In startups, speed almost always wins.

Even as you quickly iterate through multiple versions of your product, take the time to step back and ask yourself where you are with respect to your original vision. It's okay to look at your original product, the one you prototyped, and question whether it was right in the first place. In fact, if you don't find at least some parts that are no longer viable, you're probably not looking hard enough. With what you know now and with the customer feedback you've received, ask yourself, "Were the assumptions I made in creating my vision reasonable?" If not, it's all right. In fact, we encourage you to use the new knowledge you've gained to modify your vision along the way.

Be careful, though, of taking customer feedback as gospel. As Henry Ford is famously said, "If I had asked people what they wanted, they would have said faster horses."* Sometimes, the feedback you get from the early adopters of your solution may not be taking you to the place you envision. Make sure you don't have blinders on either way. Listen to what your customers are telling you, but always question the feedback, too.

Our advice is to make sure you're speaking with the right potential customers. If they are the right ones, the ones that match your persona, then their advice is likely to be golden and should be followed. If you disagree, make sure you understand exactly why you disagree and discuss it with the customer. Only then can you make a rational decision about the direction you should go. If you override the advice you get, you should be sure that you're doing it because you rationally believe you know better and you're not being blinded by your love for your own vision.

*   *   *

Most successful companies iteratively test their offering as it's developed. By creating an MVP that you can get into customers' hands as early as possible, you'll learn more about your overall business model than you could by trying to complete your offering prior to showing it to potential buyers. You might be surprised how interested customers are in being part of completing your offering, especially if you're solving a difficult problem for them. The more you involve them, the better your product will be.

Chapter 24

Making Your Customer Successful

At Innoveda, we developed complex CAD products for electrical engineering. When we founded the company, we created new technologies but also acquired existing ones from several other companies. While each individual product was solid, the combined group of them was a mess. Users couldn't make their way through them. They were confused, our support levels shot through the roof, and worst of all, customer satisfaction plummeted.

I (Will) was pulling my hair out. We were spending a lot of time and money holding it all together. Instead of investing in moving forward, we were doing everything we could just to tread water and not get sucked beneath the waves. We tried to stay close to the users by preemptively contacting them and when one would go silent, we began to really worry. Our view was that as long as people were complaining, they actually cared. When they stopped talking to us, they were likely talking to others about their bad experience with us.

Obviously, we had to make some changes. We knew that ultimately, the products would have to be adapted to work more seamlessly, but we needed to invest our resources and energy into providing as much training, support, and handholding immediately.

We rolled out startup guides, new documentation, and courses. We enhanced phone and email support, expanded it to 24/7, and visited customers physically when it made sense. We also kept a database of customer interactions so we knew who we were in contact with and, more importantly, who we weren't talking with so we could proactively contact them.

The positive impact was almost immediate. Customers don't want to *need* a vendor's help, but they like knowing that success is what they're buying, not just a product. We made it clear in all our interactions that we wouldn't sleep until they were successful.

Eventually, we built a lot of the support and guidance into the products. This didn't remove the need for everything we had put in place as a stop-gap, but it allowed us to shift our focus from being reactive to being proactive. As we moved our products forward, integration, support, and customer success became the first priority in product planning. We had higher customer satisfaction while actually spending less money on it.

Documentation, Instructions, and Guides

We find that many founders mistakenly think their products are self-explanatory and that their customers will figure out how to use their product with no difficulty. In our experience, this is never the case. Unless you want your customers to become frustrated and dissatisfied with what you're delivering, you'll need to provide instructions on how to use what you're selling.

Unless you want your customers to become frustrated and dissatisfied with what you're delivering, you'll need to provide instructions on how to use what you're selling.

Some form of documentation, including instructions, videos, and guides are a key part of your offering. Unfortunately, they are often the orphans of the product development process. Making your early customers successful is critical to your growth and your success. The best companies put their documentation on an equal footing with the product and the entire offering. It needs to be good enough to be your surrogate when you're not around to hold your customers' hands.

While having a good user interface and adopting any standards for use (say, like the consistent layout of mobile apps) is a great way to minimize the need for documentation, users still need some level of documented assistance. If you question this, check out all the Dummies books available and how many instructional YouTube videos exist on basic iPhone functions. As intuitive as you think your product is, it won't be for someone new to it and its concepts.

You'll iterate through versions of your product, so keeping the documentation virtual makes sense. That is, in an easily changeable form, like the web or downloadable PDFs. It will be changing frequently, after all. As you iterate to create your MVP, you should be testing the documentation you have, especially with new customers or potential customers along the way. It's a major part of what you're offering, so you want to make sure your customers are happy with it.

Early on, this documentation can be on your website. Having it on the web offers several benefits. It's easy to update, and the updates are immediately available to your customers. It also makes it simple to provide an interactive search function so those accessing it can find what they need quickly. As you develop your offering further and you learn about how people are using the product and where its pitfalls are, you can easily add separate documents or search functions to take them directly to the most logical resolutions and explanations.

Sometimes, the best way to answer questions and explain your product is by using videos, Q&As (Question and Answer documents), FAQs (Frequently Asked Questions documents), and knowledge bases (searchable explanations of how to do things within your product). These types of documents bridge the gap between fully written documentation and support and help your customers get answers fast and efficiently.

In some markets and with some products, printed documentation is a requirement. Sometimes, it can be as simple as an indication of the website the customer should visit to get more information. These are often found included with consumer-oriented electronic devices these days and extend to documents as complex as a printed manual describing every detail of a complex product as is found with almost any tool or machine.

As with many things having to do with your particular product or market, your need for documentation, instructions, videos, and guides will vary. Complex products will obviously need more directions, and simple products will most likely require less. Ideally, you want to include instructions with the product where possible so that customers don't have to seek out help. And, if they need it, you should provide it in the most straightforward way you can. The more implicit the instructions are—flashing lights, popup descriptions, arrows, labels, and so forth—the better.

Where possible, use images, diagrams, charts, and videos to quickly show the customer how to use the product or troubleshoot a problem. The faster they can get back to using the product for its intended purpose, the more satisfied they'll be with it.

As you think through how your customers will be guided through the use of your product, consider how their need for help might be reflected in its actual design. Consider how you can make the product easier to use to avoid problems completely, or how the design of your product might be changed in order to make it easier to use. In a hardware product, would a display with text be better than a few lights? In software, would a description of each feature when it's used for the first time make sense? In life sciences, would better labeling alleviate potential problems? When you think about your entire offering rather than separating the product from its support pieces, you can make your customers much more successful with your product.

Interactive Support

Even if you do a great job with your documentation, sometimes your customers are going to need to communicate with you to get support if they run into problems, have questions about functionality, or experience other issues. With the goal of making your customer's experience with your product the best it can be, you need to give them a way to interact with you.

Unless your market requires it—as with customers who run twenty-four hours a day with a critical reliance on your product—you are unlikely to need to jump into around-the-clock support at the beginning. People generally understand normal business hours. Still, responding to a customer's needs in a timely fashion is almost always a requirement for a solid offering.

These days, with the broad adoption of email and social networking, many paths are open to you to support your customers. This ranges from the simplest (meaning the least involvement by you) to the most complex (support is a full-time job). Following are some examples.

- **Online forums.** These are general interactive forums that are sponsored and hosted by someone else and cover multiple topics. You or one of your customers can establish a group in the forum in which your customers can communicate with each other. Sometimes, the company isn't even involved, but most often, the company scans what's going on and responds when appropriate. There are many of these specific to various industries and markets, and there are general ones like Reddit. There's also a new wave of cross-company collaboration tools that organizations are using to interact with their customers. Tools like Slack, Atlassian Stride, and Microsoft Teams, among many others, are making collaboration internally and externally even easier.
- **Q&A on your website or blog.** This is a managed discussion on your website. Again, it might be customers only, but since it's on your site, your level of involvement is likely higher. You can make this as interactive as you want. Obviously, the more, the better.
- **Direct messaging on social networks.** Most social networks offer a direct messaging feature that allows people who are in your network to communicate directly with you. Some companies have dedicated social network accounts that they use to communicate with their customers. This can work inbound as well as outbound, giving customers a way of contacting you and giving you a way to reply.

- **Email support.** Usually, the company provides a specific support email address that is broadcast to its customers. Response times can vary, but there is an expectation when your customer sends you an email that it will be responded to in a reasonable amount of time.
- **Telephone support.** With telephone support comes an assumption by the customer that someone will be at the other end of the line, at least during business hours. Or, at least, that voice messages will be returned in a timely fashion. This requires the biggest commitment to support. Not all companies will need to offer telephone support. In your early discussions with customers, you'll learn whether it's required. If you decide to offer it, you'll need to dedicate resources throughout each day to handle the telephone calls.

Of course, you can mix and match any of these that make sense for your company, but at the very least, you'll want to offer email support with fast turnaround (twenty-four hours or less) and telephone support, if it applies, for critical issues, at least during business hours. As we mentioned earlier, your goal in the early stages is less about selling a product and more about satisfying your customers. In this light, support isn't a burden; it's an opportunity. How else will the customer know how much you care about them if you don't get a chance to show them?

Fast, caring customer support alone can be a huge product differentiator. In fact, it can even make up for a lesser product. It can become the reason why people choose your product over the competition. On the other hand, poor support in this age of easily accessed customer reviews (think Amazon, Yelp, TripAdvisor, and social networks) can be a deal killer for your product's adoption. Consider how often you've relied on feedback from others to make a decision on where to go or what to buy. Customer satisfaction is critical. It's best to think of interactive support as an integral part of your offering and not treat it as an afterthought.

Planning Your Future Offering

By definition, your MVP will only offer a subset of the functionality of the product you envision. You will be picking and choosing among your product features, guided by your early customers to determine the scope of your MVP. Even though you'll work hard on your initial product, chances are your early customers aren't going to be completely satisfied with your MVP. Remember, it's a minimal product, after all.

Even before you deliver your MVP, you should think about the list of features you'll deliver next and even those that you'll deliver in the future. These lists will make up your roadmap. While it's sometimes hard to think too far ahead when you're so focused on just getting your first product out the door, it's very important that you do so.

Part of what your early customers are buying is the promise of what you will deliver. As such, you'll need to tell them about what's coming in the future and approximately when they should expect it. Additionally, you'll also need to figure out where to dedicate your development efforts for upcoming versions of your offering. Some of these efforts will take longer than others, and you'll have to make trade-offs between working on some that can be delivered in the short term and others that need more time and energy and will be delivered later. All of this takes forethought and planning.

For these reasons, you'll need to pull the team together, consolidate all the feedback you've received from customers, and take a rational view of what you can do now, what you can do next, and what you'll do after that.

Simply put, this is about prioritization, which is far easier said than done in a startup.

There are many processes for product prioritization. Some are specifically applicable to certain product types and specific markets. Below is a generalized prioritization model that we've used and have seen successfully implemented in many of the startups we've worked with, regardless of what product is being developed or market entered.

There are three major factors to consider as you prioritize products, product features, and the other components of your offering: quality, functionality, and vision.

- **Quality.** When you deliver your first product via an MVP, it will inevitably have some problems. You'll know about some of these when you deliver it, and you'll learn about more problems once it's in your customers' hands. While you'll try to find as many of the problems as possible before your customers do, inevitably, they'll run across issues you don't find yourself. Some of these problems will need to be fixed immediately, and some can wait to be addressed. When the problems are severe enough to impact the needed functionality of your product or the perception of your focus on quality by the customer, then you'll need to make fixing the product a high priority.
- **Functionality.** As we mentioned earlier, your MVP probably won't address all your customers' needs when you first release it. Since your customer likely bought your

product, expecting more than you delivered at first, you'll need to add new functions or capabilities to your product to make sure your customers' needs are met and they're happy with what you are delivering. Some of these will be required to stay ahead of your competition, others will be required to meet the needs of your existing customers, and still others will be required to expand your customer base. Each requirement needs to be ranked, so you can decide how to deliver on those parts of your product over time.

- **Vision.** After delivering an MVP, startups often become tactically focused trying to be responsive to requests for increased quality and additional functionality from their new customers. While delivering on your initial promise is important, as is responding to customer feedback, it's critical you don't forget your vision for your offering while doing so. Just being responsive to your customers is not likely to keep you ahead of your competition—in fact, it makes it more difficult to acquire new customers. You need to make sure that while you're prioritizing responsive additions to your offering that you also schedule time to deliver on the features that you envisioned from the beginning and that got your early customers and investors excited about you in the first place.

- Now that you're thinking about the factors for prioritizing how you'll spend your time moving your offering forward, you may realize it's more difficult than you originally expected. There always seems to be too much to do, and making choices can be difficult. We use three considerations to help sift through the choices and triage the opportunities. We try to get a handle on how our decisions will affect customer retention, new customer acquisition, and the financial impact to the business.

- **Customer retention.** All three of the major prioritization factors above have an impact on customer retention, but none more than quality. Problems with your product that impede its use by your existing customers is a relationship killer. Product issues will keep your customers from being able to use all the functionality you've delivered, but even worse, may indicate to them that you're sloppy or aren't concerned enough about the commitment level they're demonstrating in adopting your offering. These issues often create ill will that's hard to reverse, and that makes it difficult to retain the customers who run into problems. Making sure you retain your early customers is very important, especially when reviews through social networking are so easily broadcast, not to mention that your potential investors will be talking to your customers. Bad news travels fast, so dealing with issues, especially critical ones, is very important.

- **Getting new customers.** Your early adopter customers who agreed to work with you to develop your MVP are likely the ones with the greatest need and are among the biggest risk-takers in your market. Just because they have decided to purchase your early solution doesn't mean everyone else in your market will also jump on board. As you think about how to prioritize and schedule your development efforts, you need to think about what you should deliver to attract more customers outside of the initial group that chose to buy from you. Thinking about your new and larger customer base will probably drive you to give more weight to adding new functionality, which is likely required to bring on additional customers. Use this as a factor to influence your prioritization because you need to expand your customer base to grow quickly.

- **Cost.** The final consideration, and perhaps the most limiting one, is cost. How much will it cost to improve quality, implement new features, or execute on your vision? As a startup, you have a limited budget. If you need to hire more people to deliver on any of your prioritization factors, that will cost money. If you find a problem that is very difficult to fix and you need more time to fix it, that will cost money (and will hurt customer satisfaction). If you find that you need to work on multiple priorities simultaneously, that will cost money. Sometimes, you just can't afford to do what you'd really like to do. That's why cost is such a critical consideration when prioritizing the long list of to-dos necessary for moving your offering forward.

Implicit in these three considerations is customer satisfaction and the time it takes to deliver on any new feature or functionality. Without customer satisfaction, you won't be able to retain your customers, and attracting new ones will be difficult. You'll need happy customers to help recruit new ones into the fold, especially early on.

Time is a more difficult consideration. The longer you take to deliver on your vision for the product or to address requests and fix problems, the more negative the impact on your customers will be. On the other hand, the faster you try and do things, the more costly your efforts will be in real dollars, and the more likely it will be that you'll make mistakes.

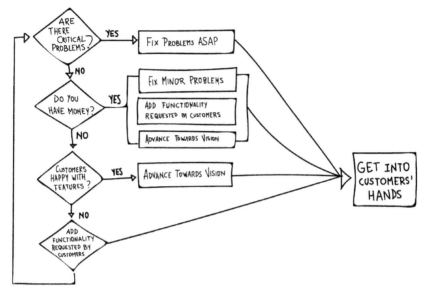

Diagram 11   A Flowchart for Prioritizing Problems

Unfortunately, there are no easy answers here, and there is certainly no perfect or absolute way to prioritize the planning for future deliveries of your offering. Not only is every product, market, and industry different, with a variety of needs and standards, but so is each situation. You'll need to dynamically balance what's best for your company, given your current situation, customer needs, and company resources.

The following diagram is a general way of thinking about the situation you're in.

Following this flowchart, your highest priority will be to handle critical problems. After that, your decisions will be based on what you can afford. Obviously, if you can afford to do several things at once, you'll want to address smaller issues, add functionality to get new customers, and make a step or two toward your ultimate vision. Without money, your hands are somewhat tied. If your current customers are happy with the functionality of your product, this likely means that it's sufficient to continue to get new customers with it. In that case, you want to bias your efforts to implementing the next step in your vision. If, however, they aren't happy, you'll want to focus on addressing small problems that remain, as well as adding specific functionality they are requesting.

As you'd suspect, this process is a loop. You still want to get whatever you've created into your customers' hands as quickly as possible, then iterate through to reprioritize your actions, based on the state of your customers.

While it's not easy, try to not get caught up in spending loads of time perfecting your list. By its nature, it's imperfect and will almost assuredly change very quickly. Use the preceding model to get the team started, and by all means, get going. It's better that customers see you as responsive than for you to spend the time trying to be perfect.

* * *

Once you get funded, you'll want to pull out all the stops to get your product to market and start making money. We'd recommend that before you go gangbusters into development, you take a step back and think about what you're doing. Your product is only one component of the offering you'll sell to your customers. Good support and documentation are critical parts as well. In the end, it's customer success and happiness that you're selling, not the tangible product that you're working on. That's just a vehicle for meeting your customer's needs and/or desires.

Once you've delivered on your initial offering, you'll want to quickly turn your attention to how and what you'll deliver to your customers to increase quality, add new features and functions, and to deliver on your broad vision. You do that by taking all the data from your early customers and getting the team together. Prioritize your efforts to make sure you're meeting the needs of your current customers. Also make sure you're doing everything you can to stay ahead of the competition and acquire new customers.

Chapter 25

How to Get Customers

Getting customers to part with their money to purchase your product can be extremely challenging, even when they love your solution. My (Rajat's) company, MobileDay, was a case study in this. MobileDay was a one-touch conference calling application for smartphones. When you needed to join a conference call, you would just tap your phone rather than having to type in up to thirty digits. Sounded great for business professionals, right?

MobileDay attracted hundreds of thousands of users, but it struggled to turn a large percentage of those users into paying customers. From the fan mail the company received, there is no doubt about the value that the solution provided to people. Unfortunately, that value wasn't enough to get the bulk of the users to pay for the app. As a result, MobileDay's original business model to give the app away to casual users and to charge power users failed.

Because of this, the company was forced to pivot and charge forward in a completely different direction. Ultimately this pivot, too, failed, and the company was subsequently acquired for its assets. The app is now a small part of a broader solution for users to join meetings whether on their phone or in a conference room. While the MobileDay app still exists and delights its users, there wasn't a clear way for us to make money from it. In MobileDay's case, a broader solution just may have been the ticket to finding a business model that worked.

Why Focus on a Go-to-Market Plan?

The popular saying goes, "If you build a better mousetrap, then the world will beat a path to your door."

In the world of startups, this generally isn't true unless your mousetrap is substantially better than any other mousetrap. Your offering has to be ten to one hundred times better than your competition to be a slam dunk to reach the point where your product actually sells itself. If you don't have that kind of product leadership, and very few startups do, you're going to have to focus on additional methods for acquiring customers. In startup parlance, those methods make up your go-to-market plan (the foundation of your sales and marketing strategy).

Of course, don't let us dissuade you from trying to create something one hundred times better. There's no doubt that it makes your life easier when you have a product so strongly differentiated from the rest of the market. Unfortunately, that's incredibly difficult to achieve when just about anyone can build a company that can compete with you. It's more likely that you'll have to find other, more efficient ways to make your target customers aware that you exist and that you can solve a critical problem for them.

So, instead of relying on just your product for differentiation, spend time creating an innovative approach to attracting and selling to customers. A differentiated sales and marketing strategy is the secret weapon for taking a great idea and turning it into a great business. Truth be told, great sales and marketing frequently beats a technically superior product.

As with almost everything else we've discussed in this book, creating an innovative go-to-market plan is an iterative process. The challenge that most startups have is being able to iterate on their go-to-market plan quickly enough, and sometimes, before they run out of cash. In our experience, more startups fail at this stage—figuring out a scalable go-to-market plan—than when building their product.

This chapter, as well as Chapters 26 and 27, cover the three major sections of your go-to-market plan: pricing strategy, marketing approach, and sales/distribution strategy. To start, we'll dust off the existing work that you did to vet your idea in Chapter 6. That work will serve as the backdrop for us to go deeper into building out your plan. We'll start with discussing various pricing strategies, including how you can use pricing and your pricing model to your advantage, and that doesn't always mean being the cheapest is the best or easiest way to get there.

The next part of your go-to-market plan is building your marketing approach. Specifically, we'll help you refine your target customer, figure out how to get them excited about your product, and then walk you through how to reach customers with a sales and distribution strategy that is in sync with your offering.

It's okay if you feel like you're jumping around while building your go-to-market plan. In the end, you won't be taking a linear path through the maze. You'll start, stop, turn around, and even meander through it. You'll likely work on pricing, marketing, sales, and distribution in parallel. A tweak in any of these parts may cause you to go back and rework other areas.

Changes in your product will also ripple through your plan. The process is highly iterative and not just in the order that we discuss in this chapter.

In Chapters 6 to 10, we talked about some of the decisions and questions that you needed to answer as you developed the foundation of your business. Many of those questions were the prerequisites for where you are now: developing the actual plan for how you'll sell your product.

Let's take stock of what you've already done:

- You have a target customer with a clear sense of why they're interested in your product.
- You understand the market landscape, including competitors and alternatives, as well as your differentiation.
- You've sketched out the overall business model for the company and generally how you'll charge for your offering.

As a reminder, here is the ideal vetting process you went through. The work you did to vet your idea feeds into the sales and marketing model that you'll leverage to get your product into your customers' hands. In fact, you likely already have an idea of what that model—your go-to-market plan—should look like.

One word of caution before proceeding: focus. Your go-to-market plan is your roadmap for getting customers, but the goal isn't to make everyone a customer. So, resist the urge to take a scattershot approach. Chasing any revenue dollar isn't what startups are about. Instead, develop a targeted plan for who you intend to reach, and then systematically test it as if you were a scientist running an experiment. This way, you'll

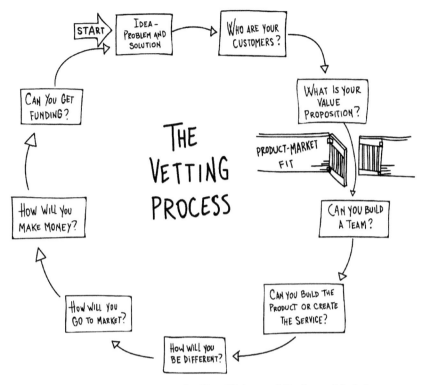

Diagram 12 The Vetting Process for Your Vision and Business Model

have a better chance of finding an approach to acquiring customers that works and that can scale the company. This is a tip we share with all new founders we advise, and one we wish someone had told us when we were just starting out. Focusing on carefully crafting how you'll generate customers is very powerful.

> Develop a targeted plan for who you intend to reach, and then systematically test it as if you were a scientist running an experiment. This way, you'll have a better chance of finding an approach to acquiring customers that works and that can scale the company.

Pricing Strategy

Although figuring out the go-to-market plan isn't linear, you need a place to start. We like to start with the pricing strategy. If you have a sense for your price point and model, that can be fundamental to the specific sales and marketing approaches you take.

A significant way you can differentiate your company is by making the pricing strategy (often called pricing model) unique. The place to start with pricing is to get a handle on the general concept. Start by investigating the following:

- **Value of your solution.** What is your solution worth to your customer? Does it help them save time or money? Is the value emotional? Does it help them generate more income? You'll need to analyze the benefit of your solution from the customer's perspective and make your best attempts at quantifying it.
- **Costs to deliver your solution.** Another factor in your pricing strategy will be your costs. While you'll likely sell your solution at a loss initially, you'll want to understand both the fixed and variable costs you'll have delivering your solution to a customer now and over time. Try to see if there are natural break points or clear decreases in cost as you scale the business. For example, most companies see a substantial decrease in selling cost when they sell more or additional products to existing customers because they already have an established relationship. Understanding the nuances of your cost model can help you get creative in your pricing model.
- **Competitive pricing.** There is generally a price point that your competitors have gravitated toward. While you don't need to sell at the same price, you need to take into

account that your customers will use competitive pricing as a benchmark. Additionally, while your competitors won't always be right, you should try to understand why they price their offering as they do. There might be a very good reason for it. You'll need to judge how best to play in the competitive landscape, but understanding what you are up against is important regardless of your decision.

- **Substitute pricing.** For many founders, the often-overlooked competitor is the substitute product. Your customers may opt to solve their problem differently than by purchasing from you or your competitors. Ride-sharing companies, such as Uber, Lyft, and Grab, among others, are viewed as competitive with the taxi industry. But, what if ride-sharing customers used their services in lieu of purchasing a car? In this scenario, wouldn't these companies be in competition with car manufacturers? The ride-sharing business model is vastly different than their substitute competition's. The challenge here is to think through all the different ways your customer can solve their problem so that you can price your solution accordingly.

- **Overall costs of implementing your solution.** Sometimes, your solution isn't everything that your customer needs. They might need to purchase additional products, or perhaps they need to pay for people to be trained or to help implement your solution. Understanding what the total costs are for your customer to gain value from your solution will also help you in the pricing discussion.

Some example models you'll want to consider are discussed in the next section. This is hardly a complete list of pricing model approaches. Ultimately, our hope is that you can develop a clever pricing model that resonates with your customer—or maybe even invent a new one. Note that some of these models can be used together, but again, the primary goal should be to find something that's natural to your customer and still represents profit for you.

- **Model 1: Premium-cost/Low-cost provider.** Many companies have built their models around being the highest or lowest cost providers. Either can work as long as you build the rest of your business around such a position. That is, are you delivering what the customer is paying for and therefore expects? Selling cheaply made products at a high price is not, generally speaking, a long-term winning strategy, and selling high-cost products at low prices isn't sustainable financially. If you're the low-cost provider, is your cost model and supply chain built for efficiency and scale? Amazon leveraged the low-cost model to compete against Barnes & Noble and other booksellers, and is now using that same approach against Walmart. In terms of premium pricing, Mercedes-Benz is a perfect example of high-end, mass market cars easily recognized by virtually anyone.

- **Model 2: Razor/Razor-Blade Model.** This is a model where the consumer purchases a core component of your product (the razor), which then requires the ongoing purchase of a consumable component (the razor blades). The core piece is frequently sold at a discount with the company generating its profits from the continuous sale of the consumable. Think of companies like HP selling printers and ink cartridges and Nintendo selling game consoles and games as excellent examples of this model. Can you lock in your customer with the purchase of a core component and then sell the consumable part to them on an ongoing basis? If you can, then this may be a model worth considering.

- **Model 3: Subscription.** Another popular model (especially in software) is to deliver your solution as a service, or said another way, on a subscription basis. Generally, the customer pays monthly or annually for you to deliver your solution, which usually occurs on an ongoing basis. This model doesn't work for one-time purchases. Salesforce, the leading sales automation company, was a pioneer of this model in the enterprise software space. On the consumer side, a number of companies are using subscription models for items that we used to buy periodically. Many web-based consumer storefronts offer subscription purchases for consumable items that are regularly needed, like household supplies or personal care items. Most large software companies like Adobe and Microsoft have transitioned to selling their solutions using monthly or annual billing.

- **Model 4: Freemium.** Another popular model frequently used in software sales is freemium. Freemium makes it easy for customers to try a product for free, then upgrade to a version with more features once they get hooked on it. Giving away your product, even a part of it or for a limited time, can be a great way to generate interest. For the startup, knowing what it costs to deliver this free solution is as critical as knowing why the customer will upgrade. Mobile phone–based games such as Rovio's Angry Birds or Supercell's Clash of Clans are a great example of this model. Many games are free, and virtual goods or features are purchased to enhance the game play.

Do your homework on models that can potentially be helpful, and then put your own spin on one. A pricing model that is seamlessly integrated with your solution approach creates a significant advantage.

As you think about your pricing model, keep in mind that startups tend to underprice their solutions. That's okay to start with, but over time, you'll want to figure out how to find the right price point for your solution.

The good news is we don't believe you should think of pricing as static. Conventional wisdom says you can't raise prices once you set them. That's untrue. While it can be hard to raise prices, it happens all the time and can be a tactic that you use to close the gap between the value that you offer and the price you charge.

Innovative approaches to pricing models have been used by a number of startups to great benefit. Take your time and figure out an approach that can be a competitive advantage.

* * *

Building the right go-to-market plan can be the difference between having a breakout success and a startup that struggles to even make it. It's without a doubt one of the most difficult components to get right. It will require incredible persistence, an ability to make the right big and small adjustments at the right time, and some very talented people.

When you have the right model, it's a little like magic. The solution sells without much friction. Sales increase quickly and without a great deal of pushing.

We urge you to take your go-to-market plan as seriously as you've taken building your product. Put in the time and effort to make it solid. Find great people to help you. Study your industry and competitors to understand what will work for you. Then, build a go-to-market plan that is uniquely tied to the strengths and weaknesses of your organization.

Chapter 26

Your Marketing Approach

Modern marketing techniques are making it easier than ever to align your marketing strategy with the rest of your business. There's been so much innovation and creativity in how to target customers cost effectively.

I've (Rajat) experienced this firsthand with our latest company, JumpCloud. We are targeting IT administrators with our cloud directory solution. Traditionally, these people weren't easy to reach, nor did they have the authority to make purchases. But now, IT admins are critical to making virtually any foundational purchase for an IT organization. We also know that this audience is incredibly discerning, and they don't like to be sold or marketed to. They also believe in trying products before they purchase them.

With that level of understanding, we now know that targeting this group has to be authentic and feel organic to the IT admin. The result? The JumpCloud team has built out a content marketing strategy that produces thousands of pieces of content that help solve problems for IT admins. As part of those content pieces, we provide the audience with options on how to solve their problems, with JumpCloud being one of these solutions.

Of course, all of these content pieces are crawled by Google, and when IT admins search for solutions to their problems, the hope is that the content we have written ranks highly. Fortunately, this strategy has played out successfully, and we have seen significant numbers of IT admins become aware of our product as a result and ultimately try it before they purchase, which is critical for our audience.

The clarity of who we are targeting and how they like to learn about new solutions has led us to this model. The alignment of the marketing strategy to put the product in front of the target audience is what has enabled us to successfully grow.

Letting Potential Customers Know You Exist

Just like the rest of your go-to-market plan, your marketing approach needs to be completely in sync with everything else. We've found that it's easy for a startup to lose its way when building its marketing approach. Founders often try to do too much too soon in this area and tend to worry about details that don't matter yet.

As a startup, your primary goal is to prove that customers want, even need, your solution. Our advice is to simplify and be laser focused on finding this initial group of customers.

> As a startup, your primary goal is to prove that customers want, even need, your solution. Our advice is to simplify and be laser focused on finding this initial group of customers.

There are three core activities you should consider in your marketing approach. Review each of the following steps, and then develop answers for each one. Remember that in Chapter 9, you developed some of these answers at a high level.

Step 1: Fine-tune exactly who your customer is.

Step 2: Build a specific message that engages your target market.

Step 3: Develop a cost-effective way to communicate your message to your target customer.

When you think through each of these steps, you'll recognize there is a lot to do, but we'll keep you focused on the core activities you should consider first. We've encouraged you to try and avoid making your initial pass perfect or final. That holds true here as well. Don't try to get it all right or even all done the first time. Iterate through these steps several times until you have an efficient, high-performing marketing model.

Who Is Your Target Customer?

Accurately identifying your customer is hard. There are no two ways about it. Unfortunately, most startups get this wrong at the start, and sometimes they can't even figure out who their customer is. Yet, when you do figure out who your ideal customer is, then the whole business becomes extremely focused.

Sometimes, your customers won't even understand their problem. Once you help them recognize their need and the pain they're suffering, they'll desperately want a solution to address it. Their problem is so pressing that they're willing to take out their wallets to purchase your product relatively quickly. The right customer is highly motivated to fix their problem once they understand it, and you can make sure it's your solution they turn to.

In Chapter 6, you identified who you thought your target customer will be. We encouraged you to create a persona and to tighten the group of potential customers to make it as small as possible. Now, as you start to build the company, you'll want to narrow that group even further by finding those who acutely feel the pain of the problem you've identified. Don't worry about it being too small at first. Your goal is to find a group of people you can learn from and build your go-to-market plan around. Then, ultimately, you'll start to target other groups that might be dealing with similar problems.

The challenge of figuring out the target customer is that founders often stay too high-level and nonspecific, and as a result, the target customer is hard to distinguish. It's very possible your solution can be used, for example, by every business professional on the planet. But, it's incredibly hard to validate a model with a group that big. Pick a small segment of those people, for example, just targeting a small group of very specific potential customers, like director-level managers of domestic manufacturing operations or something similar in your target industry. Figure out why your solution resonates with those people. This will help later in your messaging and marketing to that audience.

When you find that group of people who really care about the problem that your product solves, try to deeply understand them. Delve into what makes them tick, where they hang out, what they think about, what they care about, what they read, who influences them, and any other information that you can glean from them.

The more deeply you understand your customer, the better you'll be able to develop a thorough and accurate marketing approach.

Finding your customer is often different when you're selling business-to-business (B2B) versus to the consumer market—business-to-consumer (B2C). Each market poses different challenges in determining who is the exact customer. Sometimes, they're difficult to precisely identify. In the following sections, we discuss how you can determine who your customer is and whether it's a business or a consumer.

Business-to-Business (B2B) Customer

Identifying a B2B customer is a two-part process.

- **Step 1: Identify the organization.** You'll have an idea of the types of businesses that can use your solution from your work in Chapters 6 and 7, but now it's time to take it to another level. You want to understand what the reasons are for those organizations to be interested in your solution. What are the unique characteristics about these organizations that help you identify them as your target customer? The more detailed you can be about the profile of your target companies, the better.
- **Step 2: Identify the individuals in the company.** Once you have the target company in your sights, then you need to find the right individuals within the company who will be interested in purchasing your offering. Often, startups sell to the wrong person. We've seen founders convince someone to buy their product when that person has no power to make such a decision or the budget for it. Or, they target somebody too high in the organization that frankly just doesn't care about the specifics of the problem or solution because it isn't important enough to them.

Who you target and their level of authority depends upon the decisions you made with your solution, its cost, and complexity. For example, if the offering requires a $250,000 annual commitment from the customer, then you'll want to target someone at a more senior level who has the authority to make that kind of decision. If, on the other hand, you're looking for a $250 annual commitment, then your target will be at a lower level in the organization. As we said earlier, and as we mention frequently in this book, before you commit to a marketing approach, everything needs to be in sync. Your price point has to coincide with the perceived value that you're providing in order to get the right person's attention.

Keep in mind that as you did earlier in vetting your idea, using a persona still makes a lot of sense as a tool to understand a lot about the customer you're targeting.

There are two types of people you want to hunt for in the target organization:

- **Champions.** These are the people who believe in what you're selling, who will rally behind you, and who will encourage their organization to go with your offering. Often, these are the people who feel the most pain from the problem you're trying to address. A word of caution: pick more than one champion. People go on vacation, deals freeze, people get promoted, or they leave the company. Additionally, one of your champions may not have the gravitas in the organization to make the purchase. So, you want to find a champion, and then add a second and a third, so that you have a team of people helping you.
- **Decision makers.** These are the people who have the budget to purchase and will ultimately say yes to purchase

your offering. Often, these people are different from your champions. It's critical that you find out what motivates the decision makers to buy so you can tailor your marketing and sales efforts to them.

Be aware of the hidden influencers. Especially in B2B sales, there are people inside the organization who can influence the decision maker, but you may not be aware they exist or may not have spoken to them. This happens frequently in sales to the government. You think the people who will use your product have control over the decision, but in sales to the government, purchasing people have much more influence over whether your product is purchased.

These hidden people may have a different agenda than your champions and may be even more powerful. We often see this in larger companies as well.

Finding the real customer takes a lot of effort and time. Like most things in this book, it's an iterative process. You go into the market, gather feedback quickly, and then adjust accordingly. You're looking for consistency in a customer profile, both the target company and the individual people within it. By having a consistent group of people that you believe are interested in purchasing your product, you'll be able to more cost-effectively market to those companies and people.

Eventually, you'll have a tight profile of the company and the type of people you need to seek out as champions and decision makers.

Business-to-Consumer (B2C) Customer

With solutions that are aimed at consumers, you have a significant challenge with accurately identifying the target customer.

Consumer solutions are swimming in the sea of over seven billion people on the planet. Your goal is to identify the smallest segment you can that will love your solution. Over time, you can expand your target market to related groups if necessary and desired.

In the B2C world, there are a few different ways you can find your potential target market:

- **Geography.** Some solutions can be offered regionally. You may have a solution that ultimately will go national or global, but if you can narrow the scope to a particular geographic location, that's often a great place to start. Think Blue Apron starting their meal delivery service in Manhattan or Uber starting in San Francisco.

- **Demographics.** Many solutions can be targeted at a certain demographic. Perhaps your solution is aimed at college-age women like the startup Flare. They are selling jewelry that doubles as a self-defense solution and specifically targets college-age women. If you can start to define your first target group with such specific types of characteristics, you'll figure out how to reach them more easily.

- **Psychographics.** This area is more about the interests, values, and behaviors of potential customers. An example of products that are based on psychographics are dating apps. While geography and demographics are important in dating, the key factor is that the consumer is actually interested in dating.

These are three examples of concepts that you can use to narrow your target market. Of course, you might be wrong with your initial assumptions, but that's why you'll go test them.

Perhaps your age range isn't quite right, or some of the interests that people have may not be an indicator of their interest in your solution. At a minimum, you'll have a working hypothesis that you can more easily test.

Your Message to the Target Customer

Once you've identified your target customer, you'll need to know what you want to say to them. Your message needs to convey a lot in what is likely a short amount of time or space.

We have two specific pieces of advice for your message.

1. **When possible, use pictures rather than words.** As the saying goes, a picture is worth a thousand words. Our belief is that the right picture, graphic, chart, or symbol may dramatically shorten the time it takes for somebody to understand your message. Look at just about any billboard, magazine, or TV ad, and you will most likely see pictures being used rather than words to convey the message.

2. **Show your customer what your solution does for them rather than tell them.** If they can understand what they'll get out of your solution because they see the end result, that will help them to make a quicker decision about whether they're interested in the benefits of your product. Apple may be one of the best companies at showing what you can do with their products. Their commercials are all about showing you rather than telling you about their features and benefits.

You've already spent some time in Chapter 6, working on the value proposition for your offering. In this part of your go-to-market approach, you'll delve into how you can build a complete message that will communicate your value proposition and invite your target customer to move to the next step. That could entail a purchase, a commitment to a meeting, or an offer to try your product for free. Whatever the case, the goal of your messaging is to activate your target customer in some way.

Your message to the target customer will need to accomplish four major tasks:

1. Orient them
2. Show what can be done with your offering
3. Demonstrate why it's unique
4. Drive them to take action

Orienting Your Target Customer

As a startup, you likely haven't established any brand recognition, and one of your challenges is to quickly orient your target customer. Helping your potential customer put you in a bucket they know or understand can enable them to more quickly understand who you are.

There are many ways to do this. Some organizations will use analogies to create a first level of recognition, like 7 Up, the Uncola. Some may use competitors, and others may just identify an industry name if it's well-known and understood. It's critical for your customer to be able to place you in a position in their world of problems and solutions and do that quickly. The more time it takes them to understand your message, the greater the risk of having them move on and ignore it.

What Your Customer Can Do with Your Solution

Now that your customer has you in the right bucket of expectations, you need to show them what they can do with your solution. We aren't talking about a list of features in your product. We mean what it actually does for the customer. How does it affect their business or their life?

You'll need to start placing yourself in your customer's shoes to ask questions like, "What will they be able to do if they had my solution? Can they get a raise because they'll perform better in their job? Can they spend more time with their family because my product saves them time? Can they win more customers or save money? Can they have more fun? Will they be healthier?" Whatever it is, you're trying to figure out what they get when they buy your solution.

Generally, marketers will refer to this as your offering's "benefits." The right words or visuals describing your benefits will convey why your target customer should sit up and take notice now and how their life will be better after they've used your solution.

Why You're Unique

A key part of your message to your target customer needs to be why they should use your product. They likely have a number of choices with what to do with their time and money, so why should they spend that with you instead of with someone or something else?

This isn't an invitation to disparage your competitors, but it's a time to clearly differentiate your approach to solving their problem. To be credible, you'll need to back your claims with specifics. You can use data, testimonials from your users, or even let your potential customer see for themselves with a demonstration of what the product can do. Whatever method you use to convey your uniqueness will need to be a central part of your message.

What Action Should They Take?

Your message isn't complete without informing your potential buyer what they should do next. Do they call you, try a free sample, visit a store, or enter their credit card? In marketing parlance, this is your call to action, the immediate response you want from your customer after they finish seeing or hearing your message. You want a strong, clear invitation for your target customer of what they should do next.

> **Call to action:** The immediate response you want from your customer after they finish seeing or hearing your message.

Once you have these four components, you'll be able to implement your messaging into whatever formats are appropriate for your potential customer. You may need to summarize it in print, in an ad on the web, or perhaps, put it into a video. And, don't forget that you'll have to train your team on how to talk to potential customers live. You want everyone broadcasting a consistent message.

Reaching the Customer

Once you've identified your target customer and know what you are going to say to them, you need to reach them. People are busy, and it's hard to capture their attention. If you're selling to businesses and you've targeted senior leaders, then it will be even harder to grab their time. If you are a consumer solution and effectively on the shelf next to your competitors, how will they know to buy your product?

How you reach your target customer depends upon many of the items you've been working on in this chapter, including:

- How large and diverse is your target audience?
- What is the nature of your target customer—high-level executive, technical individual contributor, busy college student, retiree, homemaker, or urban professional?
- What is the price point of your solution?
- What is the best context for your solution? Where, when, and how will your target audience be most receptive to your message?
- How complex is your message?
- How competitive is your market?
- What is your budget?

Answering these questions will help you formulate your communication strategy. This section may be best understood by walking through two real-life examples. You'll be able to leverage the same type of thought process for your organization.

Example 1: Enterprise Customer

AWS (Amazon Web Services) has changed how IT organizations run their technology infrastructure. Previously, large enterprises built their own data centers (computer and data storage facilities) and purchased all the equipment within them. They also had to hire people to run the facilities. Data centers were a significant long-term commitment for organizations, and if circumstances changed, positively or negatively, it was difficult to adjust both financially and physically.

AWS upended this entire approach with their cloud infrastructure solution. Enterprises purchase the capabilities they need without any long-term commitment. AWS customers no longer need to build their own data centers and hire their own operations engineers. The value proposition was clear and almost too good to be true for IT professionals.

Because AWS customers entrust Amazon with some of their most critical resources, AWS's approach to the market is to engender credibility. Amazon does this through conferences, webinars, case studies, and executive visits to their largest customers. For these large customers, AWS needs to take a high-touch, direct sales approach in order to win. CIOs (Chief Information Officers) aren't about to give their business to an organization without knowing they can trust them.

For AWS, the investment to build credibility and legitimacy in the customer's mind is well worth the effort, because once the customer is hooked on AWS services, they keep purchasing more of them. The more entrenched the customers get, the harder it is for them to move away from AWS.

Example 2: Consumer Customer

Let's take an example on the other end of the spectrum. A small company out of Texas, Newtoy, created the game *Words with Friends*, a multiplayer Scrabble-like game. The game was created as an iPhone app and leveraged the network effects of mobile phones and the viral nature of games.

Like many mobile phone games, the business model is simple. A player uses the game for free, and ads are displayed in the game. If the player doesn't want to see the ads, they pay $2.99 for a premium version to have them removed. The game is viral by its nature—it's played with friends. In fact, the original version of the game didn't even allow a single user mode. Friends needed to be invited to play along.

To be successful, the game just needed to attract enough users to tip the scales for network effects to take over; that is, the game became viral and spread rapidly. One player might invite three or four of their friends to play, and then those friends might invite their friends and so on, leading to exponential growth.

A major tipping point for the game came when a prominent celebrity tweeted his enthusiasm for the game and growth took off. Zynga ended up acquiring the game and connected it to its Facebook platform, which further enhanced its viral characteristics. Zynga also added several other methods for monetizing its use, including paying for a variety of new features.

For a consumer game like *Words with Friends*, you can see how word of mouth and PR might be a great vehicle to generate users and ultimately revenue. Even online marketing on platforms, such as Facebook, can help to cost-effectively acquire users. Remember, one user may end up introducing tens or hundreds of others.

Newtoy was sold to Zynga for a reported $53 million prior to Zynga's public offering. Their success came from the fact that they figured out a clever and a largely frictionless way to deliver their online game and monetize it.

As you can see in both scenarios, we were able to reasonably analyze a number of pieces of the go-to-market plan and how they impacted the vehicle of the message. There are many conduits to deliver your message, so think about the various avenues available to you. Choose which ones are the most cost-effective to get you the sales you're looking for.

Our primary lesson for you in this section is to align the delivery of your message with everything else in your go-to-market plan. You spent a lot of time figuring out who is the right audience for your offering, and then you iterated to find the best way to convey the value of it. Make sure the method you use to reach out to that audience amplifies those factors. If you get this all right, it will make selling your product much easier.

***

Simply creating the next great product to solve a problem, speed up a solution, or make people happy isn't sufficient to build a solid startup. Nothing matters if you don't have customers, and that's what your marketing approach is all about—making them aware that you have what they need or want. As we've discussed, the marketing approach is an integral part of your overall business model, but it needs to be fine-tuned on its own.

The three main components to your marketing approach are knowing precisely who your customer is, developing specific messages that engage that customer, and finding a way to cost-effectively deliver that message. Especially at the beginning, being as focused and particular as you can with who you're targeting will be the cornerstone of your success in delivering your message.

Many startups neglect spending the time necessary to do this right. They believe that the product will sell itself or the sales channel will come up with the right messaging. This is a mistake. You don't need a team of marketing people to do this right, especially when you're starting out. The founder on the team who is best at it can take the lead (remember how we talked about diversity in the founding team?). When customers start coming to you instead of you always having to go to them, you know you've done this right. It'll make the entire selling process for your new company much easier and less costly.

Chapter 27

Sales and Distribution Strategy

When we started Viewlogic Systems, we knew we needed a direct sales force. That is, a group of salespeople who interacted with the customer on a one-to-one basis and usually face-to-face. To me (Will), this made a lot of sense. After all, it's how all our competition sold their products, and it seemed like it was the way that purchasing agents in the large companies that made up our market were accustomed to buying. So, we went with what we knew and had worked in the past.

And it worked well for us. Still, it didn't always feel right. One of our differentiators was price, and direct salesforces cost a lot. There are more people involved, and there are usually high associated traveling expenses. So, as we became more established and started to take the market lead in several areas, we added new channels. Tele-sales (sales over the phone and now often called inside sales); original equipment manufacturer (OEM) sales (other companies including our product with theirs); indirect sales (an external sales force selling our product, often with complimentary products); and reference sales (providing a commission to someone outside the company for referring a potential customer).

We didn't add them all at once and never sold all our products through all the channels. It would have been a mess. As it was, it took a lot of energy to sync up the channels and avoid overlap. Commissions for the salesforce (the compensation to the sales force based on a percentage of each sale) on its own was a major effort, as you can imagine. It was always a challenge to assign the correct level of credit to the people involved, even peripherally, in a sale.

By making the effort, though, we created more layers of differentiation for the company. We were able to reach people we couldn't with our direct salesforce, at least not cost-effectively, and customers who weren't previously exposed to our products got to see them front-and-center.

For sure, these particular channels and this number of channels are not right for every company. But startups often fall into to selling the way they know or are comfortable with. Every company should evaluate their selling methods like they do their product differentiation. It can be a key to moving faster or even the difference between success and failure.

How to Sell

The last part of your go-to-market plan is your sales and distribution approach. You've worked on how you reach your target customer with the right message and have a pricing model that you think makes sense. So, now it's time to get them to buy what you're selling.

From your work in Chapter 10, you have a hypothesis about this stage as well. It's likely that you have a vision of whether your offering requires a lot of sales effort or if your primary task will be to fulfill demand that your marketing strategy creates.

For example, a product sold through retail stores is more than likely to be fulfilling demand created by your marketing efforts, as opposed to using a salesperson who has direct contact with the customer.

Your approach to your sales and distribution is going to depend on several factors, similar to how we talked about your pricing and marketing strategies. You'll want to consider some important factors, such as the ones that follow.

- **The complexity of the sale.** Is your product difficult to understand and/or complex to purchase? Perhaps you have many customizations or options to your product, or maybe it requires many people within your customer's organization to agree to the purchase. Higher complexity selling will push you to need higher touch sales models, such as a direct sales force.

- **The implementation of your product.** You'll also want to think about how your product will be used. Can your customer use the product without any help from you or others? Do they need to have special skills or knowledge? Is your product paired with another so that it can function? The more complex the implementation of your offering, the more you'll want to be involved with your customer before and after they purchase it.

- **The price point/level of the customer.** Matching your sales model to the price point and who you sell to is important. A low-cost product that is sold to an individual or somebody at the lower levels of a corporation doesn't make sense economically with a sales model that uses direct selling, face-to-face. Similarly, an expensive product that requires trust created through direct contact is going to be a difficult sale online.

In the following sections, we'll help you to evaluate these factors and a few others. Your answers will start to guide you to the right sales model for your product. You have to do the homework to ensure that your sales and distribution strategy is aligned with your price point, marketing approach, and vice versa.

Direct versus Indirect Sales Models

You really have two high-level options when selling to your customer. You can do it directly and enable your customer to purchase right from you, or you can do it indirectly whereby your customer purchases from a representative of yours. One model isn't necessarily better than the other, just different. Some companies can and do leverage both models.

With a direct sales model, your customer sends you their money directly for the purchase of your product. There isn't a middleman between you and the customer. Direct sales models include online selling, such as on your website or through your product (usually through a software application), inside sales, or person-to-person sales.

With an indirect sales model (often called channel sales), a third party sells your product and then remits some portion of the sale to you. Many products sold indirectly are bundled with other products or services to create a more complete solution. Alternatively, your product may require some help to install or implement, so whomever implements it also resells your product as part of a larger solution, which could include services to get it up and running. Indirect sales models include retail sales, referral sales, reseller or distributor sales, affiliate sales, and embedded sales (your product is sold as part of another).

Whether or not to go directly to your customer or through a channel is a fundamental decision for your company. The decision determines the type of sales team you'll hire and how they'll work. The decision also ripples back to your price point and marketing approaches. For example, if you have a partner selling your product and you need to give them 40 percent of the price to cover their costs and give them some profit, then your revenue and cost model needs to account for that. Selling through a channel means that your marketing not only has to convince your channel to carry your product, but you'll also need to market to end users as well to create demand for your partner.

> Selling through a channel means that your marketing not only has to convince your channel to carry your product, but you'll also need to market to end users as well to create demand for your partner.

A rule of thumb that we like to give to founders is to pick one model and make that succeed first before using both. Trying to initially go direct and indirect is biting off too much. There are many conflicts between the models, and for a young company to navigate those is difficult and time-consuming. Your goal is to grow your business and prove that you have a viable go-to-market plan. Prove that you can make one path to the market work well, and then if you want to prove another, do that separately and later.

While various markets and industries have specific requirements, for most early-stage companies, we think direct sales is the way to go. We like to see founders learn how to sell their offering and become proficient at it before they try to teach third parties how to sell it. A reseller or partner is not going to care about selling your product as much as you do. And, with nascent companies, the amount of learning that needs to take place with the go-to-market plan is so significant that outsourcing that responsibility to a third-party is unwise.

Founder = Head Salesperson

In the early days of a startup, someone from the founding team should act as the head salesperson. If there isn't somebody on the founding team that can step into this role and thrive, you'll need to hire someone for it.

Founders often have an innate sense about how to sell their offering. Usually, the reason founders start a business is because they see a hole in the market. They understand the problem and have a new approach to solving it. Relating to the customer in that way often gives founders a leg up when connecting with the customer and selling to them. It's why we encourage one of the founders to be the head salesperson initially.

It's also why our preference is to have somebody on the founding team with sales experience or focus. Knowing how to sell your own offering is important, because eventually, you'll hire additional sales people and need to train them.

Hiring the First Salesperson

Even if you have the first sales role covered on the founding team, you'll likely need to hire more sales help early on and as your company grows and expands. For most organizations, this is a challenging process.

Early on, there usually isn't a repeatable sales process in place. Even if you've done what we've suggested and learned how to sell the product, a sale by a founder who deeply understands the offering and business is still hard to translate to a new, hired salesperson. That hire may not have the same technical aptitude, understanding of the market, or ability to make decisions on the fly about how to evolve the offering or message. Still, at some point, you have to figure out how to teach others within your organization to sell your solution if you want the company to scale and grow.

Regardless of whom you hire to do this, they need to possess the ability to learn. The very nature of a startup means that new problems will arise from a variety of factors like the market, the type of product being sold, and the price point. Your salespeople have to rapidly determine what adjustments to make to close the customer.

A salesperson who is used to selling with a rigid process or is used to a lot of structure may struggle in the early phases of a startup. Conversely, a salesperson who can listen well, process the feedback, and then alter the pitch on a going-forward basis is going to be invaluable early on.

You'll want to communicate what the salesperson learns while talking to customers back to the rest of the company so that you, as a group, can figure out what resonates with your customers and what doesn't. That in-the-field learning can also be used to change the price point and marketing message.

Remember, the goal is to build a model that is completely in sync, and your first salesperson is a key weapon in making that happen.

* * *

Your marketing approach brings the right type of customers to the table. Your sales process moves them to closure quickly, and your pricing model feels natural to your customer. When this happens, the business ends up growing rapidly and cost-effectively. But, when the pieces aren't in sync, you'll know it. It's the opposite of what we described above.

The business won't grow quickly. It will feel like you're pushing customers to buy, and you'll have an inefficient model. If this happens to you, don't despair. Keep working at it and tweaking various parts of your model. Test your assumptions again and again, and don't be afraid to change them. When it all comes together, you'll feel it, and the business will grow rapidly and far more easily.

We know both sides of this firsthand. On one side, it's frustrating knowing you have an excellent product but can't figure out how to get people to buy it. On the other side, when you know you have a good product and a sales model that is working, it feels like everything just gets easier.

Chapter 28

You Don't Run Your Company, Your Culture Does

At Innoveda, a company I (Will) co-founded, we knew there were two cornerstones to our success—the people who worked there and the culture we maintained. We believed that if we did well in both hiring and supporting the right people and established an ideal environment for creativity, hard work, teamwork, and success, that everything else (with a little luck, of course) would work out. And it did.

Our philosophy drove us to a stringent hiring process. We didn't care how long a job was open. We only filled new roles when we found the right person for the job and the culture of the company. And, the culture was paramount. We explained the culture in interviews and told potential hires that if they didn't like it, they shouldn't take the job. Then, once hired, we indoctrinated each new employee with classes on the culture. Further, adherence to the culture was part of the employee review process.

Yes, I *absolutely* believe that culture makes a difference.

Culture is the foundation of execution. It's not a specific culture that matters, but one that gets deeply adopted, promotes teamwork, and ultimately success. Innoveda didn't always run smoothly, but the culture and the teamwork that came from it carried us through the problems to an IPO, and later, a sale of the company.

Moving Forward

By this point in the book, you have some fuel in your tank in the form of money. You're in the process of building your product, and you're hammering through your go-to-market plan. You're in good shape. Now, you need to focus on operating the business, building it and running it on a day-to-day basis.

But, what does it mean to run the company?

It means focusing on many tasks that often aren't visible but make the entire organization work. In fact, it's this focus that is more critical to your success than your original idea or your exact business model. These areas of focus include building the culture of the company, recruiting a great team, organizing your team to execute on your vision, and then scaling to meet the demand for your solution.

In keeping with our theme of giving it to you straight, we'll tell you that this is the chapter where fortunes are made and lost. It's where most startups ultimately fail. You can have the best idea, but without executing on the everyday tasks of building a great company, you won't get there. This stage is most definitely not sexy. Get it right, though, and you'll have a business that can grow very fast, and it will be ready for the next level.

Operating the business well is extremely difficult. In fact, we'd argue that most founders struggle with this task more than anything else. We see founders with great creativity and passion for their idea and startup, but when it comes to grinding out work through a team, they flounder.

It doesn't have to be that way, though. In this chapter and the next, we'll walk you through how to think about your culture, team, operational execution, and scaling process, leaving you with the confidence to operate your startup at a high level.

Note that lessons on operating your business are worthy of an entire book, and there are already many of those out there. We'll focus on the foundational elements of how to run your startup in this chapter. This is a good starting place, but you should still seek out all resources available to make sure you become proficient at this critical part of making your business successful.

Building Your Culture

In Chapter 3, we told you that setting the culture is one of the key roles of a founder. We talked about the importance of it, but we didn't discuss what culture is in detail and how to create the right one for your organization.

There are far too many definitions of what culture is and isn't. To some extent, it's in the eye of the beholder. You can make culture mean whatever you want, but recognize that there are consequences for what you choose (good and bad). Let's get specific about what we mean. Some organizations think of culture as team unity and spirit. It's about T-shirts and hoodies, Friday afternoon beer bashes, and hanging out together after work. Others think of culture as a set of principles to abide by, posted on motivational posters hanging on walls across their office. Still, others see it as the common bond that brings all company employees together. There's no one right answer, but we'll give you some ideas about how to think about it.

We like to think of the culture as the operating system of the company. It's a framework of values, philosophies, and principles that exist to guide the behavior and decision-making of your team. In the absence of your presence, you want your team to come up with the right answer—not necessarily what you would do, but what your culture tells them to do.

We like to think of the culture as the operating system of the company. It's a framework of values, philosophies, and principles that exist to guide the behavior and decision-making of your team. In the absence of your presence, you want your team to come up with the right answer—not necessarily what you would do, but what your culture tells them to do.

Why is culture so important? Founders can't be everywhere and make all the decisions, at least if they want the startup to grow. The team needs to know the guidelines of how they should make decisions and do their jobs without having to ask. Your culture is the foundation they rely on when thinking about their jobs and the decisions they make. If you get this right, you can scale your business very quickly and in the manner you want.

We are firm believers that at the beginning, the culture is molded entirely by the founders. The founders are essentially the company in the early days, after all. The trick is to maintain that culture as you grow, even dampening or eliminating the parts of the founding team's philosophies that aren't helpful to the culture.

"Many first-time startup founders struggle to devote time to define their culture from the beginning, only to come to the painful realization that culture certainly has an impact on the operational side of business," says Corey McAveeney, founder of Kulturenvy. "Seasoned founders and CEOs who believe there is room for culture from the beginning experience less culture-related stress as they grow."*

Take the time to think through and build the right culture for your startup, and you'll maximize your chances for success.

Defining Your Culture

Culture consists of many elements that cover a spectrum from how people interact with each other on the inside of the company to how customers are treated on the outside. It includes how decisions are made, how communication takes place, and how people work together.

The challenge is how to define what is important in your culture. Most often there are too many ideas about what the culture should be, so the founding team struggles to narrow down what's important. We suggest that your culture be a mix between who you are as founders and the type of business you are building. You'll want to make sure the culture you define makes sense for what you're trying to achieve as a business.

Think about your culture as having a mix of core values, fundamental principles, and your business philosophies. Don't get too hung up on the differences or on whether you have each of these covered. Think of these three categories more as prompts to help you define the overall culture that works for you.

Core Values

Core values manifest themselves as the behaviors that your team exhibits. It is who they are, as seen through their actions. While your team will be more than just the core values that you outline, these are the non-negotiables, like trust, integrity, and respect that sit at the core of your company. Core values should be so important to you that if someone on the team doesn't exhibit them, then you'll ask them to leave. You generally don't work on core values. You either have them or you don't. You and your co-founders should agree on which ones are the non-negotiables that you convey to the world.

Amazon's core values, for example, include taking ownership, being curious, action-oriented, and frugal with the company's money. They also value healthy debate but demand a team that is committed to the decisions that have been made. These are all traits of what makes Amazon special. If their values don't resonate with an employee, that person likely leaves Amazon. And, that's the way it should be. Amazon's core values are the tie that binds their team together.

To weave values successfully into the company, you have to select just a handful. You can't have a laundry list of twenty values. That's too hard and unmanageable, and you'll never find employees who can even remember all of them, let alone demonstrate them. Your best bet is to select a few that you can easily promote throughout the organization—the ones most important to you.

Fundamental Principles

Your fundamental principles are the truths about your business. This is where you can start to bring more elements of your business into your culture. You may be in a business that is highly competitive, which requires that you're extremely efficient. Alternatively, your business may be to simplify an extremely complex problem for your customers, requiring that you be very service oriented. Or, perhaps you're dealing with legal or compliance issues where your organization has to follow specific and mandated rules and processes.

Each of these truths about your business require your company to act and perform in certain ways. These are core parts of your business that you must execute well to be successful, so building them into your culture ensures that they remain major focal points for the organization. These realities of your business need to convert into clear directions about how your team needs to operate. Note that these cultural attributes will stay with the company forever. Core fundamental principles aren't like your mission or vision or even your business model, which may occasionally change.

Some examples of fundamental principles are:

- Southwest Airlines—safety—as long as Southwest is in the transportation business, their employees must keep safety at the top of their mind.
- Twitter—open and transparent—Twitter is the embodiment of immediate and free-flowing information, so it makes sense that Twitter hires people who care about freedom of speech and open communication.
- UPS (United Parcel Service)—on-time delivery—the continued success of UPS is based on delivering packages at the promised time, which is why UPS is focused on investing in the best logistics people and technology in their industry.

When your team is making decisions about how they need to operate, your fundamental principles will be part of their guiding light.

Business Philosophies

Think of business philosophies as more like preferences for how you operate your business. For example, are you frugal with your money? Do you promote from within your organization? Both are business philosophies that can also be default actions, though neither are written in stone. You know there will be circumstances where you will not be able to follow them.

A famous example is Facebook's philosophy to go fast and break things. It's how the business biases its actions, but it isn't an absolute. There are times, of course, when Facebook will go slowly and ensure that things are buttoned down. But, the preference of the company is to be aggressive.

Your business philosophy gives more context and texture to your culture. It helps your employees to better understand how they should think about decisions and how they should work.

* * *

As you think about each of these areas, you'll undoubtedly have a long list of attributes that are important to you and your co-founders. Now comes the hard part. To define your culture, you'll need to decide what to emphasize.

As you're thinking about the cultural elements most important to you, we suggest trying to group similar items together and trying to come up with one coherent statement that either summarizes them or ensures that the other ones are adopted. For example, we talked about a business that needs to be highly efficient. It's likely you can assume that being frugal will be covered by the statement that you intend to build a highly efficient company. Of course, you'll want to say that, but those two can easily be grouped together.

As you build a manageable list or definition of your culture, you'll also want to make sure that all points are consistent and aren't in conflict. It's easy to say that you want the best team possible, but if in the same breath, you say that you have to watch what you spend, those points can conflict. Try to build a set of definitions that are mutually supporting and cohesive.

Implementing Your Culture

Once you've defined your culture, now it is time to put it into practice. As you already know, this isn't something you set and forget. It takes a great deal of work to build and maintain a culture. The sad part is that a few high-profile actions outside of your desired culture can severely damage or erode the culture. As a founder, you'll need to keep that in mind whenever you see actions or behaviors that are inconsistent with your culture. When this occurs, you'll want to address them quickly and ideally in a public way to reinforce the culture that you want.

Before we dive into how you can build your culture, here's a few words about what we are seeing in startups today. Too often, we see founders who believe that the benefits or perks they offer are the culture. Free lunches and Friday beer bashes are culture. Or, handing out clothes with the company logo on them builds the culture. While there is generally nothing wrong with leveraging these tools to help build comradery within the organization, don't mistake these for culture. They are what we called them earlier—benefits and perks. They aren't the reason why your team works at your company, and they certainly don't tell your team how to operate the business.

After defining the culture, the next thing to do is implement it based on the following elements.

Your Actions

One of the most important aspects of building your culture is your actions. Your team will be watching you and taking cues from you on just about everything. Remember when we said the culture is in the mold of the founders? This is what we're talking about. You won't be able to set a culture one way and behave a different way.

The most difficult part of this is that, at times, you won't even realize you're doing things that are counter to your culture. Or, even worse, you may think you're being consistent with your cultural attributes, but your actions are perceived differently.

Say, for example, you've established a culture that emphasizes, among other things, the importance of keeping costs low and placing value on direct customer contact. As expenses in your startup grow, you start to push back on each expense report that employees turn in. The unintended consequence that you might create is that people choose to stop traveling to see customers to avoid the conflict when they turn in their expense reports. Here, emphasizing one cultural facet may cause you to be perceived as inconsistent with another.

There's no easy answer for this, aside from vigilance. We think the best thing you can do is to have an open dialogue with your team. Make it totally acceptable for anybody to call out (in a positive way) anybody else who isn't following your culture and celebrate those who are. This goes especially for you as founders. You want your team to be able to sit with you and share where they don't think you are following the culture.

Great founders have incredible self-awareness and can sense themselves falling into traps where they end up doing things counter to the culture. If they do, those founders will readily acknowledge it and create a dialogue around how to improve. Interestingly, that, too, ends up being part of the culture.

Processes

Modeling the behavior that you are looking for as well as taking immediate action to call out counter-cultural people or actions will get you part of the way to building your culture, but that's not enough. If you want to build a truly great culture, you'll also need to implement a number of processes.

The processes will depend upon the culture you are trying to create, so you'll want to think about your cultural attributes and devise processes around them. For example, many organizations value transparency and accountability. To that end, they publish company data often and distribute it widely. They make the company's financials available to the whole team and provide regular reviews of company progress and discussions about the company's successes and failures as part of due course. They value openness and demonstrate it through these actions.

Another example is a startup that values extreme innovation in their field. If the company needs to be at the cutting edge, they send their employees to conferences, participate in working groups in the field, file for patents, or allow time for thinking and dreaming of new ideas. These are processes that should be instituted into the fabric of the organization.

Your processes will depend on the culture you are trying to build. Notice that we didn't focus on company mixers or parties, but celebrating success very well might be a core part of your culture. Building a startup is incredibly hard, so celebrating milestones along the way is important. Just put that in the context of your overall culture.

Putting the right cultural processes in place can be a lot of work, but they not only help you build the right culture; they also help you run a better business.

The culture you create becomes the driving force for how your team operates. It's the framework that allows them to make decisions, hire people, let people go, and do their jobs. As a startup, your goal is to build a scalable business. You can't do that without a strong culture that helps your business operate faster, better, and more consistently.

It's All About the People

As we discussed in earlier chapters about co-founders and early employees, it's the people you surround yourself with who will be the key to success or failure when it comes to execution. This remains true in the case of delivering your initial offering. In some instances, the founders will have the skills and time necessary to deliver the complete offering, although it's rare when that happens. Usually, several more people need to be hired in order to get it into the customers' hands and to actively and quickly respond to the feedback coming from customers.

Just how important is your team? We'd take a great team over a great idea in business any day of the week (of course, having both is even better). Why is that? Because ideas are often fleeting—markets change, technology evolves, competition is a moving target, and customers are sometimes fickle. Great teams can adapt and continually innovate. They respond, and they grow. They meet the needs of the early customers and the product vision simultaneously.

> We'd take a great team over a great idea in business any day of the week (of course, having both is even better). Why is that? Because ideas are often fleeting—markets change, technology evolves, competition is a moving target, and customers are sometimes fickle. Great teams can adapt and continually innovate. They respond, and they grow. They meet the needs of the early customers and the product vision simultaneously.

Great ideas without great teams behind them stagnate. When it's time to make your idea a reality and bring it to market, you need to have the right team of people who can make this happen. Just as you have to carefully select the right co-founders, you also have to carefully expand your initial team with the right group of people to bring the product or service to life.

***

Culture is the glue that binds companies together and has everyone working together in sync. Success in startups is tenuous. It's only when you're optimizing how everything works day-to-day that it's even possible. That's not to say you'll be getting everything right. You won't. Still, the team's ability to move forward efficiently and effectively and to weather the bumps and errors along the way rides more on cultural alignment than anything else.

Of course, you can't get that alignment without the right people. People carry the culture, not any document or poster on the wall. Making sure that everyone on the team buys into and promotes the culture is very important. Without that, the culture will wither and die.

Chapter 29

Hiring and Managing Your Team

When I started my first company, DataWare Logic, I (Will) simply didn't understand how critical hiring and managing are. As it turned out, that really didn't end up being too big a mistake since the company blew up before I could hire many people. But, when my second company, Viewlogic Systems, started growing quickly and issues from hiring errors and poor management started piling up, I learned my lesson. Not only is hiring and then managing well important, it needs to be part of the daily thought process for each founder and manager.

There was one incident that solidified this concept for me. I had hired someone for a major project that was an integral component of our first product. They had a great resume and interviewed well. After hiring him, I thought I was on top of his efforts. He seemed to be working hard and getting things done. Months later, another co-founder pointed out to me that, in fact, the person hadn't really gotten anywhere. When we dug in further, we discovered that he lied on his resume and was, in fact, lost in the project. I didn't see it. Not when I hired him and not as I managed him. It was a terrible failure that set us back.

Obviously, I had to improve as a manager, but I needed help. Even though we were a fledgling startup, we made the decision to hire a full-time HR person to take control of hiring and watching out for management issues. It worked out great. The VP of HR made the hiring process much more efficient, and he helped to quickly improve the team's management skills. While it seemed like a costly early decision in a startup, it may have been one of the best calls we made in those early days.

It worked out so well that I brought on an HR person as an early part of the team in all my subsequent companies. At Innoveda, an HR person was a co-founder. People are the core of how you build successful, scalable companies. What could be more important than finding the right ones and then managing them well?

It's the Most Important Thing You Do for Your Company

We have encouraged you to move as fast as possible when it comes to execution. That's still true, except when it comes to hiring your team. This act is so important to the success of your startup that you should do the opposite—move slowly and thoughtfully.

As a founder, hiring is the single most important thing you do. Yeah, you probably think that raising money is of greater importance. It's not. Hiring talented people will multiply your ability to execute by orders of magnitude. You'll deliver more, move faster, and have happier customers.

Errors in hiring, on the other hand, are difficult to fix and often leave behind problems that are hard to clean up. Hiring the wrong person not only means a loss of progress while they are in their position, but more importantly, it means a huge loss of opportunity that you would have realized had you hired the correct person in the first place. Also, firing people who don't work out is painful, even if it's part of your job. And then, you have to manage the rumors, emotions, and hearsay left with the remaining employees after letting someone go. Dealing with this is problematic, not to mention a distraction you don't need when trying to scale and expand your company.

Hiring the wrong people for the initial team is a common problem for many founders. We get it. It's easy for founders to grow anxious about delivering their product or service to the market quickly. Their zest to hurry causes them to make a number of mistakes, like hiring the first person they meet to join the team, recruiting a friend or an acquaintance that they force-fit into a position, or even mimicking the hiring decisions of competitors.

What we usually see, and truthfully, we've made this painful mistake many times ourselves, is that founders talk themselves into hiring someone. This happens when a founder has a need to fill a role that they're afraid will go unfilled, all while pressure is mounting to deliver their offering. They'll find someone who meets three out of the five key criteria they set for the position, and they make excuses why the other two criteria are less important. Or, they'll meet someone with the specific job expertise they're looking for but will ignore the fact that the candidate isn't culturally aligned with the rest of the team. In both instances, the founder's fear overtakes their objectivity.

If you have to talk yourself into hiring someone, then it's a sign they're the wrong person. Inevitably, these types of hires don't work out. Whether it's six months or a year later, you end up parting ways because you still need to fill the gap in their skills or because their lack of a cultural fit is a problem. Almost always, it's better to leave a position vacant than it is to rush and have the position filled by the wrong person.

Thankfully, you can avoid this situation and the potential fallout that is the aftermath of many firings. Before you interview people for the initial team, think through the key needs of the company and what you're looking for in each position. This clarity will help you to create a speculative profile of the ideal team members, including their capabilities, attitudes, and skills, as well as cultural and personality fit.

With this level of detail, you can optimize your chances of recruiting the right talent. A great place to search for the best people is by tapping into the networks of each of the co-founders. You can tell the early hires at the company, the board of directors, your advisors, mentors, investors, friends, family members, and other people you trust that you have open positions with a detailed account of the ideal hire.

The benefit to leveraging your network is that you can recruit people you trust, because of direct experience with them or because people you trust vouch for them. Bringing on trusted hires—those that close friends and co-workers have worked with before—greatly increases the chances that those people will be a good fit for the needs your company has now and in the future.

Ideal Candidate Criteria

Sometimes, it's hard to evaluate whether a candidate will be the right fit for the organization. We've found it's helpful to consider a number of factors about the potential hire. Following are the criteria we use. Go ahead and use these for your company or develop a list that better fits your startup with your fellow co-founders.

Is the candidate a cultural fit? There are entire books written about the importance of cultural fit in organizations.

We strongly believe that having people who are a cultural fit with the organization is more important than the skills they bring. Teams work more effectively than any individual can. There is a multiplicative effect to teamwork that makes everyone in the team better and more productive. Early in the life of your company, you should determine what type of culture you want, and it benefits you to make fitting into that culture paramount in the search for employees.

Is the candidate a risk taker? He or she should be. Why would you want someone who is going to move slowly and cautiously in your organization? The best people for a startup are aggressive in their actions and play offense all the time. How do you tell if someone has this characteristic? Ask them about projects they've worked on before and how they deviated from the initial plan. Or, propose a situation that's almost impossible to resolve and ask them how they would deal with it (see *Kobayashi Maru*, a test given in the 1960s television show *Star Trek* that puts characters in a no-win, life-or-death situation).* You'll learn a lot.

Does the candidate fear change? The one constant in startups is that things change constantly. The best hires for a startup are people who love change and even seek it out. Most people fear change. Some fight it actively and some passively. This will slow the organization down. If you want a fast-moving organization, you need people who welcome change, even seek it, and can quickly and easily adapt. Again, the best way to explore people's acceptance of change is to ask how they have dealt with it in the past and to create scenarios that require change and see how they respond.

Can the candidate work as part of a team? This is very difficult to discover in an interview. Of course, if the candidate doesn't look you in the eye or is a poor communicator, they are not likely to be as good a team member or someone who communicates well. The best way to check their fit is to have the candidate meet with everyone on your team. How they interact with a wide variety of people is a good indicator of how they will work as a teammate. Additionally, reference checks are a particularly good idea when it comes to teamwork. We'll also often assign an exercise for the candidate to lead a discussion or mini-project with the existing team to see how they do.

Does he or she have the skills you're hiring for? You're probably hiring because you're either stretched too thin or you need new skills in the organization. Because you have a specific need, you still must make sure the candidate can effectively get the job done. Ask detailed questions about what they've done and how they did it. Don't be afraid to dig deep to really validate their knowledge. Keep in mind that the skill set they bring should be additive to the skill set the team already has. You can't afford to double-down on the team's knowledge—breadth of knowledge is more important than depth during the early stages of the company when you have just a few people.

One final trade-off that every founder needs to consider in hiring is the potential of hiring a strong individual contributor versus a weaker team player. There are various philosophies and opinions on this point. For us, if we had the choice between hiring a brilliant person who was only great as an individual but not as part of a team versus someone with two-thirds of the intellectual talent but who worked great in a team environment, then we'd pick the team player every time.

In our estimate and in our experience, these people contribute more positively to the company, make the people around them better, and offer more to the team than one superstar. If your startup is involved in deep research where one person's efforts can make or break things, then, perhaps, the singular genius is the way to go. But in most cases, we would advise against it and opt for a solid team player.

How Much to Spend on Hiring?

Generally speaking, there is no money in a startup's budget for hiring, so recruiters and paid searches are used infrequently. Of course, if the people you need are specialized with a unique set of skills, then you may not have a choice. In this case, you should have already included this expense as part of your early budgeting and fundraising.

Financial considerations with respect to hiring remain an issue for all startups. "How should new people be compensated?" is a big question we get from all the startups we work with, and this topic has been a major issue in the companies we've founded. There's no absolute answer to this question. It's more about balancing the needs of the company with what you can afford. Sometimes, you may have to spend more money to attract key hires who have the skills, aptitude, personality, and potential to make a huge impact on the company. Other times, you'll quickly find people who are a good fit and are eager to work with you in return for a low salary and options in the company with a promise to have their compensation adjusted when the company can afford it.

The bottom line is that without a team, you're not going to get very far, and without cash, you'll die. There is no one way to solve this problem, and it's all about balance. To help you think through this balancing act, we've created the following step-by-step guidelines to help you work through this problem.

- **Step 1:** Before starting your search, take a close look at your finances and decide how much cash you can commit to fully-loaded compensation (that is, salary and benefits) for all the people you need to hire. You can check market rates by looking at online job sites to get a flavor for what other organizations are willing to pay. Additionally, being part of compensation surveys is valuable because they will share their results, which will give you insight into the average compensation offered by a broad group of companies.

- **Step 2:** Rank each position you need to fill in order of its importance to the company's progress.

- **Step 3:** While you'd like to hire people in the order of their importance, you need to be more opportunistic than that and move as soon as you find someone who fits any of the roles you're trying to fill.

- **Step 4:** If you come across someone who can fill multiple roles that you've specified, that's a bonus. This key find should then give you more room in the budget to compensate them at a higher rate, or you can use the extra budget to recruit others who didn't make your original list.

- **Step 5:** Finally, use stock options to offset cash compensation when you can, especially early on. While some people can't afford to take stock in lieu of cash, many can. You may have to give up some ownership in the company—it's generally pretty small—but saving cash is critically important in the early stages of your startup. Don't be afraid to commit to more cash for an employee later once the company gets additional financing or starts making money.

Our biggest piece of advice here: don't be overly cheap. If you miss an opportunity to hire a good person, you don't know when you'll have another. Also, don't use the levels of founder compensation in your thinking about employee compensation. It's normal for early employees to have higher salaries than the founders, but much less equity. The founders have much more ownership and are in the company for different reasons and with different goals than the initial employees being hired. Without a great team, you won't be able to deliver on your vision or achieve your goals. And, every day you waste without the right hires in place will cost you many multiples of what you thought you saved down the road.

Hiring a CEO

There's a special case of hiring that we'd like to touch on briefly, and that's hiring a CEO.

Most founders have some component of technical background, deep domain knowledge, or market expertise. The prevailing view over the last two decades was that while such a person can potentially build the product, a professional manager was needed as their partner to build the company.

Experienced or professional CEOs are skilled managers and leaders; they can also be entrepreneurial as well. These are the people who come in and start to scale and grow the business. They've likely seen various models succeed because they've been at multiple companies and are experienced operators. Founders don't necessarily always have this depth of experience and understanding.

More often than not these days, one of the founders remains in place as CEO for the life of the company. Of course that usually means, given the odds, until the company closes down. The decision on whether to bring on an outside CEO with broad experience is a difficult one and never black and white. The best way to make a decision about bringing in someone to run the company is through an open and honest dialogue among the founding team about each other's strengths and abilities to scale and grow the company. If everyone realizes that one of the biggest needs for the company is a strong CEO and no one on the founding team can assume this role, then you should go find one.

Sometimes, hiring an outside CEO isn't a choice; it's imposed on the founding team. This may come from investors, the board of directors, or advisors. If this happens to you, we counsel honesty. You need to have an honest and open discussion with the team around you, including your co-founders, board of directors (if you have one), and any advisors you have, to discuss whether the company will be fundamentally better off with a hired CEO.

When it's time to have the discussion about who should assume the role of the CEO, whether that's a founder or hiring someone from the outside, there are a number of questions that should be fully discussed among the founding team and board of directors including:

- Can the person being considered for the role of CEO do the job?
- Do they know how to do it?
- How does any particular candidate increase the company's odds for success?
- Does the candidate fit into the company's culture?
- Why do they want to take on this role?

- What's the best path that maximizes the company's economic outcome?
- Can the company afford to hire a professional CEO?
- Can someone on the founding team grow into the job over time? If the answer is yes, does the company have enough time to let this happen?

Often, this conversation is difficult and emotional. It's your company, after all, and bringing in somebody to run it can be painful. We'd offer that, generally, there is still a very significant opportunity for you financially and personally. If you've picked the right external CEO to join the company, that person will likely want to lean on and work closely with the founding team. The CEO knows that they need the founders to succeed.

Uber's leadership change is a case study in the challenges of CEO transitions. The founder and CEO was forced out after a series of highly public missteps. A fractious and divided board finally settled on an unknown candidate considered as a consensus builder after multiple high-profile candidates withdrew from consideration. The new, professional CEO has extended an olive branch to a number of constituencies to right a faltering ship, but the jury is out on whether the CEO will be successful. Leadership transitions are never easy for any of the parties involved.

Managing Your Team

One of the founder's key roles that we described earlier was executing on the vision of the company. Of course, you won't be able to do that alone. We've talked about how you'll find the right people and create the best environment to help them succeed. Once you do that, you need to get the work done. This book isn't a management book, but we do want to talk briefly about key components of great execution.

Motivating Your Team

We mentioned earlier that we routinely see companies that believe it takes lots of parties, events, trips, big salaries, and stock options to motivate your team to do great things. That's a myth. Those factors won't motivate someone, or, at least, not for long. Those types of benefits may keep people from being dissatisfied, but they won't ignite a burning passion or desire to achieve greatness within someone or at the company. Motivation has more to do with fire in the belly, thrill of achievement, pride of recognition, and passion for the work, than it does with material rewards.

Motivation is actually very complex. We often think about the model created by the psychologist Frederick Herzberg, who we mentioned at the beginning of the book. Herzberg wrote that job satisfaction is not the opposite of job dissatisfaction. He theorized that there are motivators and hygiene factors related to satisfaction. Motivators are internal to each person, but they're ignited by the environment that person is in. Hygiene factors, on the other hand, are those material rewards we mentioned. While they are great things to do, they will not, in fact, drive motivation in people.[†]

For example, being surrounded by really smart people who communicate well will motivate a person excited by learning, leading to greater job satisfaction and, likely, better effort with their job. Hygiene factors like the amount of health insurance someone receives where they work are good and important, but they are unlikely to trigger motivation in anyone.

Motivation is about deep psychological factors. You can't motivate people, but you can create an environment that makes it easier for them to motivate themselves. To do that, you need to start by learning about what drives each person on the team.

You have to understand, deeply, what they value, why they want to do a great job, what they want to do with their lives—personally and professionally—and what excites them. And, then you have to put them in a position to be able to leverage that excitement.

Figuring out what gets somebody truly excited and engaged can be incredibly difficult. Sometimes, the person doesn't even really know themselves. We like to ask people a variety of questions, and we'll do exercises that elicit more information about what gets people going. Have your team answer questions like, "How are you misunderstood? How do you like to get feedback? What are some of your quirks? What gets you excited? What makes you sad? What do you value in the people you work with?"

Share the answers with each other. That way, everyone tries to help each other achieve their goals and optimize their motivations. Sometimes, even this isn't enough because what someone says and what they do can be two different things. So, you also watch. You look for what gets a person excited.

Once you have a clear picture of the person, then you can start to connect the dots back to the organization and how this particular individual can help bring the vision and mission of the company to life in a way that also motivates them. You may need to change their role or give them different tasks. They may need to grow in certain ways that will help them fulfill their goals but support yours as well. This is the intersection you want to discover: the place where each person finds real excitement, passion, and value in solving problems fundamental to the success of the business.

Once you find that spot, you won't need to motivate the person at all. They'll motivate themselves.

Communication

We like to set up what we call a rhythm of communication in a company. This structure helps to ensure that information flows across the organization on a regular basis. As a small company, you don't need to overdo it, but scheduling various types of communication sessions with your team helps ensure that your team knows exactly what is going on with the business. From our perspective, the more they know, the better they can do their jobs.

You can create whatever rhythm and style of communication works for you, but our suggestion is to put some structure to it. In our case, we've used annual and quarterly sessions to discuss overall company direction, vision, mission, and goals. We'll do in-depth monthly updates via email relative to our goals, and then we like to have weekly team meetings where a different person in the company shares what they're working on and why that's relevant to the rest of the organization. This works especially well when your company is small, and the different meetings we just outlined are a great start for most organizations.

You can also layer in consistent communication and sessions that focus on the culture, product strategy, innovation, or departmental reviews. As your organization grows, the way you communicate will change and evolve, too. The core of this part of your management process is to ensure that your team has the information they need to get their jobs done and to build their connection to the company.

Objectives

Every startup needs a detailed list of the objectives it's attempting to achieve. This goes back to the vision and business model, and includes the time frames for meeting the objectives set down on paper. Once you know the objectives and the deadline for when you're aiming to complete them, then you can break those down even further into specific tasks. The objectives you select should be as detailed as you can make them. Be sure to include the measurements you'll use to determine if an objective was met, and who's responsible for achieving it.

For instance, we'll put together annual objectives, which include what we think we'll accomplish for the calendar year. Then, we'll break the annual objectives into quarters, outlining what we expect to accomplish each quarter that will lead us to the end of the year. Once we know our quarterly objectives, then we break those down even further into monthly and possibly weekly milestones and generate a summary.

Sample Summary

Annual objective—launch product with ten customers.

- Q1 objective—design and validate product.
    - M1 objective—initial potential customer interviews.
    - M2 objective—develop design spec and start on prototype.
    - M3 objective—complete prototype and validate with potential customers.
- Q2 objective—complete product development.
- Q3 objective—complete field-testing of product.
- Q4 objective—close ten new customers.

You can use this approach with all your objectives. It's hard, but the simple act of breaking your objectives down into their smallest parts ensures you know the steps required to accomplish your goals.

When we mentor founders, we talk about setting objectives in the context of leadership and management. From a leadership perspective, having clearly defined objectives is critically important. It helps you to figure out how to get from here to there, and it's how you rally your employees to tackle the next big hill in the journey to grow and scale the company.

From a management perspective, detailed objectives and the breakdown of how you get there will show you the roadmap of work that needs to be done. It's not only important to know what hill you're tackling, but how you'll climb it. Your team's objectives are the way to do this.

There's been a great deal written on management by objectives, and you'll find tremendous resources online about it. We happen to like this method because it paints a detailed picture of the outcome you are looking for and then forces you to work backward on how you'll get there.

Feedback

Course corrections are critical. You might not hit your targets the first time you try, and your team may not execute perfectly. Feedback is your mechanism to make adjustments to your goals and team.

You'll want to find mechanisms that help give you feedback that you're heading in the right direction. These can be market data metrics, internal interim results, and of course, customer feedback. Try to build in the places where you can get the data you need to determine if you are on track or off. Of course, including each of these as part of your objectives is a good idea.

In addition to feedback on the business results, there is also a place for you to give feedback to your team. They need to know how they are doing. Are they executing on what you want? Are they fulfilling your cultural expectations? Where can they improve? These can be some of the harder conversations you'll have with employees, but they're also critical to achieving your company goals. These conversations help employees fire up their motivational drive. Don't forget to ask for feedback from your employees on how you are doing as well.

We generally believe that people want to do a great job for their organization. Often, they don't know what that means, or they don't get feedback on where they can improve. We've found that most people are hungry for this information when it's delivered with sincerity and kindness. It's an opportunity for them to improve and be better at what they do.

Build in regular checkpoints with your team that forces this conversation. While difficult, we believe that you'll be happy you did.

Firing Employees

Try as you might to hire great people who both fill knowledge and experience gaps in your team as well as being a strong cultural fit, sometimes, it doesn't work out. It's simply impossible to explore every aspect of an individual to see if they meet all the candidate criteria we mentioned earlier in this chapter. Sometimes, however, people don't tell the truth about what they know or who they are. Other times, the organization simply can't accept the person and the work they are doing. Whatever the reasons for an employee not working out, dealing with their termination is a critical part of the management of your company.

We talked about firing a founder in Chapter 14. While firing employees isn't quite as problematic, it's nonetheless difficult. Much of how you deal with the situation is based on how you managed the employee in the first place. Did you regularly review their performance? Give them honest feedback? Explain the culture to them and tell them if they weren't culturally aligned? Did you give them specific objectives and actively communicate with them?

We find that the answers to many of the questions in startups is, unfortunately, no. When you neglect to focus on managing people, then coming up with a deterministic set of reasons to fire them is a problem. It's not really fair to fire them if they don't understand the criteria by which they're judged in the first place.

Still, sometimes the reasons for having to fire someone are quite clear. This is especially true when there is a lack of cultural alignment. There might not be anything more visible to a team than a bad cultural fit. A person who doesn't fit usually sticks out like a sore thumb. The team knows it, you know it, and it's likely the person knows it as well. This is one of the most important tests for a culture. What you do with someone who doesn't fit makes the strongest statement about how seriously you take the stated culture.

Does the person stay? Are they rehabilitated? Are they forced out? There's no right answer here. In fact, the answer depends upon the type of culture you want to build. While we can't tell you what to do, the important point is that you need to do something. Your team will definitely view it that way.

	DELIVERS RESULTS	DOES NOT DELIVER RESULTS
LIVES BY VALUES ESPOUSED BY ORGANIZATION	1	2
DOES NOT LIVE BY VALUES	4	3

Diagram 13   Jack Welch's Model for Evaluating Managers

There is a famous model created by Jack Welch, the well-known former CEO of General Electric, in which he describes the actions a manager needs to take with respect to cultural fit.[‡] We'd expand this to include all employees, not just managers. Welch describes his model:

- Type 1: shares our values; makes the numbers—sky's the limit!
- Type 2: shares the values; misses the numbers—typically, another chance, or two.
- Type 3: doesn't share the values; doesn't make the numbers—gone.
- Type 4: the toughest call of all. The manager who doesn't share the values, but delivers the numbers. This type is the toughest to part with because organizations always want to deliver and to let someone go who gets the job done is yet another unnatural act. But, we have to remove these Type 4s because they have the power, by themselves, to destroy the open, informal, trust-based culture we need to win today and tomorrow.

We made our leap forward when we began removing our Type 4 managers and making it clear to the entire company why they were asked to leave—not for the usual "personal reasons" or "to pursue other opportunities," but for not sharing our values. Until an organization develops the courage to do this, people will never have full confidence that these soft values are truly real."**

The easiest way to erode a culture is to allow countercultural behavior or cultural misfits to go unaddressed. As a founder, you'll be penalized heavily by your team for tolerating these people, their behaviors, and actions. The penalties include a loss of trust, confidence, and faith that you know what you're doing.

We should also point out that this is one of the most challenging areas for building your culture. Difficult conversations with people are, well, difficult. Parting ways with potentially high-performing people who are a poor cultural fit is the hardest decision that founders or managers make. This decision is also the one that tests your culture the most.

As a startup, you also may not have the time to work with someone who is culturally aligned but is struggling to deliver results (Type 2 in the previous chart). You likely don't have the time or potentially even the experience to train the person to be better at fulfilling their job requirements. Later, as your company becomes more established, you should try to help people of this type, but early on, it might be best to replace them.

Whatever your reasons for firing an employee, a common mistake that founders make (including us) is to focus their energy on the firing process and the person being fired. Your long-term focus should be on the people who are staying with the company. The remaining employees need to understand why someone was fired and be assured that the firing is not a trend or irrational. In high-stress situations, people first focus on themselves. If you only put your energy into the person departing, you may cause deep problems with your remaining team.

We've mentioned several times that firing is difficult and complex. Even after having done it more than we've ever wanted to, we continue to make errors in firing employees that we want to help you avoid. Simply put, we almost always take too long to fire people. At our core, we want to make it work with people. Perhaps that's because we don't want to admit to ourselves that we made a mistake in hiring them or because we want to believe we are good-enough managers to fix any problem. Neither are good reasons for not taking action in a timely fashion.

What's the downside of a delay? The other employees likely sense that the person in question is failing, and their poor performance is impacting the success of the company or even the people in the company on an individual level. It's important to note that it's also likely they've sensed this before you did because they work together on a day-to-day or even minute-to-minute basis. When other employees perceive that you're not acting on the problem, they may begin to question you as their manager and leader, asking themselves if you really know what's going on or, perhaps, if you have the courage to fire an employee.

We're not suggesting you fire people at the first sign of an issue. Your desire to work with people to improve their performance and to help them fit in is also witnessed by the other employees. It's a great cultural element in any company that encourages people to make mistakes and drive aggressively.

The key is to balance these factors and to do things in a timely fashion. As we discussed earlier, few things will be clear cut for you as a founder, but being aware of as many aspects of what is going on as possible will help guide you to do the right thing at the right time.

While firing employees is inevitable, a diligent hiring process and a communicative management style will help you avoid many of the reasons that firings need to happen. Still, even when you execute well in these areas, problems arise for a variety of reasons. If you are equally as diligent and focused on firing when it needs to happen, your actions can help enhance your culture. People will understand what is most important to you and the company. Making sure you have a high-performing team that also has a strong cultural fit with your company is what matters.

***

Most startups are founded by entrepreneurs who are not only new to startups, but also are new to management. We think it's interesting that this isn't taken more seriously. Management is a science all to itself and one that often takes years to excel at. As you grow your new company, you'll find that management issues will start to absorb more of your time than most others. People are the key to your success, so, in a sense, this is how it should be.

Learning how to deal with people-related issues and, more importantly, to avoid them, will be an important part of how you continue to grow and expand your startup. Getting better at management, especially learning how to hire the right people and keep them aligned, will help you grow your company faster and will perpetuate the culture that you've established.

Chapter 30

Scaling the Company

Will and I (Rajat) have been fortunate to have a number of companies reach the scale-up phase. There's no doubt that it is a major milestone to reach this stage. Of course, this stage has its own challenges and "playbook," if you will.

Especially in the modern era of entrepreneurship, there are more resources, people, and investors that have been through this phase. While this book is coming to a close, that doesn't mean that your entrepreneurial journey is. In fact, the scale-up phase can be just as exciting as the start-up phase, albeit very different.

Recently, our company JumpCloud reached this milestone, and we are now in the midst of this part of the journey. At this stage, we are continuing to build out the management team, finding more customers, and implementing systems that will help us scale, such as financial and billing tools.

Before we started to aggressively scale the company, we spent a great deal of time to ensure that the signals we were getting were legitimate. Perhaps the most important was product-market fit. We knew that if customers were purchasing regularly and sticking with the product over the long-term, we could be ready to scale. We also made sure that we could add customers cost-effectively and once we confirmed this, we knew it was time.

Luckily, at JumpCloud we were able to find an excellent financial partner in General Atlantic to help us take the company to the next level. We also have recruited additional team members and advisors who have been through this stage numerous times to help support us on this part of the journey.

To Grow Fast, You Need to Scale

Now that you've put in all the hard work to run a great business, we hope you are starting to see and feel some success. Soon, you'll be entering the phase we like to think of as scaling up.

In this phase, you're starting to get past the point of being a pure startup with all the early stage challenges. You'll start to enter a period with many new types of challenges. In general, going through that stage is for another book, but we'd like to set you up for it before we let you go.

When to Scale

As you start to think about whether you're ready to start stepping on the gas and growing a bit faster, you'll want to make sure you're really ready to do it and the signals that you're receiving are the right indicators.

A few startups are so flush with cash and support that they don't need the market to tell them when they should start to rapidly scale. They can simply afford to do it at any time. For most startups, though, you'll want to pick the right time to start the scaling process. Too early and you'll burn through a tremendous amount of money, and you may hire the wrong people. Too late and you may miss the market opportunity or let a competitor take over your leadership position.

If you thought the beginning of a company is fraught with peril, you should understand that more than a few great companies have died during the scaling process.

So, when is the right time to scale your startup?

Like everything else, there is no easy or right answer. You'll have to feel your way through it. But, we've made the following list of several key milestones you'll want to achieve before scaling.

- **Product-market fit.** Before you start spending a lot of money, you should determine if your offering is what your market truly needs and what they'll pay for. You'll almost always want to do more with your offering, but are most of the prospects you're talking to buying your solution as-is? If they are, then this is a good indicator of product readiness and fit.
- **Pull versus push.** Is your potential customer base seeking you out (pull), or are you having to push your offering to customers? This is somewhat subjective, but your prospects should be driving you versus you driving them. If they're driving you, then that tells you they have a burning need they want to solve.
- **Small tests working.** Before you scale, you are going to want to test in small quantities or dollars to make sure you have at least an indication of whether you can see scale. We often see this with marketing spending or hiring additional sales people. Don't add ten sales people; add one and see how it goes. Then add another. If the new

sales people are adding sales at the pace you want and you feel that continuing to add people will result in more sales, then that's a great signal.

- **Solution usage/feedback.** While you may have great signals on the front end—people interested in your offering—you'll want to make sure your offering delivers over the long haul. The last thing you want is to scale up only to be stopped because your offering fails in some manner with more customers. As you roll out your offering to new customers that weren't closely involved with your MVP or early versions of the product, speak with them to make sure they're happy and the product works according to their expectations. It's important to understand whether your product is ready to stand on its own or whether it still requires the level of support you gave the early adopters.

People, Process, Technology

Now that you are scaling your organization, you'll witness a lot of change in your company. You'll want to manage that change proactively, so you're in control of the process. As we discussed earlier, change is hard, and the uncertainty it brings often frightens people. Even if you had this in mind as you hired new employees, the rapid pace of change in expansion might still shock them. It can be a time for transition where people move on, roles morph, and jobs narrow. For some, this can be a time of consternation and for others an opportunity.

As you scale, it's critical that you involve your team, build smart processes, and leverage technology where possible. Let's look at these areas in greater detail.

People

As founders, you should assume that your roles will change and morph during the scaling process. Some founders will become more focused on management, and others may end up having a boss that isn't a founder. Either way, as the organization grows, founders should stay flexible and embrace the changes. Not only is that important for you personally in order to stay with the organization, but it sends a very important signal to the rest of the company: the founding team is embracing the scaling process and its changes, and so should you. Besides, scaling is a great milestone; it means your creation is growing.

Recruiting new people to the team will end up being critical to the success of this phase. There will be nonfounders in important, influential roles. Those people, more than ever, need to fit the company culture and be great at what they do. They also need the support of the founding team.

The pressures of the scaling process can lead to shortcuts in hiring. Take the time to do it right and be as diligent as you were in the early phases. Misfires in hiring can have significant downside consequences. Entire functional groups within the company can be stunted, great people may leave, and the culture may be negatively impacted. As your team expands and the founding team loses control, keeping your culture intact and strong will ensure that it grows in the direction you want.

Process

Scaling is a time to go from having one-off solutions to problems to addressing issues with systematic processes. Processes are predefined sets of actions that help you drive repetitive tasks to a consistent result. They are often an anathema to entrepreneurs, but they help you grow and scale. You simply can't grow quickly without having some systems in place.

> Scaling is a time to go from having one-off solutions to problems to addressing issues with systematic processes. Processes are predefined sets of actions that help you drive repetitive tasks to a consistent result.

Another reason that processes are important is that, as a management team, you can't be involved in every one-off decision and conversation that takes place. Once you create a process, it can be followed to address a problem or capitalize on an opportunity by almost anyone in your company. Without processes, the management team will always need to be involved, and this slows the business down.

A good example of an early process to build is how to follow up with a potential customer. After an inquiry, you'll want to have a solid process on how your team will respond, how frequently, and with what message and content. Perhaps, the first step in the sales process is to respond via email with basic information about your solution and inviting the prospect to share more about their problems. Your second step then may be to offer an online demo of the solution, which will then lead to their third step, an evaluation. Once the evaluation is successfully completed, you'll work on closing the sale with contracts and legal documents. This is a simple but effective process on how to deal with each prospect in a consistent manner.

Don't shy away from building strong processes to solve problems when you are at this stage. Balance a focus on repeatability with the magnitude of the problem that you're solving.

Technology

As you begin to grow, you have the opportunity to put systems and technology in place to help you. We think that part of scaling is instituting some of these systems. You often can't scale processes and people without some technological solutions.

The right technology can save your team time and money. It can also help you better deliver for customers, so embrace how technology can help solve your problem. There are many tools to help with communication, prioritization, task management, and tracking. Some even automate tasks that previously required direct human action, like support, product testing, and scheduling. Most are easy to use and relatively inexpensive.

A common set of technology solutions that startups use is email and productivity solutions like G Suite from Google or Office 365 from Microsoft, that both include email, spreadsheets, word processing, and presentation solutions. Collaboration tools like Slack, customer and prospect tracking technology from Salesforce, accounting software like Quick-Books, and website hosting from WordPress are also broadly used to speed the operations of startups.

Just as the founding process is challenging, so is the scaling process. But, it's also rewarding and almost like a rite of passage to get to the other side. That other side can be a large, powerful company in your market space.

* * *

Scaling your startup will be fundamental to its success. As we talked about early in the book, scaling is, in fact, part of the definition of a startup after all. But, it's not just a byproduct of selling more of your initial product. You should think of your first offering as a pedestal for building a bigger and better company. The more stable the pedestal, the better a scaled company you can create.

You won't just be selling more of your initial product to new customers. You'll also be selling additional product to existing customers. Even more, you now may be able to sell to people who didn't know about you or weren't satisfied with your initial offering.

It's a whole new world as you scale. You'll not just be doing more of the same thing. You'll actually be doing more things. Each one of those will need efforts similar to what you did to make your first product a success—the same planning, customer involvement, and teambuilding.

Yes, they should go much faster now. You'll have some money, more people, and some success to ride. Still, don't just assume that because you were able to do it the first time, you'll automatically win as you scale. Learning from what made your initial product a success will offer a great guide for the future. We're sorry to say, though, it never gets much easier.

Conclusion

Even after starting nine companies, I (Rajat) still find the process to be challenging and rewarding. The experience helps me to know what to do, but that doesn't change the fact that each business is very difficult to get to the scaling stage. My latest startup, JumpCloud, is yet another example of this.

I started the company several years ago, and Will is a board member, investor, and advisor to the company. Our friends at Foundry Group, OpenView Venture Partners, and General Atlantic have funded the business, so we have a wonderful team of people and strong backing to make the business work.

And yet, the process has still been difficult. I've had to go through several iterations of vetting our product and go-to-market plan. I've had challenges finding and recruiting the right team, building the product, and figuring out the best ways to reach customers. I've struggled with pricing (and the pricing model), positioning and messaging, and the sales model. Despite doing this before, I still need the tips, hints, and advice from this book for my company.

Lessons

There's no doubt that starting companies is hard. The odds are stacked against you, after all. To rebalance the scales and shift the odds in your favor, the most important thing you can do is surround yourself with people who have done it before—physically or virtually—and learn everything you can from them. That's what *The Startup Playbook* is all about. It's our way of giving you a step-by-step playbook, sharing what we've learned from building many startups and helping you build your own.

Of course, there's a lot of detail throughout the book, which we hope you'll find applicable and valuable. Almost everything we've discussed, we've learned through trial and error and, sometimes, through some pretty painful experiences. We've tried to provide shortcuts, secrets, and advice as well as guidance on how to decode situations and what people say to you and ask of you. That alone should make your path much easier to navigate.

Still, there are a few cornerstone principles and actions from the book that we'd like to reiterate as we conclude here. It's not so much that these are more important than the rest of what we've discussed, but what makes them worthy of recognition is the fact that we've found them to be the most impactful lessons we've learned in our careers. They're the points that make us smack our palms to our heads and mutter, "If I had only known that before I screwed up x, y, or z." They are, for us, the highest-leverage lessons we've ever learned.

Look Before You Leap

We've all had the experience where the reality of the outcome is completely different from our expectations of it. Startup companies used to be that way, but now, there is so much data and information available to potential founders that understanding what you're getting into before you start a company is not only possible, but mandatory if you want to create a success.

Start by talking to everybody you know who has founded a company and those who work at startups. Then, check in with mentors, investors, and executives who are involved in the startup community to glean every bit of information you can from them. And, of course, read everything you can. Then, after that, take the time to honestly reflect on what you've learned.

Once you're armed with information and advice, carefully consider, is starting a company the right thing for you? Do you have the skills and personality to build a startup? Are you prepared to make the sacrifices to make the company successful, even when things are difficult? Are you ready to step into a long-term commitment that will leave you exhausted and drained most nights?

Our advice: take the time to discover whether being a founder is right for you. It's all right if it isn't. There are lots of cool entrepreneurial opportunities available for you aside from being a co-founder.

Diligence Is Your Friend

Having a great idea is just the first step. But, to make sure your idea has real potential, it's imperative that you vet everything about your vision. Use the business model validation loop from Chapters 6 to 10 to keep you on track and save you from making big mistakes.

The core of vetting your idea and business model is to research everything. Analyze every part of your plan and talk to potential customers every step of the way. The more you talk to potential customers, advisors, investors, and others in the startup community, the more likely you'll be able to get to a validated model that will improve your chances of success.

But, remember, you'll want to do this quickly. It's easy to be paralyzed from too much analysis. No business model is going to be perfect.

Our advice: do the homework of vetting your business model as quickly and deeply as you can and make bold, clear decisions that form the foundation of your company.

Doing the Right Thing with Your Co-founders

You'll have plenty of battles to fight externally, so don't waste your time dealing with internal issues if you can avoid them—they're a startup killer. You can get out ahead of any potential issues by being clear, honest, open, up front, and direct about how you'll work together with your co-founders.

Spend the time discussing the tough problems of roles, responsibilities, equity, and decision-making. And then, document everything possible. You'll be surprised that while your co-founders as a group may not agree on everything, the process of deeply discussing the issues will put you all on the same page and keep you moving forward together. Everybody will feel like there is a solid foundation from which to build upon.

This is also a great time to leverage mentors, advisors, lawyers, executive coaches, and your extended network to get your entire team working together well out of the gate.

Our advice: form deep relationships with your co-founders early, but don't stop after you make key decisions about roles, responsibilities, and equity—continue to make your founding team a tightly knit group as you build your company.

Raising Money Improves Your Business

We've encouraged you to raise money to move fast and beat the competition. Interestingly, it's not just the money that helps; it's also what you'll learn during the fundraising process.

The preparation work required for raising money will help you build a better business. Remember the vetting you did in Chapters 6 to 10? You'll need to hone your business model, financial model, and your overall vision for the company. The byproduct of all that work is that you'll have a better chance to raise money, and you'll have a better company because of it.

If you're successful in raising money, you'll likely add a group of investors that will actively help and support you as you grow and even when you stumble. Smart, savvy investors have seen a lot and will be on your side helping, supporting, cajoling, critiquing, and encouraging you to build a better business. Find the right investment partners, and you'll create a powerful dynamic to improve your business.

Our advice: use the process of raising money to not only get money, but to fundamentally improve your overall business.

Execution Turns Ideas into a Company

Thus far, you've likely been doing a lot of planning: vetting your business model, talking to potential customers, and even raising money. Now, it's time to pull all the parts of your company together to go out and build a product and generate customers. Without an intense focus on execution, all you have are ideas and plans on paper. Execution is what turns them into a company.

Execution is about getting the right things done consistently. That means managing a team by clearly setting objectives and milestones, tracking their progress toward those goals, and communicating clearly to create feedback loops to better complete and improve the work.

There's a science and process to execution that can be very different from the early creative stage of building out your vision and business model. For most founders, execution is a learned skill, so we suggest getting support and help from mentors and advisors.

Our advice: learn how to execute well. It's what wins in the end.

It's All About the Team

Solid execution can only happen if you have the right people in place. That includes the co-founding team, of course, as well as everyone you hire. The group of people you surround yourself with and the culture you create is what makes great execution possible, after all.

Recruiting the right team actually starts with your culture. By clearly defining your values, principles, and business philosophies, along with your vision and business model, you'll better target and attract the right talent for your startup.

A brilliant employee who doesn't fit the culture of the company can be a startup killer, while a cohesive team of dedicated professionals that embody the culture can move mountains for you. And, not only that, your high-functioning team will attract other like-minded people to your startup.

Our advice: surround yourself with the best people you can. Choose people you can learn from and who fit the culture that you want to build. Great teams are almost unstoppable.

* * *

We hope this book has been helpful in your journey to become a founder. We also hope you'll come back to it time and again. It's inspiring to us to see so many people taking the leap to build startups.

We wish you the best of luck and look forward to one day reading your stories.

Acknowledgments

This book is based on what we've learned starting, running, advising, and investing in companies. The vast majority of that education came from the experiences we shared with other entrepreneurs, mentors, advisors, family members, and friends. We learned more from the people around us than we could have ever learned on our own. All those many people who were so patient with us and held our hands along the way deserve our eternal thanks. In an entrepreneurial sense, they helped us become who we are.

The actual process of writing this book was more challenging than we expected. Not surprisingly, as novice authors, we found we had a lot to learn along the way. We were helped by so many people who played pivotal roles in assisting us form this book into its final product. Lorne Cooper, Brad Feld, Pete Birkeland, Paul Foley, Ben Einstein, Dave Jilk, Shawn Broderick, Laura Medina, Chris Kiyan, Larry Middle, Jason Jacobs, Greg Keller, Seth Levine, Noah Kagan, Elisabeth Vezzani, Travis Coggin, and Sara Schaer all invested many hours helping us out by reviewing the book and providing truly great feedback. And, Ben Casnocha supplied valuable input on the practice of writing and publishing a book.

Alexandra Antonioli and Sandra Herman, who both had the patience to read our first written chapters—and the kindness not to laugh about them in our presence—have our

427

enduring love not only for their valuable feedback, but for their understanding during the creation of this book.

Dharmesh Shah, Alex Rigopulos, Jason Jacobs, Katie Rae, Ben Einstein, Brad Feld, and David Cohen each deserve our gratitude for their kind reviews of the book. And, we'd like to thank Matt Golden and Nikhil Kalghatgi, who gave us early feedback on the concept of the book.

Additionally, we thank Zach Obrant for his continued help and support, and his invaluable contributions to the original edition of the book.

About the Authors

Rajat Bhargava is currently co-founder and CEO of Jump-Cloud, a cloud software company building technology for organizations to securely connect their employees to IT resources. An MIT graduate with over two decades of high-tech experience, Rajat is a ten-time entrepreneur with six exits including two IPOs and four trade sales.

* * *

Will Herman is an entrepreneur, active angel investor, corporate director, and startup mentor. He has started and managed five companies, resulting in two IPOs and three corporate sales. Will has also invested in over 80 startups, sat on the boards of twenty five companies, and has advised hundreds more.

Notes

Introduction

* Erin Griffith, "Why Startups Fail, According to Their Founders," *Fortune,* September 25, 2014, http://fortune.com/2014/09/25/why-startups-fail-according-to-their-founders.
† "2015 Exitround Tech M&A Report: What Happens in Tech Under $100 Million," Exitround, http://exitround.com/data (*accessed February 17, 2020*).

Chapter 1

* Steve Blank, "Steve Blank: The Six Types of Startups," *The Wall Street Journal,* June 24, 2013, http://blogs.wsj.com/accelerators/2013/06/24/steve-blank-the-6-types-of-startups-2.
† Natalie Robehmed, "What Is a Startup?" *Forbes,* December 16, 2016, http://www.forbes.com/sites/natalierobehmed/2013/12/16/what-is-a-startup/#208b77514c63.
‡ Alyson Shontell, "A Startup Is a State of Mind, Not a Word That Can Be Defined," *Business Insider,* February 27, 2014, http://www.businessinsider.com/what-is-a-startup-2014-2.
** Jules Maltz and Parsa Saljoughian, "How Fast Should You Be Growing?" *Techcrunch,* August 24, 2013, https://techcrunch.com/2013/08/24/how-fast-should-you-be-growing.

Chapter 2

* Scott Shane, "What Slow Exits Mean to Startup Investors," *Entrepreneur*, December 3, 2015, https://www.entrepreneur.com/article/253459.
† ECOMMERCE GENOME by Compass, "73% of Startup Founders Make $50,000 per Year or Less," January 14, 2014, http://blog.compass.co/73-percent-of-startup-founders-make-50-dollars-000-per-year-or-less.
‡ Ibid.
** Griffith, "Why Startups Fail."
†† Frederick Herzberg, "One More Time: How Do You Motivate Employees?" *Harvard Business Review*, January 2003, https://hbr.org/2003/01/one-more-time-how-do-you-motivate-employees.

Chapter 3

* Paul Graham, "The 18 Mistakes That Kill Startups," October 2006, http://www.paulgraham.com/startupmistakes.html.
† Adam Callinan, "Thinking of Going Solo? 7 Reasons You Need a Co-Founder," *Entrepreneur*, November 20, 2014, https://www.entrepreneur.com/article/239945.
‡ Business Dictionary, accessed June 18, 2016, http://www.businessdictionary.com/definition/organizational-culture.html.
** First Round Review, "80% of Your Culture Is Your Founder," http://firstround.com/review/80-of-Your-Culture-is-Your-Founder.

Chapter 4

* First Round Review, "80% of Your Culture Is Your Founder," http://firstround.com/review/80-of-Your-Culture-is-Your-Founder.

Chapter 8

* "Lean Startup," Wikipedia, accessed November 16, 2017, https://en.wikipedia.org/wiki/Lean_startup.

Chapter 9

* Clare O'Connor, "How Alli Webb Grew Drybar from Her Backseat to a $70 Million Blowout Chain," *Forbes*, March 3, 2016, https://www.forbes.com/sites/clareoconnor/2016/03/08/how-alli-webb-grew-drybar-from-her-backseat-to-a-70-million-blowout-chain/#54cd2ce63b96.

† Ibid.

Chapter 12

* Cromwell Schubarth, "First Round Capital Shares Secrets of Success: One Is Backing Female Founders," *Silicon Valley Biz Journal*, July 30, 2015, http://www.bizjournals.com/sanjose/blog/techflash/2015/07/first-round-capital-shares-secrets-of-success-one.html.

† Jennifer Alsever, "Fighting Co-Founders Doom Startups," *CNN Money*, February 24, 2014, http://money.cnn.com/2014/02/24/smallbusiness/startups-entrepreneur-co-founder.

Chapter 15

* "QSBS (Qualified Small Business Stock)," Investopedia, accessed November 16, 2017, http://www.investopedia .com/terms/q/qsbs-qualified-small-business-stock.asp.

† "Section 1202," Investopedia, accessed November 16, 2017, http://www.investopedia.com/terms/s/section-1202.asp.

Chapter 17

* Tatjana De Kerros-Budkov, "This Is Why 2017 Is Going to Be a Hell of a Tough Year for Seed Startups," *VentureBeat*, January 8, 2017, https://venturebeat.com/2017/01/08/ this-is-why-2017-is-going-to-be-a-hell-of-a-tough-year-for-seed-startups.

Chapter 18

* Techstars, "Frequently Asked Questions," accessed on June 20, 2017, http://www.techstars.com/faq.

† Tom Mickey, "One-Third of U.S. Startups That Raised a Series A in 2015 Went through an Accelerator," *Pitchbook*, February 5, 2016, http://pitchbook.com/news/articles/ one-third-of-us-startups-that-raised-a-series-a-in-2015-went-through-an-accelerator.

‡ AngelList, accessed June 20, 2016, https://angel.co/help/ syndicates.

** SBIR-STTR, "Frequently Asked Questions," accessed November 16, 2017, https://www.sbir.gov/faq/all.

Chapter 19

* Stephan von Perger, "How Much Should Your Startup Raise and at What Valuation?" November 15, 2015, https://medium.com/entrepreneur-toolkit/how-much-should-your-startup-raise-and-at-what-valuation-d15df45cfcf5.

† "The Global 2016 Tech Exits Report," CB Insights, 24, https://www.cbinsights.com/reports/CB-Insights_Global-Tech-Exits-2016.pdf?utm_campaign=Report%20-%20Content%20Emails&utm_source=hs_automation&utm_medium=email&utm_content=41630619&_hsenc=p2ANqtz-8x4H7y4XPEE37IzAuIbLse6t6Pzm0S9ChT4S6zcUleG1MlnYP7-PI1CVjFF-8uVSEXuv_0PMzxPEdjLrvMDK6eB1Q7qA&_hsmi=41630619.

Chapter 20

* "Seed Accelerators," Seed-DB, accessed November 16, 2017, http://seed-db.com/accelerators.

Chapter 22

* "The Anti-Portfolio," Bessemer Venture Partners, https://www.bvp.com/portfolio/anti-portfolio.

Chapter 23

* Patrick Vlaskovits, "Henry Ford, Innovation, and That 'Faster Horse' Quote," *Harvard Business Review*, August 29, 2011, https://hbr.org/2011/08/henry-ford-never-said-the-fast.

Chapter 28

* Corey McAveeney, "How Do You Define Startup Culture?" *Wired*, September 2013, http://www.wired.com/insights/2013/09/how-do-you-define-startup-culture.

Chapter 29

* "Kobayashi Maru," Wikipedia, Accessed June 1, 2017, https://en.wikipedia.org/wiki/Kobayashi_Maru.

† "Herzberg's Two-Factor Theory of Motivation," Management Study Guide, accessed February 13, 2020. http://www.managementstudyguide.com/herzbergs-theory-motivation.htm.

‡ Robert Slater, *Jack Welch and the G.E. Way: Management Insights and Leadership Secrets of the Legendary CEO* (New York: McGraw-Hill, 1998).

** Ibid.

Index

NOTE: Page references in *italics* refer to figures